SETH

I

SETH

DREAMS AND PROJECTION OF CONSCIOUSNESS

JANE ROBERTS

STILLPOINT PUBLISHING

WALPOLE, NEW HAMPSHIRE

1986

This book is manufactured in the United States
of America. It is designed by James F. Brisson,
cover art by Garrett Moore and published by
Stillpoint Publishing, Box 640, Meetinghouse
Road, Walpole, NH 03608.

Published simultaneously in Canada by
Fitzhenry & Whiteside Limited, Toronto.

Library of Congress Card Catalog Number:
86-60443
Roberts, Jane
Seth, Dreams & Projections of Consciousness
ISBN 0-913299-25-1

0 9 8 7 6 5 4 3 2 1

SETH

~

CONTENTS

PREFACE

*T*he television camera lights were warm on my face. My husband, Rob, and I sat with Sonja Carlson and Jack Cole, who were interviewing us on the Boston "Today's Woman Show" on television station WBZ. It was 10 A.M. on the last day of our first tour to promote my book, *The Seth Material*. This was our fifth television show. I tried to look composed and confident, though I still found it difficult to face strangers so early in the day, much less the world at large — particularly when I was expected to explain my own psychic experiences and the philosophical concepts of *The Seth Material*.

As he began the interview, Jack Cole told the unseen audience that I was a medium who spoke for a personality called Seth. He emphasized that my presence on the show didn't necessarily mean that he or Sonja accepted Seth's independent existence. I smiled, somewhat ruefully. Many people feel duty-bound to express skepticism as if it were an automatic badge of honor and intellectual superiority. I'd done the same thing in the past, so I could understand the attitude.

During the interview Jack asked me if Seth would come through. I replied that it was up to Seth. Actually, since I hadn't gone into trance on any other programs, I doubted I would now. Instead, Jack began to play a taped Seth session. As I heard those deep resonant tones of his, I knew that Seth was present.

For a moment I was appalled. All kinds of doubts filled my mind. I hadn't held a regular Seth session since the tour. Suppose the lights bothered me or the trance wasn't deep enough? I had a horror, too, of putting on any kind of display. Regular Seth sessions in the privacy of our living room were one thing. Going into trance on television was something else again. "Oh, Seth," I said mentally, in consternation.

Just then I felt an enormous sense of reassurance, good will and confidence. At a level beneath words, I knew that Seth was right: this *was* the time. Wholeheartedly I gave assent. I reached over for Rob's hand. "It's Seth," I muttered quickly. My face must have begun to change even then, the muscles rearranging themselves into Seth's characteristic expressions, because in that last moment I saw what seemed to be a gigantic camera lens coming in for a close-up. . . .

When I came out of trance, Rob was smiling, Jack and Sonja looked dazed, the camera crew were staring at me and the program was over. "Seth was great," Rob said to me. I was overwhelmed with relief. It was over, then; Seth had come through on television. Hadn't I alternately hoped that he would and been reluctant at the same time?

"Are you okay? Can I get you anything?" Jack asked. He looked so concerned that I laughed automatically.

"No. I feel fine. I always come out of trance easily. I'd love a bun and some coffee, though. Now I'm starved."

A small group surrounded us — the producer and assistant producer, Jack, Sonja and the camera men. I looked at Rob with a touch of dismay because while I'd reassured Jack that everything was quite normal, actually something *was* different this time: I felt as if I'd been in a plane going incredibly fast, only to be yanked suddenly to a halt. Such a tremendous amount of energy surged through me that I didn't know what to do. For a moment it sent me reeling, and Jack caught my arm. This only embarrassed me further. I could feel my cheeks flush. I always tried to behave very sensibly to show that a trance was not a strange but a very natural phenomenon, and so my momentary stagger caught me by surprise. Rob was beside me in a moment, and I explained how I felt. A taxi was already waiting to take us to our next show, a radio program. I grabbed my bun and coffee and took them with me.

What actually happened while I was in trance? Jack and Sonja described some of the session to me in our brief conversation afterward, and Rob filled me in as we rushed to the next program.

First of all, as always, my face changed expression drastically, and I began to speak in a deep male-like voice. My own characteristic gestures vanished, to be replaced by Seth's. He turned toward the camera, speaking directly to the viewers for perhaps ten minutes. By then, Sonja and Jack recovered from their surprise, and Jack asked Seth if he would speak about reincarnation.

Immediately Seth launched into a discussion of Sonja's past life experiences. In the time available, he dwelt on one life in particular, during which he said Sonja had a cleft palate that impeded verbal communication. According to Seth, this partially accounted for her interest in the field of communications now. He also said that Sonja loved color and fabric and that she used these as a method of communication in the past life as well as in this one. Some names and places in fourteenth-century England were given, and these are being checked out.

After the program, Sonja said that the character analysis given along with the reading described her beautifully. She also told us that she had used both color and fabric to communicate with children on an educational television program — a fact unknown to us.

A few days later, I received a long distance call at home from a woman who told me that Seth's appearance on the "Today's Woman Show" convinced her of life after death, though she had never believed in it before. She also said that listening to Seth had been the most profound religious experience of her life, although Seth had not talked in specific religious terms. Since then, we have received many calls, letters and visits from people who saw that show. They were astonished by the program, yet in a strange way, so was I. It taught me several things.

Above all, it deepened my trust in Seth and in his psychological insight and impressed me once again with the remarkable abilities of the inner intuitive self, for it is this part of me that makes communication with Seth possible. For another thing, because of the program format the trance was cut short, and this gave me the opportunity to study the trance phenomenon from a different angle.

Usually a session runs for several hours, and the energy is used up by the time the session is over. On the show, the session lasted only twenty minutes or a half hour, at most. When it was cut short, all that energy was still available, and subjectively I was aware of its full strength for the first time.

People have often asked me how I know when Seth is present, and I have had some difficulty in answering. Examining my feelings after the program and finding myself face to face with that energy, I realized that the same sort of energy, to a lesser degree, is one of my main cues that Seth is ready to come through.

It is not a neutral energy but one of strong emotional impact, reassurring, and in an odd way, personified — warm and amazingly immediate. Perhaps it envelops me, but I do not fall asleep or lose myself in nothingness. I am myself, but very small. I seem to fade into a distance that has nothing to do with space but more to do with psychological focus. Yet I am upheld, supported and protected in the midst of this pervading energy that seems to form about and within me.

I was disappointed that I wasn't able to see the television program, because I've never seen myself as Seth in trance except in a few photographs. Seth manifests through me, addressing himself to others who feel the impact of his personality, but I can't see this as they do from the outside, objectively. To observers, Seth's otherness from me is apparent in the way the open eyes are used, in the gestures and rearrangement of facial patterns. We simply use the body in a different way.

Seth's presence is felt instantly, not esoterically, but in the way we perceive a magnetic personality of power and ability. Though the objective effects of this phenomenon largely escape me, I'm trying to learn all I can about the subjective aspects involved, for surely no one is in a better position to do so. Because of the emergence of Seth, I've become increasingly aware of many other states of consciousness besides the normal daily state that all of us know.

While I'm writing this book in the three-dimensional world, for example, the source material for it comes from the other side of consciousness — that dimension that is revealed to us in dreams, inspiration, trance states and creativity. This book is about Seth, dreams and "astral projection" — all aspects of a different kind of consciousness than the objective one with which we are usually occupied.

You could say, if you wanted to, that Seth intruded himself from some unconscious dimension into my conscious life, yet now he is such a part of my professional and personal experience that much of my time is spent studying and interpreting his theories. His appearance on television seems to represent a further step in his "objectification," which is to me, an astonishing one.

Certainly my life has been vastly enriched by an odd subjective mobility. I write this book during the day in my study, looking out the wide bay windows at the street and at the mountains and river just beyond. But when I want new material for a particular chapter, I turn the focus of my attention from the exterior world to the interior one. Then my physical environment does not concern me, and my normal waking life is the dream.

It wouldn't surprise me to learn that in dream life I'm writing a

book about waking consciousness just as, with my waking consciousness, I'm writing about the reality of dreams. It wouldn't
astonish me either to learn that Seth in an entirely different dimension speaks for a personality called Jane. In fact, I sometimes
amuse myself by imagining a situation in which Seth wonders if
Jane is a secondary personality with an obsessive belief in some
improbable physical reality. Seth, however, is far more knowl-
edgeable than I am, so if he were speaking for me, then I'm afraid
he would get the lesser end of the bargain.

And, as far as I know, Seth has no imprisoning body. He projects part of his consciousness, at least at times, into mine. Curious
thought — I can also imagine some good-humored game of musical chairs in which I try to get out of my body, while Seth tries to
get into it. While this presents a rather hilarious image, it is actually unfair. Seth doesn't have any great interest in taking over my
body for any length of time, while I have an insatiable curiosity
about the experience of getting out of mine.

I have been speaking for Seth in twice-weekly sessions since late
1963. At the very least, this has given me personal experience with
altered states of consciousness and glimpses into subjective areas
largely unexplored. Certainly, it was because of Seth that I found
myself studying the dream reality that comes into focus while the
body sleeps.

Following Seth's instructions, my husband and I first learned to
recall and record our dreams. Through later experiments, we discovered that we could bring our normal waking consciousness into
the dream state and "come awake" while dreaming. Later we began to take bolder steps into these inner areas, learning to manipulate consciousness in what was for us an entirely new way.

The relationship between Seth and myself snaps into focus by
prearranged appointments, as suggested by him in the early days
of the sessions. Each Monday and Wednesday at 9:00 P.M., I sit in
my favorite rocker. Rob sits across from me on the couch with his
note pad and pen, ready to take notes. Normal lights are lit. I may
feel very unpsychic, or even cross. I may feel tired, or really want

to go dancing. Yet at nine, the session begins, and Seth "comes alive."

I don't "become" Seth. Instead, I seem to bask in what he is, or in his presence, if you prefer. Sometimes I am distantly aware that my facial muscles are being rearranged as they mirror Seth's emotions rather than mine. But then, for me, the reality of the room vanishes. Though my eyes are wide open, it is Seth who looks out and smiles at Rob; Seth who speaks through my lips, discussing the nature of reality and existence from the viewpoint of someone not confined to the three-dimensional world.

On Tuesday nights I hold an ESP class, and often Seth addresses the students, explaining his ideas in terms of every-day life, relating them to personal conduct. Often he speaks to individual students, encouraging them to use their own abilities and solve their own problems. His psychological understanding is excellent. He seems to be a personality enjoying the full richness of experience and potential.

For this reason alone, I would like to believe that his abilities were mine, that in the trance state, my own latent talents were operating without obstruction, freed from the normal hang-ups and distractions that annoy us all and hamper our development. I would like to think that for a few short hours a week, at least, I was operating at optimum capacity — that Seth's energy and knowledge were really mine. Lovely thought, and possibly true to some extent.

Fortunately or unfortunately, however, I suspect that our relationship is far more complex. One thing I know: Seth does not have his present basic existence in the three-dimensional world, and I do. He *has* given us instructions that allow Rob, my students and myself to take our own sometimes faltering steps out of our usual physical reality. He initiated our exploration into the universe of dreams, for example, and is therefore largely responsible for this book. But we must return to our normal daily dimension of actuality. And Seth returns to his.

Even without a physical form, Seth is highly effective in our world. Through me, he is producing the Seth Material, a continuing manuscript dealing with the nature of reality, consciousness and identity that now totals over fifty notebooks. He is also dictating his own book: *Seth Speaks: The Eternal Validity of the Soul.* To date, we have held nearly six hundred sessions. In fact, he seems to operate more efficiently in his contacts with physical reality than I do in my journeys into dimensions more naturally considered his.

My out-of-body experiences are not nearly as well directed, deliberate or effective as Seth's behavior is here, for example. Seth dictates one final draft of his own book, while I do at least three drafts of my own. (This present book is my third since the sessions began, so Seth is hardly "stealing" any of my creative energy.)

Seth calls himself an energy personality essence no longer focused in physical reality. Whoever or whatever he is, he is well equipped to discuss the nature of nonphysical existence and to serve as a guide through the other side of consciousness, for it is his natural environment. He comes as a visitor from levels of awareness beyond those with which we are usually acquainted.

In *The Seth Material,* I told the story of my psychic initiation and introduction to Seth as I understood it at that time, and gave a sampling of his ideas on a wide variety of subjects. I also emphasized the "evidential" material we had received — spontaneous clairvoyant demonstrations given in sessions and in the envelope tests that we conducted for over a year. Seth has given correct clairvoyant descriptions of people and events in other parts of this country and Puerto Rico.

Here I will stress subjective experience itself as it is turned toward the dreaming state in particular, and deal with Seth's conceptions of the dream universe through excerpts from his continuing manuscript. This book will also serve as a journal of our own subjective excursions as first Rob and I, and then my students, used Seth's ideas as maps into that strange inner landscape. We have become involved in the keenest of adventures in which ordinary obstructions do not exist while the usual suppositions of physical life do not apply.

According to Seth, dreaming is a creative state of consciousness, a threshold of psychic activity in which we throw off usual restrictions to use our most basic abilities and realize our true independence from three-dimensional form. In dreams, Seth says, we write the script for our daily lives and perceive other levels of existence that our physical focus usually obscures.

Seth maintains that the dream universe has its own basic laws or "root assumptions" — mental equivalents to our laws of gravity, space and time. In other worlds, dream reality only seems discordant or meaningless because we judge it according to physical laws rather than by the rules that apply within it.

Dreams, then, are not just imaginative indigestion or psychic chaos. We are not temporarily insane when we dream, as some theorists maintain. To the contrary, we may be far more sane and alert during some dream states than we are ordinarily. Certainly we are more creative. We may even be more "alive," as you will see from some of our own experiences.

While the main emphasis of this book will be on Seth's dream concepts, the reader is invited to test them out for himself or herself. Seth told us early in the game that many dreams were precognitive, for example, but personal experience is a great convincer, and we discovered this ourselves as we followed his instructions — recalled, dated and recorded dreams and then checked them against events.

Many of Seth's concepts, on probabilities or on, say, the nature of radio stars, cannot be checked out except by specialists. Most of the data on dreams, however, can be proven by anyone with enough curiosity, determination and sense of adventure to follow the guidelines that *The Seth Material* provides. In one of his early statements on dreams, Seth said:

You think that you are only conscious while you are awake.

You assume yourselves unconscious when you sleep. In Freud's terminology, the dice are indeed loaded on the side of the conscious mind. But pretend for a moment that you are looking at this situation from the other side. Pretend that while you are in the dream state you are concerned with the problem of physical consciousness and existence. From that viewpoint, the picture is entirely different, for you are indeed conscious when you sleep.

The locations that you visit while dreaming are as real to you then as physical locations are to you in the waking state. What you have is this: In the waking state, the whole self is focused toward physical reality, but in the dreaming state, it is focused in a different dimension. It is every bit as conscious and aware.

If you have little memory of your dream locations when you are awake, then remember that you have little memory of your waking locations when you are in the dream situation. Both are legitimate and both are realities. When the body lies in bed, it is separated by a vast distance from the dream location in which the dreaming self may dwell. But this, dear friends, has nothing to do with space, for the dream location exists simultaneously with the room in which the body sleeps.

In the 28th Session, he used an analogy to explain this dual conscious focus:

There is, of course, an apparent contradiction here, but it is only apparent, your dilemma being this: If you have another self-conscious self, then why aren't you aware of it? Pretend that you are some weird creature with two faces. One face looks out upon one world [the dream reality] and one face looks out upon another world [the physical one].

Imagine further this poor creature having a brain to go with each face, and each brain interprets reality in terms of the world it looks upon. Yet the two worlds are different, and more, the creatures are Siamese twins. At the same time, imagine that these two creatures are really one, but with definite parts equipped to handle two entirely different worlds.

The subconscious, in this rather ludicrous analogy, would exist between the two brains and would enable the creature to operate as a single enity. At the same time — and this is the difficult part to explain — neither of the two faces would ever 'see' the other's world. They would not be aware of each other, yet each would be fully conscious.

Actually, this is a simple analogy and only carries us so far, but in the beginning Seth used it as a way of giving us some idea of man's current (and artificial) relationship to dream reality. Later, by following the material and Seth's instructions, we discovered that we could dissolve these barriers to some extent. We have been able to prove, to ourselves at least, that dream events are quite real. Flying dreams are not all disguised sexual fantasies, as Freud maintained, for example. In many of them we *are* flying, and the destinations we reach are quite physical. Our records show clearly that what we saw in some such episodes were not imaginary places, but locations we visited while the body slept. Some are described in this book.

In other words, while most books are written about events that occur in waking reality, this one will be mainly concerned with events that happen precisely when consciousness is turned away from normal objective life. Much more is involved than even the nature of the dream state and man's fascinating ability to withdraw consciousness from the body. These phenomena are only evidences of the greater creative consciousness that is inherent and active in each of us — the interior universe of which we know so little.

Today I received scientific corroboration by mail from James Beal, a NASA scientist, for some of Seth's data on the units that Seth says underlie all physical particles. This information, given to us in sessions, was published in the appendix of *The Seth Material*. The paper Jim sent was so professionally oriented that I could hardly understand it, couched as it was in specialized mathematical language. Yet through Seth, we had received the same data. Someone — my own unconscious or Seth — had access to it; that much is certain. The creative consciousness was at work far "beneath" the consciousness I call my own.

We all have access to this creative consciousness, particularly in dreams and dissociated states when we are not so obsessed with physical sense data. Often, evidence of it emerges into consciousness in the guise of sudden hunches or creative inspiration.

It often seems to me that only when we close our eyes do we begin to see, literally and figuratively. This is somewhat of an exaggeration, and yet my experience, Rob's and my students' makes several facts clear. Our ordinary consciousness shows us only one specific view of reality. When we learn to close off our senses momentarily and change the focus of awareness, other quite valid glimpses of an interior universe begin to show themselves.

This is most obvious in dreaming, of course. Dreams may well represent us at our most creative, for not only do we process the past days activities, but we also choose tomorrow's events from the limitless probable actions that are presented to us while the waking self is still.

It's tricky to play hopscotch back and forth between various stages of consciousness, to travel into little-understood subjective realms, explore those inner landscapes and return with any clear clues as to their nature. Such explorations are highly important, however, because they bring us in touch with that basic inner reality that underlies our individual conscious thought and existence and which is the bedrock of our civilization.

To some extent, I do this in each Seth session — lay aside my usual consciousness. A strange letting-go that I still do not understand is necessary along with a simple but profound trust. It is, perhaps, the same sort of trust we have when we dive into the ocean — the faith that we won't sink. (Knowing how to swim helps.)

The water analogy intrigues me, though it can't be followed too far without leading to distortions. A scuba diver, for instance, explores what he finds on the ocean floor and brings us clues from this vast, submerged area. I try to do the same thing, salvaging instead clues from the hidden layers of our inner being. But if he goes far enough, the scuba diver must somewhere come to the bottom of the ocean, and I don't believe there is any bottom or boundary to this inner reality. Instead, I suspect that there are even stranger chasms and openings into other worlds of whose existence we are quite unaware — pools of creativity, consciousness and experience, from which not only our three-dimensional reality but also others spring.

INTRODUCTION

~

It seems incredible to me that my wife, Jane Roberts, has been dead for more than thirteen months. It's late October 1985 as I begin this Preface for her *Seth, Dreams and Projection of Consciousness*. As I have informed many correspondents, Jane died at 2:08 A.M. on Wednesday, September 5, 1984, after spending 504 consecutive days in a hospital in Elmira, N.Y. I was with her when she died. The immediate causes of her death were a combination of protein depletion, osteomyelitis, and soft-tissue infections. These conditions arose out of her long-standing rheumatoid arthritis. I'll be discussing Jane's illnesses — her "symptoms" — much more thoroughly in other work. Indeed, I plan to eventually write a full-length biography of her, and am doing research for that project now.

Ater Jane's death I became extremely busy. I had to cope with my grief, and one way I chose was to immediately begin keeping elaborate records in and writing essays for a series of "grief notebooks." I told no one about the notebooks, or the three drawings I had made of Jane as she lay in her bed right after her death. I was obligated to spend many months finishing a Seth book — *Dreams, "Evolution," and Value Fulfillment* — that we had started way back in September 1979, long before she went into the hospital; as I had planned to, I resumed work on that project the day after she died. (Jane was cremated the next day, in a process we had agreed upon several years ago.) I also worked upon two other books we collaborated upon after she had been hospitalized. There were many legal matters to attend to, much mail to answer, and more to keep up with.

I couldn't believe it when I realized that my wife had been dead for a week. As I lived and worked in it, our house looked the same as it ever had. In spite of my sorrow, I presented a cheerful face to the world; I talked and joked, and did everything I was supposed to do. I also discovered what must be a very common phenomenon: Those who knew of Jane's passing became instantly self-conscious when we met. I felt their embarrassment at their damned-up sympathies, and their fear of the same thing happening to them. They didn't want to hurt me further. Amazingly, I found myself offering comfort to them, to help them surmount such barriers so that we could talk. My visitors reminded me anew of how private an event Jane's death is for me, yet how universal it is. How many uncounted quadrillions of times has that transference from "life" to "nonlife" taken place just on our planet alone? And I don't believe that anyone has tried to cope with questions of life and death any more valiantly than Jane did.

As the physical time passed, however, I began wanting to do a little formal writing about Jane's death, so last month when Jim Young of Stillpoint Publishing gave me the chance to do so in this Preface for *Seth, Dreams* . . . I accepted at once.

"To me," Jim wrote, "it would be a special opportunity for you to make whatever statement you might wish about Jane and her work. It would also be nice for the many readers of Jane's books to have a chance to hear from her partner, who so beautifully and critically assisted in the birthing of the Seth books.

"Finally, [I ask] if you have a photo of Jane that you particularly enjoy that we can use on the flap. Once again, many of her fans would enjoy such a photo as a personal remembrance. It would also [let] us show a photo that does not exploit her channeling. Incidentally, this photo need not be recent. Simply one that you like."

I don't care for the term "channeling," since I think it too all-inclusive and already trite. However, I liked both Jim's ideas of my doing the Preface for Jane's book, and of publishing a photo of her. And Laurel Lee Davies, the young lady who's now helping me carry on my publishing activities, at once intuitively picked out from my files the one right photograph of Jane to us for *Seth, Dreams . . .* Jane's father, Delmer Roberts, took the snapshot when she was on vacation with him in Baja, California in 1951. She was twenty-two years old. Jane and I didn't meet until 1954. That little picture, then, was taken some twelve years before she began "coming through" with the Seth material. Yet, I find in it all of the ingredients that made up the Jane I knew — her great beauty, personality and creativity, her love of manipulating within her physical environment; I see her "steering herself" toward extraordinary accomplishments.

As soon as I took Jim Young up on his word that I could make whatever statement I want to about Jane's work, I knew that this Preface would contain relatively little about *Seth, Dreams and Projection of Consciousness* itself, and I wrote to Jim about this. The book stands perfectly well on its own. These notes, then, will contain material not only about Jane, but my own involvement with her, her work, and her death. I trust that even though physically she's no longer with me, my wife agrees with my choices, for she helped me learn that the one truly unique thing I have to offer the world is my own creation of it.

Many people know of Jane's death by now, and this makes it impossible for me to deal with that event in chronological order

within her books. By rights, I shouldn't be mentioning it sequen-
tially until I publish the two books that Jane and I had finished
while she was hospitalized — then it would be all right to annouce
that she is dead! But for convenience's sake, in *Seth, Dreams* . . . I
bring together certain events in chronological time; I feel that its
having been written some time ago makes this book the ideal place
for me to discuss Jane's death, to unite the "past," the "present,"
and the "future'; I regard it as being next in line after *Dreams,
"Evolution," and Value Fulfillment*, which Prentice-Hall, Inc. is
publishing in two volumes in the spring and fall of 1986. In
Dreams, "Evolution, " . . . I stuck to Jane's production of the Seth
Material for that work, plus a strict chronological account of our
personal lives while she delivered it. I made no leaps in time to
write about her physical death, for to me that sad event lay too far
in the future — over two and a half years — from the time she
finished dictating *Dreams, "Evolution," .* . . in February 1982.

In more specific terms, I'm organizing this rather short exploration of Jane's death around these items; a loose chronology surrounding her writing of *Seth, Dreams* . . . in 1966-67, and our
unsuccessful attempts to sell the book; my acceptance of the survival of the personality after physical death; a waking experience
involving my sensing Jane very soon after she had died; a metaphor I created for her death; a dream in which I not only contacted her but gave myself relevant information; another metaphor for Jane's death; my speculations about communication
among entities, whether they're physical or nonphysical; a letter
that could be from the discarnate Jane — one that was sent to me
by its recipient, a caring correspondent whom I'll call Valerie
Wood; a note I wrote to Sue Watkins about the death of her
mother; some quotations from a published letter of mine; Jane's
notes concerning the relationship we had; and, finally, the poem
in which she refers to her nonphysical journeys to come.

How *Seth, Dreams* . . . eventually came to be issued by
Stillpoint Publishing, how it can even be thought of as a "lost

manuscript," makes a most interesting account that I'll just out-line here. First, though, I remind the reader that Jane spoke in a trance or dissociated state for a discarnate personality who calls himself Seth; by his own definition he's an "energy personality essence," no longer focused within physical reality. Last July my agent, Tam Mossman, phoned to ask that I search Jane's papers for a manuscript he remembers her submitting to him some seventeen years ago, when he had been a young editor just beginning a ca-reer with Prentice-Hall. That manuscript is *Seth, Dreams and Projection of Consciousness.* As soon as he'd reviewed it back then, Tam had asked Jane to do a book on Seth himself. The result? *The Seth Material*, for which Jane signed a contract in December 1968. The book came out in 1970; and in it she had used certain portions of *Seth, Dreams . . .*

My own imperfect recollection following Tam's request that I look for it was that *Seth, Dreams . . .* was an unfinished collection of records, ideas, and chapters that Jane had struggled with for several years, without selling it. Instead, what I found in a box in the basement was, to my amazement, a completed manuscript — a full book ready to go, one as fresh as it had ever been, and my wife had struggled with it. What emerged as Laurel Davis and I searched Jane's and my records, including early Seth sessions, was a long story of our doubts and gropings in an area in which we had no guidance except for our own explorations. *Seth, Dreams . . .* was rejected by three major publishers while Jane worked on it during 1966-67. She was still an unknown in the field; by mid-1966 she'd had only one small psychic book, *How to Develop Your ESP Power*, published. Our subject of interest itself was largely denied validity by the social, psychological, and scientific estab-lishments. We were still operating alone, then, even though Jane had been speaking for Seth for about three years. In spite of all of her questions, however, her strong creative vitality — her intuitive insistence upon using her most unusual abilitites — kept her focus-ing ahead, and I helped her as much as I could. I'm still astonished when I think of what Jane was to accomplish in the next few years.

Jane began dictating *Seth Speaks* in January 1970. In March, Tam signed her to a contract for *Seth, Dreams* . . . on behalf of Prentice-Hall. *The Seth Material* was published. Jane was on a creative roll. She kept changing and adding to the portions of *Seth, Dreams* . . . that she hadn't used in *The Seth Material*, while at the same time her new work kept crowding it out. Finally, in 1971 Tam converted her contract for *Seth, Dreams* . . . into one for *Seth Speaks*. Jane didn't keep on trying to sell *Seth, Dreams* . . . Neither did I, and somehow that perfectly good book ended up packed away. Tam left Prentice-Hall for other employment in 1982; he became my agent after Jane's death in 1984. When at his request I rediscovered *Seth, Dreams* . . . three months ago, and examined it, I couldn't believe that that finished manuscript had never been published. I'm most pleased that Jim Young accepted it at once for Stillpoint Publishing — just as I know Jane is!

Without taking into account here the essences of other life forms, do I think the human personality survives physical death? Considering the loving, passionate "work" that Jane and I engaged in for more than twenty years, of course I do. No other answer makes intuitive or consciously reasonable sense to me. I think it quite psychologicaly and psychically limiting to believe otherwise, for such beliefs can only impede or postpone our further conscious understanding of the individual and mass realities — the overall "nature" — we're creating. I think that all of us seek answers, and that our searches are expressed in our very lives.

In those terms I have my own proofs of survival, just as Jane had — and as she still does. We always had far too many questions about such matters to be satisfied with the very restrictive "answers" that our religious and secular establishments offer. I cannot believe that in matters of life and death my psyche would be so foolish as to indulge in wish fulfillment, relaying to me only those ideas it "thinks" I want to consciously know. Each time I may feel my own ignorance about even our own physical reality, let alone other realities, I fall back upon my own feelings and beliefs. I have nowhere else to turn, really, nor did Jane. As Seth told us in a number of ways (and to some extent I'm certainly paraphrasing him here), "Never accept a theory that contradicts your own experience." Jane and I found much better answers for ourselves, even if they were — and are — only approximations of more basic, and perhaps even incomprehensible, truths. My unimpeded, creative psyche intuitively knows that positive answers to its questions exist, that otherwise it wouldn't bother to ask those questions within nature's marvelous framework, that nature is alive and, as best we can sensually conceive of it, eternal. My psyche knows that it makes no sense within nature's context for the human personality to be obliterated upon physical death.

I think that I've had a number of waking and dreaming experiences in which Jane and I have communicated with each other since her physical death thirteen months ago. So have others. I'm offering two such events of my own, and one from the friend I've never met in person, Valerie Wood.

My first conscious contact with Jane took place less than two hours after she had died. After making certain funeral arrangements for her by telephone, before leaving the hospital, I drove home at about 4:00 A.M.

'It was a warm starlit night,' I later wrote to a friend, 'just beautiful, and as I got out of the car and looked up into that depthless sky I felt Jane right there, above the car. She'd followed me home. "Thank you, Jane," I said aloud, and went into the house.

'I went back to work on a long-overdue Seth book the next day, but don't let my determination to carry on Jane's work fool you. A cave has opened up inside me, and I can only trust that the wound would heal itself. I still cry for my wife several times a day, fifty-seven days after her death. From watching Jane for 504 consecutive days in the hospital, I learned that human beings have tremendous, often unsuspected reserves of strength and power, yet I still don't understand how I can feel such pain and live.'

Along with my conscious contacts with Jane, I created a number of metaphors, or implied comparisons, revolving around her death. I'll describe one now and work in another one later. These constructs, which are sometimes quite effortless, show how I began to express my longing for my wife very creatively even during a time of great stress. I've often become aware of the one to follow; it reminds me of certain speculations and truths that I think will always be with me.

But first, the beautiful little house that Jane and I bought in 1975 sits near the top of a moderately steep hill at the western edge of Elmira. We soon came to call it the "hill house," in person and in our books. (Eventually mail began to arrive addressed to us simply at "The Hill House, Elmira, N.Y." The people at the post office still see to it that such pieces are delivered. I'm grateful.)

Rewritten from the entry I made in my grief notebook on September 26, 1984 — or sixteen days after Jane's death.

Last night was the fifth night in a row that I've slept on the screened-in back porch in my new sleeping bag. I didn't start doing this to avoid the bedroom that Jane and I had shared in the hill house for the last nine years, but because I'd always wanted to and now can. Jane is no longer here for me to be so close to, night and day, to leap to take care of when she needs me. She'd never been able to sleep on the porch — one of the reasons we'd had it added onto the house to begin with.

The night was so warm that I unzipped the bag all the way down to my feet. In the half-dark I spoke aloud to my wife, telling her that I wished she was with me. I fell asleep. Around 4:30 A.M. I woke to the sound of a heavy wind and the feel of much colder air creeping in around my body. The wind chimes hanging in a corner of the porch were clashing together repeatedly. I zipped up the bag as spatters of rain began to blow in on me. The woods come down over the crest of the hill in back of the house, to the north, and with a sound like an ocean tide the wind was racing through their treetops, plunging south past the house and into the valley. Jane and I had always loved that great roar. The trees thrashed in my neighbor's yard across the road. The whole scene was one of change and energy and mystery.

Oh, sweetheart, if only you were here with me to see this,' I said aloud to Jane. And as I talked to her I suddenly found myself crying for her again there in the semi-dark night while the wind seethed and roared. Deep wrenching sobs began in my legs and stomach and rose up through my chest. I tried to keep talking to her, but could not. 'It must be better where you are,' I finally gasped, 'but you should see this. It's so wonderful . . .' And as I spoke I intuitively understood that the motion of the wind was an excellent creative metaphor for the motion of Jane's soul, that its cool feel upon my face could be the physical version of her caring for me 'from where she is.' The storm of my grief eased after a while, but the wind and the light rain continued. I dozed. When I woke half an hour later the wind had diminished a great deal. I felt drained. I went into the kitchen for a glass of water. Was Jane's soul resting from its earlier great commotion, or had she moved away for the moment while exploring other aspects of her new reality that were perhaps out of range to us earthbound creatures? I crawled back into my bag and slept until dawn.

And I often feel this metaphor return as I step out on the back porch of the hill house and listen to the wind in the treetops to the north.

I had this meeting with Jane, partially wrapped as it was in dream elements, thirty-five days after she had died. The following is revised from my dream notebook.

October 10, 1984. Both of us had jobs at the large hospital in my home town of Sayre, Pa., eighteen miles southeast of Elmira, N.Y. The setting and the buildings weren't like those of the "real" hospital in Sayre, though. It was a gorgeous summer day. Jane was much younger than she'd been when she died at the age of fifty-five. She still had her long jet-black hair, slim active figure and exuberant personality. I could have been my own age, sixty-five. We relaxed upon a large, sloping, very green lawn beside a brick hospital building that was several stories high. Then with great surprise I saw that on top of the near end of the building there sat an old, flat-sided, two-story house with steep roofs, weathered a drab gray and with all of its windows shuttered. Caught in one shutter was a filmy pink garment like a negligee, fluttering in the breeze. Curiously, Jane and I stared up at the house perched so incongruously there, and we talked about trying to get up into it to see what it was like inside.

At the same time I knew that Jane had some sort of deep commitment. However, this didn't stop her from giving me a series of face-to-face hugs, very close, smiling like she does in some old photos of her that I'd found in a file yesterday. I was leery of responding too openly to her advances, though, since I didn't know what her commitment was. A beautiful arching stone bridge was to my right as we talked and hugged. The lawn extending underneath the bridge was an extremely rich green — glowing and pulsing as though it was alive.

Then I was in an elevator car inside the building, and rising toward the house on the roof. Jane wasn't with me. Another, older lady was having trouble repairing a small mechanism that was fastened to the wall beside the car's door. I offered to fix it for her; this involved my turning some large screws into place by hand. While I was doing so, the elevator stopped at a floor and the door opened. The lady left, and I hurriedly inserted the last few screws while the door stayed open. Just as I finished — or perhaps nearly so — the door began to close. I leaped toward it. I wedged my shoulder between the door and its frame and forced the door open enough so that I could squeeze out into a hallway of the hospital. The door shut behind me.

When I got up at 6:15 A.M. I hurried to write down this most significant account, and begin my interpretation of it. (Seth wasn't available, so I couldn't ask him to do it for me!)

"Since I trust my feelings," I wrote, "I just know that I've met Jane again. In this 'adventure in consciousness' she leaves the choices up to me — and I very clearly tell myself that I'm not ready to leave this mundane world. The experience is full of highly creative images.

> Why do we have jobs at a hospital, when Jane was so afraid of them while she was physical? I interpret our employment there, and her joyful mood, to mean that from where she is now she no longer fears hospitals and the medical establishment — that she's moved beyond that deep apprehension she began to build up around the age of three, as her mother became gradually, and permanently, incapacitated with rheumatoid arthritis. I think that my own much more pleasant earlier experiences with the hospital in Sayre, including my doing free-lance art work for some of its doctors, helped me place the locale for this adventure there, rather than at the hospital in Elmira, where Jane died. In addition, we lived very happily in Sayre for several years following our marriage.
>
> 'The appearance of the old house stands for our ordinary physical reality — but its high location and closed shutters prevent me from looking inside it, into another reality; the negligee represents my knowledge that Jane is in that new dimension. Our meeting is her message to me that she is well, rejuvenated, with her abilities and personality intact after her death. My reluctance to fully return her hugs is a sign that I'm not yet ready to join her. Her youth also stands for the plasticity of time.
>
> 'The glowing, very beautiful and alive grass also represents Jane's new reality. The bridge arching over the lawn symbolizes another connective between that universe and my physical one. Jane doesn't ask me to cross the bridge now. I think that the structure also stands for the 'psychological bridge' upon which she met Seth during her sessions with him. (Seth wasn't in this experience, however.)

'My bursting out of the elevator car, which was lifting me toward the house on the roof of the hospital building, and a new reality, is a close thing as I force my way free. I'm delayed by fixing the mechanism; repairing it means I still have things to do on the earth, as does the lady who was with me in the car. My almost waiting too long to get out of the car also stands for my grief for Jane, and for my intense questioning and speculating about 'where she is' now. I'm sure that she lives. I want to know more — yet I'm not ready to die now in order to find out. I feel sad, writing this and thinking of her.

'The hospital obviously represents the jumping-off point into another reality for Jane. She died in such an institution. But more often than not people go to hospitals to prevent their physical deaths, to stay away from realities like the one Jane is in for as long as possible. I also think that at this time in our history the hospital — any hospital — is a powerful social symbol for our species' strengths and weaknesses. I use the hospital in a positive way by plunging out into the hall; I signal myself that I mean to keep on living physical.

Now here's the second of the metaphors I referred to earlier — those intuitive comparisons I searched out as I kept on trying to grasp that Jane is truly, temporally dead. I created this one just three days after having the hospital adventure in consciousness.

A block to the west of the hill house, the main road drops straight down into the outskirts of Elmira. Opening off the road to the left like a series of steps are short, level sidestreets upon which I often run late at night. In the beginning the running helped me physically handle my grief over Jane's passing; I cried often as I ran, and tried to comprehend where she is now. I'm a natural runner, but had been unable to do more than a little jogging in recent years because of the pressures of work and of taking care of Jane as she became more and more ill. After her death I could run nightly if I chose to. I find that activity still secret and evocative. The streets are lined with trees arching up to meet overhead; periodically those intersecting patterns of leaves and branches are punctuated by bursts of light from the streetlamps. At certain times the moon follows me along in its phases. The only sounds might be the wind in the treetops and the chug-chug of my shoes on the asphalt. A dog may bark in the distance. When I do it right I float effortlessly along. And amid my tears I finally permitted the obvious to become obvious to me. The following is revised from my entry in my grief notebook.

> October 13, 1984. Jane has been dead for thirty-eight days. It has finally come to me that the dark tunnels of those streets I run on, with their mysterious implications of the unknown, and the fear of the dark that such streets can generate, are physically oriented metaphors for the transition Jane has made to another reality. In our terms, the tunnel shapes lead to an unfathomable new reality that is supposedly filled with the light of the universe. That light is symbolized by the streetlights shining through the tunnels every so often, and hinting at that great brilliant reality beyond. This metaphor is perticularly apropos at this time, with the trees still carrying their thick growth of leaves — yet later in the fall it may become even more applicable as the leaves drop and the streetlights, poor as they may be in comparison to the light of the universe, can shine through a little more brilliantly.

My hospital adventure is still symbolic and literal to me in the most intimate of terms. It's made me think often about the tremendous variety of reassurances the "dead" can choose to offer the "living." A number of Jane's readers have sent me communications they claim to have received for me from Jane in her after-death state. I'm making a collection of these for study. In the midst of my worroying for my wife, how did I — and how do I — know which of the communications are really from her? Or whether any portions of some of the messages may be? I soon learned that in each case I had to rely upon my own sensual and psychic equipment to intuitively know what to believe, or to be moved by, sometimes to the point of tears. Obviously, I can judge my feelings about what's right and not right in my own experiences with a discarnate Jane much more easily than I can gauge the outside of someone else's communication. But since I believe the Seth Material is valid, it would be very arrogant of me to think that none of Jane's readers except me had legitmately tuned into her where she is now or perhaps touched upon her world view.

(See the considerable world-view material from Jane and from Seth in Volume 2 of "Unknown" Reality. *A world view is the body of an individual's personalized interpretation of the physical universe; emotions are necessarily involved. "Each person has such a world view," Seth tells us in Session 718, "whether living or dead in your terms, and that 'living picture' exists despite time or space. It can be perceived by others.")*

So if I insist that I've communicated with Jane at times, then I'm obligated to consider statements from others claiming the same thing. But in ordinary terms, even if my wife's death has left me more open and vulnerable to psychic possibilities, I still shrink from offering any sort of blanket assurance. ("Yes, I'm convinced that you have reached Jane, just as I have.") I'm not contradicting myself when I note that perhaps — and I've suspected for a long time that ultimately this is correct — it is true that on some far levels of consciousness and communication that we do not (or even cannot) understand at this "time," each person who is so inclined to do so has at least touched a Jane who responded clearly enough. She will continue to do so. In this view, those elements in such messages that have no meaning for me can be only distortions on the part of the medium or the letter-writer or the poet. I do think that communication among entities, whether they're physical or nonphysical, is always going on, and from every conceivable angle and in every way. Hardly a new thought, yet grasping it, or even speculating about it, is to touch upon a portion of the mystery of life. (And from where you are, Jane, what do you think of my very cautious approach?)

I first heard from my unseen correspondent, Valerie Wood, not long after Jane had died thirteen months ago. I sent her one of the cards I'd had printed, giving a few details about Jane's death and stating my determination to carry on with our work. Valerie responded with some poetry relative to Jane's passing, and my reactions to her death, that I interpreted at once as being very evocative of Jane and me. At the time I didn't know what to believe about the source of the material, even while I found it reinforcing my own contacts with Jane. Were Valerie's messages from her own subconscious? From Jane's world view? From Jane herself?

I wrote Valerie that she was gifted psychically and suggested that she might cautiously proceed with learning more about her abilities, to whatever extent she chose. Valerie is thirty-eight years old, and lives with her husband in a western state; they have two children. She works part time in the field of education. She is developing her gifts through study and practice. During the year she sent me a number of messages "from" and about Jane. Some of them subjectively feel right to me; they effortlessly mirror or echo the way the Jane I lived with for almost thirty years often talked and wrote. In fact, at times I found the similarities between the contents of those messages and my ideas of Jane's own ambience to be striking.

Valerie's material raises as many questions as it gives answers for, of course. Are her messages really from Jane, or is she "only" telepathically picking up from me what I want to hear, and flashing it back to me from her trance states — as communications from Jane? An unbelieving scientist would say that Valerie is hardly in touch with a discarnate Jane, since science doesn't accept survival of death. Nor would the idea of reaching Jane's world view be considered, or telepathy from me, for both of those concepts are scientifically unacceptable. The most parsimonious view — the simplest, stingiest one — would be that through studying the Seth Material Valerie subconsciously divines the replies I want from my dead wife, and in all subjective innocence comes through with her trance messages for me, to fit my own stubborn belief in Jane's survival.

I may be projecting my own fears here, but I don't agree with the scientific rejection of all portions of the schemata listed above.

The objections don't feel right to me. They question not only Valerie's sincerity and performance but my own, as well. I keep thinking about the twenty years of ideas and study that Jane and I put into the Seth Material. Surely my contacts with her, and the work of gifted, dedicated people like Valerie, show us human potential in very challenging ways, hinting at how much we have yet to learn about our individual and collective consciousnesses. And out of my own selfish need and longing for my wife, who is dead, I want people to read her books so that they can understand her great contributions.

Right now, though, I want to present a message from Valerie that she received upon awakening at 6:30 A.M. on September 6, 1985 — some six weeks ago, in other words, and a year and a day after Jane died.

(But first this note, In Appendix 19 for Volume 2 of "Unknown" *Reality, I offer material from Jane and from Seth about that atonal, very distant-sounding Seth Two. I quote myself as writing that* "Seth Two exists in relation to Seth in somewhat the same manner that Seth does to Jane, Although that analogy shouldn't be carried very far.")*

Just as received from Valerie Wood, and with her permission,

For Rob

You will join me as I have joined others.
No physical form or physical thought
can express my existence.
The term love, with its message
of caring for another,
is the most important of our
messages in the physical.
Seth Two is to me now what Seth was to you.
I am a step higher but not removed.
Yet, I have changed enough since "my
death" that it is difficult,
at times, to relate to your existence.

The love and the emotions you feel are
the connectives between us.
My love for you has not changed but expanded
in a way you do not comprehend.
Physical needs are for physical beings,
and I understand and know this.
Touch is important at your level.
My new or returned mind loves you more
deeply than in our earth time together,
but it is also much more
understanding of physical need.
When I said, "Be for me as I would
be for thee," I didn't mean to limit you.
Be the physical person you need to be,
as you are physical for a limited and
for a purposeful reason.
Enjoy physical reality between others,
for the mind endures and exists
beyond your understanding and existence.
I love you as you were
and as we will be.
Your now is for you to enjoy.
I never judge your actions, and this
I repeat with love and utmost understanding.
Be yourself and in being yourself
you will be for me as I would be for thee.
You do well and I watch you often.
Continue to love physical life
while you are physical.

Until later.
(Jane.)

"Rob," Valerie wrote at the end of her material, "I hope this has meaning for you, and whether it is Jane's, or my subconscious words, it is beautiful, wise and useful — best to you until next time."

Indeed. A commitment is required upon my part in this case: I think that Valerie's message for me is from Jane. A possible qualification of that belief can be that the material is interwound with data Valerie picked up from Jane's world view, where Jane wouldn't have necessarily been involved — only the body of her personalized and emotional experience in physical life. I cannot objectively prove either of those propositions. Yet I have my own intuitive proof, because I strongly feel that the contents of Valerie's message fit very well both the physical and the nonphysical Jane Roberts.

Aside from the obvious reassurances Jane is quoted as offering to me, as a physical creature, I could comment extensively upon some of the other points she makes — especially the two I briefly refer to below; the reader may enlarge upon portions of the message also, depending upon what he or she understands of the Seth-Jane philosophy. Jane remarked, "Yet, I have changed enough since 'my death' that it is difficult, at times, to relate to your existence." And, "My love for you has not changed but expanded in a way you do not comprehend." How interesting these statements are! Does Jane contradict herself in them? No — yet the meanings within them require intuitive exploration and conscious comprehension. They're very personal observations that at the same time echo that mystery of life I'm always referring to. I was quite aware of those statements and their implied challenges in connection with the ingredients I bring together in the next paragraph.

I began thinking about and working upon this Preface for *Seth, Dreams* . . . late in October 1985. As I reread the book I learned that Jane devotes considerable portions of several chapters to material involving our friend, Sue Watkins — her adventures with dreams, projections, and probable realities — and also refers to her in other chapters. Sue published her two-volume work, *Conversations With Seth*, in 1980-81; her father died two years later.

I've already referred to Laurel Lee Davies, the young lady who now works with me (and is helping especially with proofreading and answering mail). Ever since she arrived from the West Coast in August, Laurel had wanted to meet Sue, who lives in upstate New York. The three of us finally did meet — a few days after Sue's mother had died on October 19. Two nights earlier, Sue had had a very strong precognitive dream concerning her mother's death; she plans to discuss that event in the book she's writing. Laurel made a card for Sue when we heard about the demise of her mother, and left room inside it for me to write a note. Here's what I spontaneously produced.

> Dear Sue:
>
> There's little I can say that will offer comfort to you about your mother's death. On the other hand, I can say everything — for her life encompassed the world, the universe, just as much as yours does, or mine, or Laurel's. She lives then, as I'm sure you know. From my own experience I can say that she'll surely communicate with you, expressing new and unfathomable facets and attitudes of the universe — always brilliant, perhaps inexpressible in ordinary terms, yet reaching you and touching in unexpected ways. I think I know my own parents better now than I did when they were 'living.' I understand so much more about them now, and with compassion see and feel their strivings and hopes, loves and successes and failures in ways I was not consciously aware of before. I think this kind of heightened knowledge and awareness always comes to those still 'living' — but also, that those who have 'died' are more alive and adventurous than ever, and at least sometimes in ways we just cannot comprehend. I know this is the case with Jane. So, I think, it will be with you and your mother and father. My love to you and your son.
>
> Rob.

To me, even thinking about an entity who has died is a form of communication with the essence of that departed one, whatever its nature, shape, and complexity "was." We must have much to consciously learn here. Imagine our planet swinging through its orbit independently of the sun's illumination. I've often thought that if each birth and each death was signalled by a flash of light, an observor in space would see an earth that was always bathed in a flickering gentle glow because of all of the activities of consciousness going on there. What a profound and revealing sight that would be!

That vision reminds me of a letter of mine that has just appeared in *Reality Change*, a magazine its editor is devoting to the Seth Material, and publishing in Austin, Texas. At her request last September, I briefly described my feelings a year after Jane's death. I mentioned how worthwhile it would be to throughly study the continuous global healing processes that I believe constitute one of the earth's major forces, so that we could consciously use them to "help our species lead itself into new areas of thought and feeling." Now I enlarge upon that idea by stating that such processes should be studied amid the earth's even larger life-and-death cycles — those making up that "flickering gentle glow" my mythical observor would see from space. I think that eventually we'll regard all life upon our planet — or upon any other — in such terms, that we'll be led to do so by our own needs and creative curiosity. Beyond that will lie our exploring, as Jane did, the more basic nonphysical nature of reality.

Obviously, my life has been enriched in numerous and unexpected ways by knowing Jane, and I feel myself still growing, still asking questions. I was blessed, then — a situation that in my youth I'd hardly dared hope for in conventional terms, yet had been open enough in my beliefs to create. The cave that I'd felt open up inside me after Jane's death is closing and healing itself, while leaving its inevitable psychic imprint.

'These days I dream about Jane,' I wrote in my article for *Reality Change*, 'and feel her presence just as much as ever, yet my mourning is inevitably enlightened by new forces and experiences. This is just the way Jane wants it to be; she told me not long before she died that she didn't want me to spend my life in grief and alone. I agreed with her when she said those things but had little idea of the emotional depths of sadness and yearning that one must face and live with before becoming free enough to turn one's thoughts outward into the world again.'

Seth remarked many times that each person sends out invisible signals of need and desire that are picked up and reacted to by those who have similar challenges. In our own case, Jane and I were always acutely aware of the difficult personal working-out of the interchanges that followed our getting together. Here are her rough notes for September 29, 1976, just as she wrote them in her journal.

Considering Rob's and my relationship — the challenges, joys, hopes, strains and our own personality characteristics. Maybe the whole thing is — reacting to ourselves individually and to the other person — experiencing our own personal reactions and then reacting to them — then reacting to the other person who experiences the same processes in himself. We . . . creatively keep altering ourselves and our mates. We can't be 'perfect' at the start because the processes include changing events. There's bound to be some lopsidedness to our growth, as we form psychological 'art' throughout our entire lives — or learn to live . . . artistically. Each person in such a relationship changes constantly in relationship to himself and the other person, until — hopefully? — by death you've used the characteristics of your own personality the best you can. Merged them with your mate's so that between the two of you, you get a new creative mixture in a kind of psychological multiplication . . . You try different ways of using your own traits, etc.

Some seven and a half years later, Jane had been hospitalized for over ten months. We worked together during most of those days of treatment; by then, also, she had carried nearly to the limit her exploration of both her personal life and her "psychological 'art' " of living. She very creatively considered those journeys and her new goals in the untitled poem that she spontaneously dictated to me from her hospital bed on March 1, 1984. It took her just seven minutes, spanning as it did two interruptions by nursing personnel,

> *My history is filled*
> *with kingdoms lost and kingdoms found,*
> *with magic mirrors that open up*
> *into brand-new cosmic maps,*
> *and within my head*
> *glittering worlds are spread*
> *enough to fill*
> *a thousand books.*
> *Multiple vision leads me on*
> *over paths that form*
> *new worlds of fact.*

Six months later, on September 5, 1984, Jane was dead — gone to one of those "glittering worlds," these "new worlds of fact," that she had told me she knew about and that she so wanted to see.

Robert F. Butts
Elmira, N.Y.
November 1985

PART ONE

Intrusions from the
Interior Universe

A Subjective Journal

1

Dreams, Creativity
and the Unconscious

*Excerpts from "The Physical Universe
as Idea Construction"*

My First Glimpse into the Interior Universe

Three particular dream-events high-
lighted my psychic initiation and led, indirectly, to this book. The
first was a comparatively minor dream that was surprising to me
when it happened, but it could easily have been forgotten. The
second was an amazing experience resulting from a dream that I
could not remember. The third was a dream that gave me a startling glimpse into another kind of reality.

The first dream occurred in July 1963, before I knew anything
at all about psychic phenomena. The third occurred in February
1964, shortly after the Seth sessions had begun. Between these two
dates, I found myself propelled into a dimension of experience
that had been completely unknown to me before.

The initial dream involved a neighbor, Miss Cunningham, who
lived in this apartment house long before we knew it existed.
When Rob and I moved here in 1960, she had already spent a
quarter of a century in her three small rooms, surrounded by
books of poetry and drama. As we came up the front steps, we

often saw her sitting in the upstairs window, watching the traffic below. But the year we arrived, her life began to shrink. She retired from her position as a high school drama teacher and spent more and more time in her little apartment.

In the beginning, Rob and I only saw her face to face in the dark apartment house hallway, usually at the mailbox. She was fiercely independent, tall and slim, with neatly coiffeured hair and tailored clothes. Her English was flawless. She had an excellent reputation as a teacher, and now and then she was visited by former students to whom she served tea. During the holidays, her mailbox was stuffed with cards.

These small facts were all we knew of her, and we never became close friends. Yet my first precognitive dream involved her, and, in a strange way, my psychic experience became bound up with her life. I seemed to keep track of her in my dreams. As her world became physically smaller, she seemed to reach out into mine.

That summer, Rob and I vacationed in Maine. We hadn't communicated with Miss Cunningham at all. But on the night of our return to Elmira, I awakened suddenly with the memory of a disquieting dream which bothered me so much that I awakened Rob. He sat up, astonished. Neither of us remembered dreams at all.

"I saw Miss Cunningham, of all people," I said. "We were in a hospital. She wore a black suit, and her eyes were terribly red and sore. She was crying, saying over and over, 'Oh dear, I have to go away, and I don't want to go.' There was a glassed-in area to the left in the hospital lobby, where you could buy gifts for the patients. It was all so real."

"Maybe you should write the dream down and date it," Rob said.

This upset me further. "Why? You don't think that it's symbolic or something? Or that it might come true? And why should I even dream of Miss Cunningham? We hardly know her."

"Well, it won't hurt to write the dream down, will it?" Rob asked.

"No," I muttered, "But I had the strangest feeling, as if recording the dream would give it some kind of undue importance. Anyway, I'd rather just forget it," I said. "I wish that I hadn't remembered it at all." But I got sleepily out of bed, wrote the dream down and dated it.

In the morning, I was still upset. Our television set hadn't worked the night before. We didn't have a phone then, so I decided to ask Miss Cunningham if I could use hers to call a repairman. Actually, I thought that if I saw her, hale and hearty as always, I'd feel better. Then, I reasoned, I could just dismiss my dream and forget the whole thing.

The minute I knocked on the door, Miss Cunningham opened it. Her hands reached out for mine, supplicatingly. Usually she was primly polite and rather distant. The change in her manner instantly alarmed me. Startled, I drew back for just a moment before asking what was wrong. "Oh, I'm so glad to see someone," she said. "I'm so upset. I've just learned that I have cataracts, and I'll need operations on both of my eyes. It's so depressing." Her voice wavered. With a gesture of despair, she waved at the floor-to-ceiling bookcases and at the magazines piled on the coffee table. "I read so much . . . so much. What would I ever do if I lost my sight?"

I didn't know what to say because I was still so startled. Her eyes were very red and sore-looking, as they had been in my dream. I stayed with her for a short time, trying to be as comforting as I could. Finally I returned to my own apartment, distressed both because of her condition and the connection with my dream of the night before.

Yet, later in the day, I managed to convince myself that only coincidence was involved. "After all," I said to Rob, "she wasn't wearing black. And we weren't in a hospital. Maybe I just noticed *subconsciously* that her eyes were failing and then made up the dream."

"Maybe. We haven't seen her in nearly a month, though," Rob said.

"Well, it has to be something like that," I said. "I admit that the whole thing is . . . evocative, but it irritates me, too. I mean, think of how much more difficult life could be if we could see the future in dreams? I've got enough to handle as it is."

As the days passed, the dream was more or less forgotten. Only now and then did it nag at me with its disquieting connotations. I felt, uneasily, that a small but significant tear had been ripped in the nature of things. Looking back, I'm sure that I sniffed danger as surely as any animal who senses something strange and new in his environment — or as any adult when threatened by a change in the status quo. So for all general purposes, I put the dream out of my mind and went on my way. I later mentioned this dream in my first book in the field, *How To Develop Your ESP Power*. Even then, I had no idea that it would be only one of a series of psychic events involving Miss Cunningham, nor did I see its true significance in my own development.

Summer passed and autumn had begun before the next experience, one that was to change my life. I awakened one September morning with the feeling that I'd had a most unusual dream during the night, one that would affect me deeply. Yet I had no memory of the dream at all, and as the day went on, the feeling vanished. That night I sat down to write poetry for an hour as usual, and, suddenly, the small rift that had opened so slightly with the first dream now yawned wide open.

I described that experience in *The Seth Material*, but because it rose from the world of dreams and is so connected with unconscious activity, I want to examine it from a different viewpoint here. The Miss Cunningham dream had startled me. This time, I was swept away by the most awe-inspiring event of my life to that date; yet, I was not afraid.

One moment I sat at my desk with my paper and pen beside me. The next instant, my consciousness rushed out of my body, yet it was itself body-less, taking up no space at all; it seemed to be merging with the air outside the window, plunging through the treetops, resting, curled within a single leaf. Exultation and comprehension, new ideas, sensations, novel groupings of images and words rushed through me so quickly there was no time to call out. There was no present, past or future: I knew this, suddenly, irrevocably.

Then, gradually, I became aware that my consciousness was settling back in my body again, but slowly, like dust motes descending through the evening air down to where my body sat upright at the table, head bent, fingers furiously scribbling notes about what was happening as if they had a mind of their own.

But then, as I returned, the intensity of the experience began to fade. The miracle began to withdraw. Three hours in all had passed. I was left with a pile of scribbled notes, written and titled automatically: "The Physical Universe As Idea Construction" — all that was physically salvaged from that remarkable experience. And I knew beyond all doubt that those ideas had been given to me initially in the forgotten dream of the night before.

Since those notes were born so directly from that event, and since they represent the first strong intrusions from the interior universe into my own life, I still find them intriguing. I am looking at them now, as I work on this chapter some five years later. They seemed charged with a fierce vitality that leads me to consider the ambiguous nature of creativity, for if those ideas and the experience itself initiated a new kind of consciousness in me, they also possessed an explosive force powerful enough to considerably dismantle the previous frameworks of my thoughts and ideas. The ordinary surface of my world literally quaked open, and I had no conception then of what was still to emerge.

In *The Seth Material*, I included only a few brief quotes from "The Physical Universe As Idea Construction," but here I will go into that manuscript somewhat more thoroughly, since it is so close to the "raw form" that erupted from that experience and represents, in embryo, I believe, the material that Seth would later be giving us. The manuscript itself consisted of approximately forty pages of scribbled notes written during the height of the experience. Later I wrote fifty more pages as I tried to recapture the feelings and insights I'd had at the time.

I'm including here only some of the passages that were written by my fingers without my knowledge while I was out of my body. To some of my readers these ideas will be far from original. I discovered later that many of them have appeared in "esoteric" manuscripts throughout the centuries, though to me they were not only completely new but also were accompanied by such intense certainty that I would never be able to doubt their validity.

Following are excerpts from "The Physical Universe As Idea Construction." In the original manuscript, this entire portion came to me as definitions.

> **Energy** *is the basis of the universe.*
>
> **Ideas** *are mental transformations of energy by an entity into physical reality.*
>
> **Idea constructions** *are transformations of ideas into physical reality.*
>
> **Space** *is where our own idea constructions do not exist in the physical universe.*
>
> **The physical body** *is the material construction of the entity's idea of itself under the properties of matter.*
>
> **The individual** *is the part of the entity or whole self of which we are conscious in daily life. It is that part of the whole self which we are able to express or make "real" through our idea constructions on a physical level.*
>
> **The subconscious** *is the threshold of an idea's emergence into the individual conscious mind. It connects the entity and the individual.*
>
> **Personality** *is the individual's overall responses to ideas received and constructed. It represents the emotional coloration of the individual's ideas and constructions at any given "time."*
>
> **Emotions** *are the driving force that propel ideas into constructions.*

Instinct *is the minimum ability for idea constructions necessary for physical survival.*

Learning *is the potential for constructing new idea complexes from existing ideas.*

Idea complexes *are groups of ideas formed together like building blocks to form more complicated constructions in physical reality.*

Communication *is the interchange of ideas by entities on the energy nonphysical level.*

Action *is idea in motion. The senses are channels of projection by which ideas are projected outward to create the world of appearances.*

Environment *is the overall idea constructions with which an individual surrounds himself.*

Physical time *is the apparent lapse between the emergence of an idea in the physical universe (as a construction) and its replacement by another.*

The past *is the memory of ideas that were but are no longer physical constructions.*

The present *is the apparent point of any idea's emergence into physical reality.*

The future *is the apparent lapse between the disappearance of one idea construction and its replacement by another in physical reality.*

Psychological time *is the apparent lapse between the conception of ideas.*

Aging *is the effect upon an idea construction of the properties of matter of which the construction is composed.*

Growth *is the formation of an idea construction toward its fullest possible materialization following the properties of matter.*

Sleep *is the entity's relative rest from idea construction except the minimum necessary for physical survival.*

The physical universe *is the sum of individual idea*
constructions.
Memory *is the ghost image of "past" idea constructions.*

Each evolutionary change is preceded and caused by a new
idea. As the idea is in the process of being constructed onto the
physical plane, it prepares the material world for its own
actuality and creates the prerequisite conditions.

Evolution is energy's movement toward conscious expression
in the physical universe, but it is basically nonphysical. A
species at any given time is the materialization of the inner
images or ideas of its individual members, each of whom forms
their own idea constructions.

At no point can we actually say that one construction
vanishes and another takes its place, but artificially we adopt
certain points as past, present and future, for convenience. At
some point, we agree that the physical construction ceases to be
one thing and becomes another, but, actually, it still contains
elements of the "past" construction and is already becoming the
"next" one.

Though the construction of an idea seems to disappear
physically, the idea which it represents still exists.

Sleep is the entity's rest from physical idea construction. Only
enough energy is used to keep the personal image construction
in existence. The entity withdraws into basic energy realms and
is comparatively free from time since idea construction is at a
minimum level. The entity is in contact with other entities at a
subconscious area.

After death, the entity will have its ghost images (memories)
at its command, though their apparent sequence will no longer
apply. Memories are properties of the subconscious energy entity
and, as such, are indestructible (though they may be
unavailable to the individual under various circumstances).

The next plane of existence will involve further training in energy use and manipulation, since the energy of which the entity is composed is self-generating and always seeking more complicated form and awareness.

Each material particle is an idea construction formed by the individualized bits of energy that compose it.

Each entity perceives only his own constructions on a physical level. Because all constructions are more or less faithful reproductions in matter of the same basic ideas (since all individuals are, generally speaking, on the same level in this plane), then they agree sufficiently in space, time and degree so that the world of appearances has coherence and relative predictability.

The Fabric of Physical Matter

All physical matter is idea construction. We only see our own constructions. So-called empty space is full of constructions not our own that we cannot perceive. Our skin connects us to other physical constructions, and through it we are involved in the complicated fabric of continuous matter. The action of each one of the most minute of these particles affects each other one. The slight motion of one grain of sand causes a corresponding alteration in the distribution of the stars and in all matter's fabric, from an atom in a man's skull down to the slightest variation in a microbe's action.

All matter is idea construction, woven together; each construction is individual and yet cohesive to the whole. The smallest particle is necessary to the whole, forming part of matter's design.

The Universe as a Physical Body
(see diagram)

The matter of the universe can be conceived of as a physical body, an organism of individual cells (objects) held together by

connective tissue (the chemicals and elements of air). This
connective tissue is also alive and carries electrical impulses.
Within it, as within the connective tissues of the human body,
there is a certain elasticity, a certain amount of regeneration
and a constant replacement of the atoms and molecules that
compose it. While the whole retains its shape, the material itself
is being constantly born and replaced.

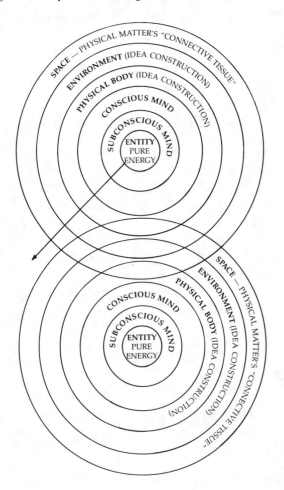

This rough diagram "came" with the above material. It was supposed to represent the energy of the entity as it flowed outward through the subconscious to the conscious, in order to construct the physical image and environment in response to the self's idea of what it was.

I was involved with the "pure" experience behind the diagram and words with which I was left. The revelation was that there were no real boundaries to the self; skin did not separate us from others but connected us in a webwork of energy; what we thought of as Self and Not-Self were interrelated; and that, in this life at least, ideas were constantly being transformed into matter.

Here are some further excerpts from "Idea Construction."

The ability of the entity to transform energy into an idea and then to construct it physically determines the entity's place on the physical evolutionary plane. Simple organisms are capable of "picking up" fewer communications. Their range is less, but the vitality and validity of their constructions is excellent. In simple organisms such as the paramecium and amoeba, the few sharp ideas received are constructed almost simultaneously, without reflection. The organism needs no other mechanism to translate ideas. What it has is sufficient.

More complicated organisms — mammals, for example — have need of further mechanisms to construct ideas because they are able to perceive more of them. Here memory is an element. Now the organism has a built-in ghost image of past constructions by which to perfect and test new ones. Reflection of some sort enters into the picture, and with it the organism is given more to do. Slowly, within its range of receptivity, it is given some choice in the actual construction of ideas into physical reality.

The reflection is brief, but for a moment the animal partakes of a new dimension. The shadow of time glimmers in his eyes as the still imperfected memory of past constructions lingers in his consciousness. As yet, memory storage is small, but now the instantaneous construction is no longer instantaneous, in our terms. There is a pause: the organism — dog or tiger — can choose to attack or not to attack. The amoeba must construct its small world without reflection and without time as we know it.

Entities with still broader range need more complicated structure. The scope of their receptivity is so large that the simple autonomic nervous system is not enough. The amoeba constructs each idea it receives, because it is able to receive so few. All must be constructed to ensure survival. With man, the opposite becomes true. He has such a range of receptivity that it is impossible for him to construct all of his ideas physically. As his scope widened, a mechanism was necessary that would allow him to choose. Self-consciousness and reason were the answers.

Suddenly, time blossomed like a strange flower in his skull. Before this he was transfixed in the present. But memory produced another dimension in the animal and man carried it further. No longer did memory flicker briefly and disappear, enclosing him in darkness again. Now it stretched brightly behind him and also stretched out ahead — a road on which he always saw his own changing image.

He learned continuity. And with his focused memory at his command, man's ego was born, which could follow its own identity through the maze of blazing impulses that beset him, could recognize itself through the pattern of continuing constructions and could separate itself from its action in the physical world. Here you have the birth of subject and object, the I AM who is the doer or constructer, and the construction itself.

This new dimension enabled the species to manipulate and recognize its own constructions and freed it to focus greater energy in projecting some ideas over others. In other words, conscious purpose became possible, physically. Somewhere along *the line, however, man began to divorce himself almost completely and artifically from his own constructions. Hence his groping, his sense of alienation from nature, his search for a Cause or Creator of a creation he no longer recognized as his own.*

It's impossible to describe the impression that this manuscript made on me, much less to verbalize the experience that accompanied it. All of these ideas were completely new to me and quite contrary to my own beliefs. I had never written anything like this before. Rob was painting in his studio at the time. When he came out, I was so excited and amazed that I could hardly speak.

We stayed up late that night, talking. I tried to explain what had happened, realizing for the first time the vast gulf between words and subjective feelings. So I showed Rob the manuscript. Without it, incidentally, I would have been left without any tangible evidence at all. Yet when it was all over, my intellect was on its own again. What did the whole thing mean? I knew beyond all doubt that the ideas I'd received were true, yet, intellectually, they shocked me completely.

Now, seven years later, I realize that this was an excellent example of the ways in which the inner self can suddenly regenerate and revitalize the personality, open up new methods of perception, shatter barriers and flood the personality with energy that sets it right, reorganizing it in more meaningful directions. It is a second birth. Such events are like geysers that erupt suddenly, bringing us close to the center of our being. They come from subjective rather than objective reality, and, in my case at least, they become objectified, their force propelling them into physical actualization.

2

A Note of Subjective Background

The Impetus Behind Unconscious Intrusions

*B*ut what initiated the "Idea Construction" experience? Even when I wrote *The Seth Material*, I didn't clearly understand why it happened or connect it in any way with my previous life or beliefs. It seemed like a complete intrusion. This present book, devoted to dreams and subjective experience, led me into deeper self-examination. In preparation, I reread my own records and poetry. The poetry itself provides a clear record of subjective thoughts and emotions. And it was through reading this old poetry that I found clues that showed me the points of continuity between my life before my psychic initiation and after it.

Looking back, it is obvious that I had unknowingly reached a crisis of development — a crisis that comes to each of us in our early adulthood. The rest of our lives depends upon what happens. Either we grow to a new understanding of the meaningfulness of existence, or we lose much of the force and purpose with which our youth automatically endows us.

I'm including in this chapter a few poems as notes of a subjective autobiography, to show what events triggered this first release of unconscious material on my part, opening the doors to the interior universe; for now I believe that certain personal conditions are characteristic prerequisites for such developments, that the channels of intuitive knowledge are opened according to the intensity of individual need. This need might not be *consciously* recognized, as it was not in my case, but it must be present.

The poems show my attitude toward life in general just before my psychic experiences began. When you see the type of poetry that I was writing then, you will understand immediately why the ideas in "Idea Construction" were such a revelation to me. Incidentally, I considered these poems as aesthetic creations. I made no effort at the time to examine my own subjective states — I simply expressed them as best I could and then criticized the poems on their aesthetic merits. The way I saw life was the way life was! It never occurred to me that my own attitudes had anything to do with it.

These poems were all written in spring and summer of 1963 and concern life in general:

One and One

One and one makes nothing.
Arithmetic destroys us all.
Subtraction is the answer
To our hypothesis.

Morning makes sense
To any animal,
And each one feels
Death's decimal.

We've never learned to add
For all our numbers' worth.
Division and subtraction
Will total up to death.

I remember writing this poem on one of a series of dreary afternoons in which it seemed that life in general had little meaning.

On This Hazy Day

On this hazy, lazy day
All thoughts drop to sudden end,
As if the sullen air
Into itself a puncture drew,
So trees and houses and all we know
Were gently drawn to follow through —
Then quickly, like a holocaust,
A container tipped at end at last —
All our thoughts slide away
Into a hole that time has made.

Rob always enjoyed excellent health, but in 1963 he came down with severe back trouble. Certainly this frightened me and was probably partly responsible for the feelings expressed in the following poem — feelings, I think, that are quite prevalent during early adulthood:

Magic Was

Magic was my middle name,
I was so brave and tall.
No one knew who I was then,
Myself least of all.

I was untouched ten years ago,
By love and even pain.
The world touched me or touched me not.
To me it was the same.

But then the flesh knew it was flesh,
And howled out its defeat,
And I was flamed to life
By vulnerability.

This next is not as good a poem, aesthetically, as the others, but it was written to Rob and clearly shows the growing sense of panic with which I viewed the passing years. I remember writing it — half in tears.

To Rob

Let's cut loose, you and I,
Zig-zag like fools beneath the sky,
Follow the crazy plunging moon
Through secret towns like crying clowns,

See the wide world circus spread
Upon the earth's great sacred ground.
The masks at midnight tumble down
And the great stone faces stare.

Beaches sparkle under stars.
They'll be there for a million years.
Seas leap up in endless waves,
But we live far briefer lives.

Let's cut loose, you and I
Before we grow old and scared,
Too timid to breathe, too fearful to blink,
Too cautious to cross a quiet street.

No magic then will move our blood,
Nor moonlight rush through brittle bone.
Then let us plunge while there is time
Through worlds to look back upon.

In other words, my poetry finally revealed to me my state of mind before "Idea Construction" and Seth. Little by little, using it as a guide, other memories came back to me — all trivial in comparison to real tragedy and yet, to me, bitterly depressing. The death of a kitten that year led me to write:

Death came in and took my cat
And passed right by my dog.
He chased her through the living room
Over the woolen rug.
I sat right there and never knew.
I sat right there and never saw.

A small household tragedy, the death of a cat, yet to me it contained the question of the uniqueness of life and the value of consciousness. Didn't anyone or anything care that one cat had died? I felt guilty even considering the question. In a world where humans slaughtered their own kind constantly, who in their right mind would give a moment's thought to a cat's consciousness? Yet either all life was sacred, or none of it was. So I brooded.

And when I looked around me, it seemed that for all of man's good intentions, he only transmitted the errors of his race; that each man or woman unknowingly perpetuated the peculiar sins and failings of their families. I wrote one of my most pessimistic of poems:

Old Hates

Old hates lie in wait for the infant
As he grows into a man,
Then they leap upon him
When he puts his father's coat on.
When the father's bones drop into the grave,
The lice flock up as the dark earth falls
To feed on a son's guilt love.

No man can look in his son's face,
What was done to him he does in turn,
For he carries the hate in his blood.
Ghosts of days forgotten,
Tragedies unseen, unspoken,
Wait in the past's proud flesh,
And nothing can shake them off.

And en masse, for the race, I saw only one answer:

The Terms

I dig my own grave
With dignity.
We are all gone.
There is nothing else to say.

Doom was a toy ball.
We toss it high
And laughed to see
The rockets rise.

Our ashy laugh
Scattered over the countryside.
We never understood
The terms.

Now I remember that spring, recall sitting at my desk writing poetry, caught up in a feeling that nature was betraying us all with its promise of hope and renewal. It was almost mechanical, I thought, as if some second-hand god kept reusing the same leaves each year, over and over again, and we were too childish to see beneath the subterfuge.

Yet that same May, while I was writing the most pessimistic of poetry, I also remember a break in my mood, a quickening of spirit that was reflected in two poems of quite a different nature. The first was written on my birthday.

Birthday

I shall never be adult
But I am growing wise
Like some crazy holy child
With ghosts inside its head.

At midnight I rush to the river's edge.
I'd bay at the moon if I could.
And fish and birds and sky and sand
Cascade in a splash in my blood.

My fingers are leaves that rustle and drop.
Birds fly through the eyes of my skull.
Clouds float atop my spinning head
And stars burn the moons of my toes.

Mountains and hillsides cut through my arm.
Rivers fly past my pulse
Generations of ghosts laugh at my talk
While my tissues burn and go up in smoke.

Two days later, I sat at my desk, idly watching the sunshine on my bare arm, and was suddenly astonished by the miracle of skin. I wrote the following poem which is mentioned later by Seth as an indication of the inner knowledge that was almost ready to burst into consciousness.

Skin

Though this criss-crossed fleshmesh
Tastes like peach and feels like peach fuzz,
All utterly mergings of gold and green and red,
Sunnily rendered, dizzy and delicious,
Still, touching it with eyes is like peering
Through a fence
With wires cunningly connected,
A million to an inch.

The wind on the arm blows the hair,
And at the base, a golden mole,
Such a speck as a peach might have,
But the hair arches back to show a gaping hole,

And each ounce of flesh is a fence,
Erected roundly and snug
About hidden landscapes, suns, and shadows,
Inroads laced with prickly shrubs.
Peer through. The holes are not big enough to see much,
But dreams travel wondrous wires.
Fires brighter than autumn moons
Throw leaping shadows on the arm.
Days and nights burn like stars
In the twinkling meadows of the skull,
And through the fence of peach-blooming flesh,
Other fruits blossom, beyond reach.

I think that my "Idea Construction" experience was initiated, then, at least in part, by the need that is apparent in these poems. The last two show early indications of emerging intuitive knowledge. I believe that I had gone as far as my intellect and normal creativity could take me and that new channels were opened when I needed them most. Generally, I think, these other channels open when we have ceased to rely upon most of the answers that have been given to us by others and found wanting. (Along these lines, I wonder if tranquilizers often cut us off from such intuitive breakthroughs by preventing us from coming to grips with the true "darkness of soul" that can precede such experiences and by allowing us to accept temporary, objective and artificial solutions.)

I suppose that the "Idea Construction" experience could have gradually faded from memory, losing much of its vitality if the manuscript did not exist as a constant reminder; but this is difficult to imagine. Instead, the theories were made manifest in my life, becoming facts of my existence. I never would have been able to accept Seth and the sessions without that initial introduction to nonphysical information. That experience, then, led to the sessions and to this book, containing enough energy and motive force not only to change my life but also to affect the experience of others.

I have dealt with this extensively here because creative, unconscious energy is so often a part of the dream state. Apparently, in my case at that time, the "intrusive" unconscious material had to be propelled through to my consciousness during my waking state, since I never regained memory of the initial dream in which the information was originally given.

Time and time again, the inner centers of our being come to our aid through subjective promptings — either in waking, dream or trance states. Through the dream experiences related later in this book, this will become quite clear. Dreams, inspirations, experiences in mystic consciousness — all, I believe, have their prime source outside of our usual consciousness and mode of activity.

This book is concerned mainly with dreams, but it will also stress the true mobility of our consciousness which makes possible dreaming (and astral projections) and those unconscious abilities that are so vital to our functioning.

At the time of the "Idea Construction" experience, the Seth sessions themselves were undreamed of, of course. So while this book is devoted to Seth's theories on the nature of dreams and his instructions on their use, it is not meant to be a definitive statement. Seth continues to deliver material on dreams, along with other subjects. Those of you who want a more general idea of Seth's views can refer to *The Seth Material*. Here, I'll give the material on dreams as it was given to us in succeeding sessions — particularly in the early part of the book. This automatically presents the material in order, preserving the sense of continuity, and serves as a progressive, subjective journal of dream experiences as Rob and I, and later my students, followed Seth's suggestions. This method of presentation also gives the reader a built-in opportunity to try the experiments for himself, just as Seth gave them to us as we went along.

Before Seth began a discussion of dreams, and as a preliminary, he explained the natural mobility of human consciousness and outlined the main features of the "interior universe" that could be glimpsed in both waking and dream states and which underlie physical reality. This introduction offers a natural pathway into the area of dreams (part of the interior universe) and to the other states of consciousness possible within the dream framework. The first portion of this book will therefore deal with this material and with our first explorations into that inner reality.

3

The Introduction of Seth

Further Steps into the Interior Universe

*D*uring the rest of that September in 1963, I reread the "Idea Construction" manuscript many times, trying to understand it and hoping to recapture some of the feelings I had had during its delivery. Now and then, flashing insights came to me in response, but more often than not, I just sat there, frustrated. My intellect just could not get beyond certain points, and I knew it.

Suddenly, however, I entered a period of intense creative activity, ending a dry spell that had lasted for nearly a year. Ideas for poetry, in particular, came so quickly that I hardly had time to write them down. It wasn't too difficult to trace most of these to the "Idea Construction" manuscript. Also, I began a new book.

Because of the Miss Cunningham dream and the "Idea Construction" experience, Rob suggested that I try some experiments in ESP and expansion of consciousness and do a book on the results — negative or positive. Those of you who read my two other books in this field know that the experiments were astonishingly

successful and led, through the Ouija board, to our first contact
with Seth.

I have described those early sessions elsewhere, but here I'm
including, instead, a poem that is a dramatic, intuitive statement
about my feelings at the time. Actually, several episodes are condensed into one in the poem. Seth didn't really announce himself
until we had worked with the Ouija board four times. And it was
in the middle of the eighth session that I began to speak for him.
Almost from the beginning, however, I did anticipate what the
board was going to "say," and the poem is as valid as any strictly
factual statement I could make about those sessions — if not more
so.

The Visitor

We tried the Ouija board one night,
My husband Rob and I.
The cat sat on the bright blue rug.
Hot coffee bubbled on the stove.

"This thing will never work," I said.
"We must be out of our minds,"
But we weren't, at least not yet.
The cat smiled but didn't say anything.

Then the little pointer moved,
As if a thousand molecules grew legs,
And carried it upon their backs,
Lightning-fast across the board.

"You're moving it," I shouted.
"Hon, that isn't fair."
"What a riot." I tried to laugh.
"I'm not doing it," Rob said.

"You may call me Seth," the letters spelled.
Rob looked up but didn't speak.

The cat strolled about in the warm lamplight.
"The coffee must be done," I cried.

I ran into the kitchen. "Do you want some now?"
Rob shook his head.
"There's something that wants you back at the board.
You'd better sit down again."

I stared at him. He meant it.
I knew him well enough to know.
I said as defiantly as I could, "It's only a game.
Besides, we don't know any Seth."

But my mind felt crowded out of itself,
By thoughts not its own,
As if someone were settling down in my skull
That I hadn't invited in.

Then my visitor sat with my husband,
And smiled out through my eyes at the cat.
With me out of the way, he seemed quite at home.
"Good evening. I'm Seth," my lips spoke.
He began walking my body about
As if getting accustomed to arms and legs.
I'd never been so astonished,
To be locked out of myself like that.

But he was benign and jovial as a bishop
Someone might ask in for an evening of tea,
And when he let me peek out through his eyes,
The familiar living room seemed very strange.

Now as seasons come and go,
He visits twice a week,
From worlds that have no wind or snow,
But still have promises to keep.

Actually, the board first gave a few messages from a personality called Frank Withers, who insisted that he had known our neighbor, Miss Cunningham. I didn't take this very seriously at first, but he also said that he knew an elderly woman who worked with me at the local art gallery where I had a part-time job. When questioned, this woman told me that she *had* known such a man, though he had merely been an acquaintance.

This was enough to send me to Miss Cunningham's apartment, hoping to bring up the name in conversation. (I wasn't about to tell anyone about the Ouija board messages.) It struck me odd, also, that Miss Cunningham would be in any way connected with our Ouija activities. This tie-in immediately reminded me of the July dream, of course.

It was the first time Miss Cunningham and I had really talked together in some time, and I was shocked by the change in her. Her hair was unkept. She plucked nervously at her dress. As she spoke, she would suddenly stop in the middle of a sentence, begin to hum a tune and then would forget what she had said. The next moment, she would be herself again. Then the cycle began all over.

"Did you ever know a Frank Withers?" I asked finally. "His name came up the other day. Someone said you knew him."

"Withers? Withers?" She said. "Hum." And off she went into a little tune.

"Frank Withers," I said, feeling guilty at disturbing her.

"Yes. Yes." Her voice trailed off, disappeared and returned. "I had many students by that name . . . there were several . . ."

I waited for more.

"What were we saying? Did you want something? How nice to see you," she said brightly. But already, the opaqueness was ready to settle back, so I knew it was useless. Disquieted, I returned to my apartment.

As the days passed, I was nervously aware of her, wandering through the hallways, and made it a point to look in on her now and then. But we were so taken up with our own affairs that I saw her infrequently.

It was a strange time. The assassination of JFK took place just after our sessions began. The familiar physical world did not seem to be a very secure place. The old ways of thought were bringing appalling fruits. An uneasy December followed — bitter and dreary and discouraging on the national scene — and locally the weather was dark, with snow piled high. And yet, inside our small, lighted living room, we both felt we were making important inroads, gaining invaluable insights and finding a point of sanity amid a chaotic world.

In the meantime, we held our board sessions twice a week. By the time I returned from the art gallery on those winter afternoons, it was already dark. After supper, I did the dishes and worked on my poetry for an hour, and then Rob got out the board. Often these sessions lasted until midnight. Rob took verbatim notes from the beginning. Most of the first ten sessions dealt with reincarnation and included some fascinating material on Rob's family.

"They're great tales," I said.

"I notice we've been using the insights about my parents and relating to them better than we ever did before," Rob said.

"Sure . . . glad to," I said. "And reincarnation is a terrific theory to play around with. Remember my first published short story, "Red Wagon," in *Fantasy and Science Fiction*? It was based on reincarnation. But that doesn't mean that I believe in it, or think it's true or fact."

"Maybe underneath you knew it was true even then," Rob said.

"Oh, Hon," I retorted, with uneasy and quite unconscious scorn. So the early sessions intrigued me, but, intellectually, I couldn't accept reincarnation. Interestingly enough, reincarnation wasn't a part of the "Idea Construction" experience. *Those* ideas were imbedded in me so thoroughly that I would never doubt them.

By now, we were also trying other experiments for my book, which I was writing during the mornings. And in our 12th Session Seth gave what I still think of as a cornerstone that served as a preliminary framework upon which the rest of *The Seth Material* would be built. I have quoted parts of it in other books, yet the analogy Seth gave us is such an excellent introduction to the interior universe and to his ideas that it is almost indispensable. Each time I read it, I gain new insights.

I had only begun speaking for Seth a few sessions earlier. Before the eighth session, all replies came through the board. The whole thing seemed so wild to me. "Just turning into someone else like that!" I used to say. The session was held on the evening of January 2, 1964 and lasted three hours. We locked the door and closed the blinds but always left the lights on for the sessions. We began this one with the Ouija board, but after only a few moments, I shoved it aside and began dictating as Seth. Here is a brief excerpt from that twelfth session:

As far as fifth dimension is concerned, I have said that it is space. I will have to try to build up the image of a structure to help you understand, but then I must rip down the structure because there is none there.

Consider, then, a network of wires somewhat like, though different from, Jane's conception of "Idea Construction" — a maze of interlocking wires endlessly constructed, so that looking through them there would seem to be no beginning or end. Your plane could be likened to a small position between four very spindly and thin wires, and my plane could be likened to the small position in the neighboring wires on the other side.

Not only are we on different sides of the same wires, but we are at the same time either above or below, according to your viewpoint. And if you consider the wires as forming cubes . . . then the cubes could also fit one within the other, without disturbing the inhabitants of either cube one iota — and these cubes are also within cubes, which are themselves within cubes, and I am speaking now only of the small particle of space taken up by your plane and mine.

Again, now think in terms of your plane, bounded by its small spindly set of wires, and my plane on the other side. These, as I have said, have also boundless solidarity and depth, yet in usual terms, to one side the other is transparent. You cannot see through, but the two planes move through each other constantly.

I hope you see what I have done here. I have initiated the idea of motion, for true transparency is not the ability to see through but to move through. This is what I mean by fifth dimension. Now remove the structure of the wires and cubes. Things behave as if the wires and cubes were there, but these are only constructions necessary, even to those on my plane, in order to make this comprehensible to our faculties, the faculties of any entity.

We merely construct imaginary lines to walk upon. So real are the wall constructions of your room that you would freeze in the winter time without them, yet there is no room and no walls. So, in a like manner, the wires that we constructed are real to us in the universe, although . . . to me, the walls are transparent. So are the wires that we constructed to make our point about the fifth dimension, but for all practical purposes, we must behave as if the wires were there . . .

Again, if you will consider our maze of wires, I will ask you to imagine them filling up everything that is, with your plane and my plane like two small birds nests in the netlike fabric of some gigantic tree . . . Consider, for example, that these wires are also mobile, constantly trembling and also alive, in that they not only carry the stuff of the universe but are themselves projections of this stuff, and you will see how difficult it is to explain. Nor can I blame you for growing tired when after asking you to imagine this strange structure, I then insist that you tear it apart, for it is no more actually seen or touched than is the buzzing of a million invisible bees.

"Let me read you some of the material you just dictated," Rob said, and he read several pages. (Only a few excerpts were given here.)

"It makes more sense to me than anything I've ever read," I said. "But where did it come from? Now, in my ordinary state of consciousness, I can only appreciate it or even criticize it. The source is gone."

"Is it?" Rob asked. "Or do you only permit it freedom — with great caution and under certain definite conditions?"

When he said things like that, I'd get upset, and the familiar living room seemed strange. The table, chairs, the couch and rug looked satisfyingly normal in the warm lamplight. Yet I felt these shapes were highly significant, only intrusions of other realities that were invisible but always active.

"If you were doing this instead of me," I said, "you'd be cautious too."

But Rob only grinned. "Would I?"

During all of this time, Rob and I were having our first experiences with mobility of consciousness. What else could consciousness do? What could mine do? The questions filled me with wonder, and we tried all kinds of experiments.

One of the most fascinating was an experiment we tried alone one night. I'm including Rob's notes of it to give you an idea of the various things we were trying. I'm convinced that this sort of exercise is most valuable in that it helped to shake our consciousness out of its usual focus in objective, ego-oriented reality.

For me, the episode was amazingly vivid, the scenes clear and bright in my mind's eye. It was something like attending an inner movie. (Or, someone might say, like dreaming vividly while awake.) But, for me, then, it was simply a completely new state of consciousness and awareness, a psychological experience like none I'd known before.

I'm rather embarrassed now by the fact that we turned the lights off, since our sessions and classes are always conducted in normal light. In those days, though, we didn't know how to proceed, and we had read that such affairs were conducted in near-darkness. Rob and I sat at my wooden table with only a small electric candle lit. After quite some time, I began to see pictures, and as Rob took notes, I spoke aloud in my own voice, describing what I was seeing and experiencing. This was the resulting monologue:

"I see the name: Sarah Wellington. She was in a cobbler's shop . . . It was 1748 in England. There were huge cowhides hanging up in the back room of the cobbler's shop and dried cowhides hanging in another room. It was very cold in there, where the first cowhides were. It wasn't ventilated, and there were no windows.

"There were windows in the front room, though, and benches and a stone floor. It was a stone house with a fireplace; September, damp and foggy in the afternoon, about four o'clock. Sarah Wellington was blond. She had stringy hair. She wasn't very pretty, but bony. She was seventeen.

"Her parents weren't there, and Sarah didn't live there either!"

I paused. Rob waited for a few moments, wondering whether or not to interrupt me. Finally, he asked quietly, "Where did she live?"

"Three doors away."

"How long did she live?" he asked.

I paused again. Then I saw the whole thing very clearly, and I said, excited: "She died, at seventeen, there in the cobbler's shop. She died from burns. The cobbler came out of the back room, and there she was, all in flames and screaming. He shoved her out into the street and rolled her over and over on the stones and in the dirt; but she died.

"She . . . she lived three doors down the street, in a dark front room. She had two brothers, one off someplace; he was a sailor. The other was younger. Sarah's father did something for the cobbler, and, in return, he made shoes for the younger brother, and Sarah was in the shop to get them."

Another pause. "What?" Rob said. "Can you make that clearer?"

"It was a craft," I said. "Something Sarah's father bartered for the shoes . . . something to do with fishing nets. The village was right by the sea. The cobbler's shop was the only one around, though there were other villages. Sarah's father made fishnets out of seaweed, dried seaweed. They wove it together like rope, then made the nets.

"The fishermen had plain wooden boats and piles of fish on a good day. Black fish, some of them only a few inches long, some much longer, averaging maybe a foot in length. There was fishing all year long. It wasn't seasonal. The water was warm in the winter. That's why it was so foggy. They didn't farm too much because the ground was poor and rocky, very hilly; so they depended on fish."

"Do you know the name of the village?" Rob asked.

I had been seeing everything that I'd been describing, and now the name just appeared in my head. "Levonshire. It was fewer than three hundred people, on the northeast coast of England. The people also got some of their food from another village further north. For some reason, the land was better there."

I kept seeing more. I would think that I was telling Rob about each scene as I saw it, but then he would ask a question, and I'd realize that I hadn't said a word for some time.

"What crops did they grow?" he asked, and I tried to rouse myself enough to keep on speaking while still retaining focus on these strange shifting scenes.

"I see tomatoes, but even as I say it, it seems to me once that I read that people didn't eat tomatoes in those days. But yes, the people in the small villages did; and wheat and barley. They had cows.

"The cobbler was an old man. He was also the sexton of a small church, the Church of England. He used to ring the bells. His wife was fifty-three, Anna. She wore glasses and had grayish white hair and was very stout and messy.

"There was a boy in the shop, too — not their son, an apprentice to the cobbler. He slept in the kitchen. His name was Albert Lang. He was eleven, I think. The cobbler and his wife had no children.

She had trouble with her glasses . . . most people didn't wear any. They were handmade; they had to grind the glass. They were like magnifying glasses, in a frame on her nose . . .

"The cobbler was comparatively well off, though not wealthy. He was fifty-three when he died. The boy, Albert, was too young to take over the shop, and for a couple of years the village had no cobbler, and the boy was a fisherman. Then another cobbler came and Albert helped out in the shop again . . . He finally married. His wife's name was also Sarah. She was a cousin of Sarah Wellington's. Most of the people in the village were related in one way or another; they had no other place to go."

I stopped speaking again for a few minutes. I don't know if my eyes were open or closed, and, in any case, the room was so dark that Rob could just manage to see in order to make notes. All I saw were the vivid places and people, and I spoke in jerky quick sentences, sometimes with no effort to make complete sentences.

"What do you see now?" Rob asked.

"The main street."

I laughed out loud, because I saw it so clearly. "I see houses and a couple of shops, then a narrow cobbled walk raised up high — it was a partly dirt road built up of rocks and stones that ran around an inlet from the sea. But it was never flooded; the road kept the village dry. There wasn't any sandy beach, though."

"Would you know it if you saw it in physical life now? If you took a trip to England?" Rob asked.

"No. It's not there now. I don't think I'd know the spot. It was just this little inlet, with the rocky hills and not much grass. It wasn't a seaport. Big ships couldn't get in close. There was just enough room for the little boats to go out for fish . . ."

My inner gaze traveled up the hills beyond the village. I felt myself climbing. But Rob interrupted: "How far was it from London?"

And suddenly I "knew" the answer and saw a dark landscape from above. There were other flurries of images that I also described.

"It was two days overland by stage, two days by horseback. They made about twenty miles a day. They didn't like to travel after dark. It was too dangerous; there were too many robbers. So they always stayed at an inn that was about halfway there. It was called Sedgewick. They'd get there by the evening of the first day.

"In the inn there was a huge fireplace. Their dishes were made of earthenware. They had ale . . . it was served with meals. Their meat was ribs — mutton ribs — and something called 'braunsweiger.' They had bread . . . barley bread and soup . . . fish soup and mussels. They didn't have salt. They had beans; I don't know what kind.

"They always carried pistols. The pistols were black and long, much longer than pistols today. There was a jigger at the top that they kept powder in — I don't know what for."

Suddenly I started laughing. I was seeing this pistol very clearly. But I have absolutely no interest in guns and no knowledge of them at all, so it was difficult to explain how the pistol was made. I didn't know the names of the parts. It seemed incongruous that I could have a "vision" of such a simple object and then not have the vocabulary to describe it.

Yet I seemed to know everything about the gun. Part of me was aware of the strangeness of the situation and of the flickering candlelight in which Rob was furiously taking notes. But another part of my consciousness was focused on the gun, and I was intent upon describing it as well as possible.

"They . . . they made bullets and put powder into them. The powder and bullets were kept separate until they were put into the gun, though one or two bullets were always kept ready. They saved the bullets if they could find them, after firing. The metal was hard to get. The guns were awfully heavy. These bullets were something new. They didn't last; they stopped making them. For some reason I don't understand, the bullets might explode. The men didn't want to keep the powder and bullets together. Sometimes the powder was rusty and sometimes whitish. They were big bullets — one of the reasons the guns were so large.

"The people didn't go to London often. Some never went at all.

The first Sarah, who died at seventeen, never went. Albert's Sarah went. King Edward was in London then. Albert and Sarah did well and could afford to go. When Edward was crowned, they made the trip. They didn't see the coronation. She was forty-one and he was forty-six at the time. They had two or three children. I don't know what happened to them.

"Albert liked to hunt, but he couldn't get much because the ground was too rocky . . . deer and rabbits, a special kind of rabbit, no big tails, gray hares of some kind. And there were gray squirrels."

Then the images dispersed, and for a very brief moment, there seemed to be a gray fog, and through it I seemed to see the town in a still more distant past. "The town had been there for at least 350 years. I told you the name before — Levonshire. Before that, it had a different name. . . .

"There were invasions. A lot of them came along that coast earlier, the Norsemen and, I guess, the Gauls. The Gauls looked French, swarthy; and they were little men. Everyone knows what the Norsemen looked like. . . ."

Then suddenly, I was back again, seeing the later time. "In London, I don't know why, Albert's wife liked to go to the bakery shops. They had fancier breads there than in the village. And Sarah . . . the first one . . . if she hadn't burned to death, she would have died anyhow at seventeen, of tuberculosis. One lung was bad. It was a bad place to live. The village wasn't sunny, and they kept the windows closed. There weren't many windows anyway. The land was so rocky . . . and they would build a house on a slab of rock, and it was always damp. . . . Sarah's dress was dirty. It was woolen, a brown natural color because it wasn't dyed. It wouldn't have burned so, but it had grease on it, and the grease caught the flames. . . ."

I shivered, seeing the dress catch fire and watching once again as the cobbler rolled the girl out to the street, beating at the flames. Then I seemed to be above the town again, looking down, but dimly. "The descendants of the invaders lived in the village too. There was the Laverne family, and De Nauge, and the Breims. They slept on hay. It was so damp and goffy, and the hay was never dry . . ."

I was quiet again. Rob didn't know exactly what to do, so he just asked the first question that came into his head. "Were the people happy?"

"That's a silly question," I retorted, but with a great impartiality; it didn't seem that it was me replying at all. "They were as happy as anyone else then. They didn't like their babies dying, but they just thought that . . . that was life. They drank a lot. Most of them couldn't read. Well, the sexton could some, not much. People didn't think it was necessary. They didn't have books, so what good did it do to learn to read?

"A few could write their names, but usually they couldn't read other people's names. . . . They didn't have water to drink. There was salt in the ocean — that's why they washed there. But they thought that drinking water was unhealthy. It was hilly and rocky behind the village, but there was a stream up there, and they went up with horses and buckets. But they didn't drink the water. They drank ale. They made soups from the water, though, and they were lucky that the stream came down from a high place. Otherwise they'd have had to dig down too far.

"They boiled the water for soups; this killed a lot of germs, so they were actually healthier than other communities who had more water, since a good deal of it was polluted. They used natural liquids from animals when they made stews."

I stopped. Suddenly all of it was gone. I told Rob, and he switched the lights on.

"That was something!" I said. "Did I somehow go back in space and time, or did I hallucinate the entire episode?"

"What did it feel like? What do you think about it?"

"I don't know," I said. "I saw so much, so clearly. And I seemed to change position in the air or in space, though I knew I was here, in this room. Could I have seen an old movie when I was a child, forgotten it, and then hallucinated scenes from it, all without knowing?"

"It's certainly possible," Rob said. "Even that would show the mind's fantastic abilities. But I have something to tell you, too. Just before you got started, I had a vision of my own."

"Why didn't you tell me?" I asked.

"I couldn't. Just as it vanished, you started to go into the English thing."

"Well, what did you see?"

"Well. I saw the . . . feet of a man. He was walking along a flat, dusty, reddish road. I think he was barefoot, though now I wonder about some kind of rudimentary sandal. He had a brownish, long robe flapping about the calves of his legs. The legs were thin."

"What was his face like?" I asked.

Rob grinned. "I couldn't see his head, shoulders, or even waist. The land was very flat — reds and browns. There was nothing in the far distance on the left, beyond the feet. For a moment, though, I thought I saw a group of pyramids far ahead on the horizon to the right. They were in cool brilliant color, blues or greens. I couldn't see the bases of these, though, and I'm not even sure they were pyramids. But I saw the soles of the man's feet, wrinkled and brown and, yes, without shoes, lifting after each stride. They were covered with dust."

"My experience was great," I said. "But it was something like a moving picture I was looking at from some crazy angle. The scenes would change too. I'd be looking at that main street, and then suddenly I'd be in the hills beyond the village. Not really there like I'm in this room now . . . but . . . partially floating. Very dim at times. But your vision was quicker, more limited, but very precise."

"I'm going to do a sketch or painting of it," Rob said. "The colors were terrific."

"Do you know who the man was?" I asked.

"I'll ask Seth," Rob said, smiling. "Or maybe he wasn't anyone."

"I wonder if my town was real. To me it was . . ."

"Then isn't that enough for now?" Rob said. I nodded; at the very least there was enough material for a good short story on the whole thing, I thought. Yet the village and the scenes lingered in my memory. "We've only been involved in this stuff a little over a month," I said. "I'm content for now. But we're going to have to try and check some of this out if it keeps on."

"We will. Don't worry about that. In the meantime, it is what it is," Rob said.

"Yeah . . . but is it what it is, like Willie our cat is?"

Rob began to laugh. "That's part of the fun of it," he said. "Finding out."

4

My First Glimpse of Dream Reality

A Blundering Trance

Two Fugitives from the Dream World

Seth did mention Rob's vision in the next (thirteenth) session on January 6, 1964. We began this one with the Ouija board. Rob said, aloud: "Seth, can you tell me anything about the vision I had two nights ago?"

The pointer spelled out *LOREN, THE MAN WAS A MONK ON A PIL-GRIMAGE.*

"My brother, Loren? Where was he traveling to?"

HE WAS ON HIS WAY TO THE HOLY LANDS. HIS SHOES HAD BEEN STOLEN AS HE SLEPT. THE BUILDINGS YOU SAW WERE NOT PYRAMIDS BUT THE RUINS OF MONASTERIES IN THE DISTANCE.

"In what land was this?" Rob asked.

The pointer replied: *ASIA WAS WHERE YOU SAW HIM, THOUGH HE WAS IN MANY OTHER PLACES, TRAVELING IN HIS MIDDLE YEARS, DO-ING PENANCE FOR HIS SINS ACCORDING TO THE CUSTOMS OF THE AGE.*

"Was I alive then?" Rob asked.

NO.

"Will you tell us what mental enzymes are? You mentioned them once before in a past session. I guess I'd rather learn more about that right now," Rob said.

Now, as Seth, I shoved the board aside and began to dictate:

As mental genes are behind the physical genes, so to speak, so are mental enzymes behind the physical stuff you can examine on your plane. Chlorophyll is such a mental enzyme, and there are more which I will describe to you at a later date.

In a sense, any color or quality of that nature could be considered a mental enzyme. There is an exchange of sorts between the mental and physical without which, for example, color could not exist. I use color here as an example because it is perhaps easier to understand how this could be a mental enzyme than it is to perceive the same thing about chlorophyll. Chlorophyll is green in more than color, incidentally.

Nevertheless, there is an interaction here which gives chlorophyll its properties. I hope to make this clearer to you, but it involves part of a larger concept for which you do not now have the proper background. . . . Chlorophyll is a mental enzyme, however, and it is one of the moving forces in your plane. A variant exists in all other planes. It is a mental spark, so to speak, that sets everything else into motion.

This also has to do with feeling, which is also a mover. You must try not to categorize things in old ways, but when you open your mind, you will see a similarity between chlorophyll, as a mental enzyme or mover, and emotion which is never still. Emotion 'solidified' is something else again and is perhaps a framework of other worlds. . . .

And really, Jane, you're giving your subconscious an awful lot of credit. Let's see credit where credit is due. I suggest you take your break.

Rob laughed at the remark about my subconscious, but instead of giving us our rest period, Seth went on for a moment:

Perhaps I may be able to make mental enzymes clearer. . . .
In your own experience, you are familiar with steam, water
and ice. These are all manifestations of the same thing. So can
a seemingly physical chlorophyll be also a part of a seemingly
immaterial emotion or feeling, but in a different form — and,
of course, directed into this form or caused to take various forms
in response to certain laws — as your ice will not exist of itself
in the middle of your summertime. And if I am not to be
compared to a symphony, Joseph, you must admit that I do
well with a figurative baton.

Here, we took our break. Rob always enjoyed Seth's sense of
humor, and he was still smiling at the last remark when I came out
of trance. "He called me Joseph again," he said.

"Serves you right," I said, grinning. Seth referred to me as Ruburt and to Rob as Joseph, saying that these were our entity
names. The entity is the whole self who experiences many reincarnations. I didn't like either name too well, so we used to joke
about them. We didn't have time to say much, however, because
Seth came back in about ten minutes. During the break, Rob had
made a remark about solidified emotion, and Seth began by saying:

Why do you find the phrase 'solidified emotion or feeling'
outlandish? You both understand now that your plane is
composed of solidified thought. When your scientists get
through with all their high fiddle-faddle, they will also discover
that this is the case.
When I told you earlier to imagine the wire structure
penetrating everything that is, I meant you to imagine these
wires as being alive, as I am a live wire myself. Joking aside, I
will now ask you to imagine these wires as being composed of

the solidified emotion of which I have just spoken. Surely you must know that the words feeling or emotion are, at best, symbols to describe something else, and that something else comes extremely close to your mental enzymes.

Actually, a counter-action within a mental enclosure occurs. A mental enclosure divides itself in two, splits up, multiplies, acts upon its own various parts, and this produces a material manifestation. The 'material' is material, yet it is mentally produced. The mental enzymes within the enclosure are the elements that set off the action, and — listen to this — they are also the action itself.

In other words, the mental enzymes not only produce action in the material world, but they become the action. If you will read over the above three or four paragraphs, you will come close to seeing where mental and physical become one.

You both know what love and hate are, but as I told you earlier, try to think in new ways. Love and hate, for example, are action. They are action and they both imply action in physical bodies . . .

These mental enzymes, to go back to them, are solidified feeling, but not in the terms that you usually use . . . I have said that our imaginary wires that seem to permeate our model universe are alive; and now if you bear with me, I will say that they are mental enzymes or solidified feelings, always in motion, and yet permanent enough to form a more or less consistent framework. You could almost say that mental enzymes become the tentacles that form material — though I do not find that a very pretty phrase . . .

The framework, again, is only for convenience, as your physical walls are for your convenience, as I mentioned earlier. The walls are not there as such, but you had better act as if they were or suffer a possible broken neck. I must still respect many like frameworks in my own plane, but my understanding of them renders them less . . . opaque. . . .

Intellectual truth will not make you free, you see, though it is a necessary preliminary. If this were the case, your walls would fall away, since, intellectually, you understand their rather dubious nature. Since feeling is so often the cohesive with which mind builds, it is feeling itself which must be changed if you would find freedom from your particular plane of existence at your particular time. That is, changing feeling will allow you to see variants . . . These discussions now are, of necessity, of a simple and uncomplicated nature. If I speak in analogies and images, it is because I must relate with the world that is familiar to you.

This session actually lasted from 9:00 P.M. until midnight, so only excerpts have been given here. The material on mental enzymes intrigued us. Looking back, we can see what a chore it must have been for Seth to introduce us to ideas that were very basic — to him — and quite new to us. Much later, he was to give some excellent material on the nature of physical matter and its "mental" components. But at the time of this session, he told us all we could understand, while he began slowly to build up the necessary background and concepts.

The sessions had begun on December 2, 1963. This was still only the middle of January of 1964. We were trying other experiments on our own, some like the example given earlier, some entirely different. Mornings, I worked on my book. Afternoons were spent at the gallery. If it wasn't a session night, after dinner and an hour's poetry, we tried other experiments. Rob spent a good deal of time typing the sessions, as he still does. He couldn't do much more without cutting down on his own painting hours, so I often did experiments on my own while he was in the studio.

By now, we were both convinced that the human mind or consciousness had abilities and methods of perception far beyond those we had thought possible. If this was the case, then my consciousness possessed these potentials, and I was determined to discover their nature and extent. I never considered them supernormal, or rather, supernatural. On the other hand, it never occurred to me that there was any other way to study consciousness except by studying my own — a journey into subjectivity seemed, and still seems, as valid as a journey into objectivity.

Because we were so innocent about psychic literature, we weren't hampered by superstitious fears about such phenomena. I didn't believe in gods or demons, so I didn't fear them. I wanted to learn. Rob and I had discovered a whole new world together, and we were going to explore it.

There was a constant battle, though, as some of our results ran full tilt into my intellectual ideas. In the beginning, I took it for granted that Seth was a subconscious fantasy, personified, because I simply couldn't accept the possibility of "spirits" or, for that matter, life after death. Then, after it became obvious that the Seth sessions were going to continue, we kept constant check on my personality characteristics and went to a psychologist — as any sane, red-blooded American would do under such circumstances in those days. Seth seemed far more mature and well-balanced than the psychologist, so finally I stopped worrying. Besides, my personality showed no adverse signs of instability. If anything, I was more competent in handling physical affairs. This is not to say that the experience did not cause certain strains and stresses that could accompany any worthwhile venture in an entirely new field.

One episode in particular is funny in retrospect — looking back it was certainly undisciplined — but at least it was not overshadowed by superstitious fears about demons; and it led to the episode with which I will close the first portion of this book. The event was a deep trance experience into which I blundered. A second experience convinced me of the high validity of dream existence, for in it a dream was split open while I watched.

One night while Rob was busy in the studio, I decided to experiment with a crystal ball. Since I didn't have one, I substituted a lovely blue bottle which was filled with water and into which I stared intently for a good half hour. Just as I finished, Rob came out to see what I was up to. According to him, I had been too quiet.

I laughed and said, "Well, there's nothing to crystal-gazing. All I saw was what you could expect — lights and reflections and things. I guess you can't win them all, as they say," and I plunked myself down in our wooden rocker. In the next moment, a fascinating series of events occurred that were to culminate in the third dream-state experience mentioned earlier in this book. I'm going to quote the notes I wrote the following day. In this way, our attitude towards the events *at the time* becomes obvious.

After staring into the bottle, I began talking with Rob in the living room. I mentioned being able to put myself in a dissociated state at the gallery when things got sticky and said that this saved lots of effort on my part. As I spoke, my voice seemed to get hoarse and husky. I laughed and commented that I hoped Seth wasn't going to start using my voice whenever he wanted to.

As nearly as I can recall, it was then that I began to feel strange — as if something were going to happen. I put the feeling down as due to imagination. Almost at once, I felt drowsy and sat in the rocker — without rocking. My eyelids were very heavy; my head slumped sideways. I could hardly keep awake, but my senses were extremely acute; I could hear every sound in the house.

Rob asked me what was wrong. I answered that I felt odd and unlike myself. My body then was very light — weightless to me, anyway. I wasn't conscious of any muscular weight or pressure at all. My arms and shoulders felt like water or air. Rob told me to get up. He was beginning to look worried. But I could hardly rise from the chair. He had to help me to the couch. I didn't feel physical enough to move.

I could tell that I was heading into a very deep trance state. On the one hand, I was tempted to go along with it, since I was supposed to be experimenting. Along the way I was able to maintain my present state, without going deeper, but I didn't know how to snap out of the present state.

Rob made coffee for me. I didn't believe I could lift the cup. When I finally did, my motions were extremely slow, as in a slow-motion motion picture. Rob made me drink two cups of coffee. He had me stand with my head out of the kitchen window in the cold night air, but nothing seemed to help. I just seemed to be in a weightless body in which I had little interest. By now I was rather frightened, yet I thought that I could snap out of it if I really exerted all of my will power — or knew how.

Rob thought the concentration of writing a statement of how I felt would help. Instead, my efforts showed what a crazy state I was in. My handwriting just wasn't my own. Hardly any pressure was exerted on the pen. The writing was wavery, small and grew progressively smaller. The prose expression was nothing like mine; it was very childish. Thoughts or messages poured to mind, and I wrote them down in this weird (unedited) script:

I was sitting at my desk when I began to feel funny. I don't know how. Then I sat in another chair and felt funnier. My hands felt very light and so did my shoulders. Light, then as if they were not there at all.

I do feel strange though, no doubt about it. Rob says I'm just wiggling my fingers.

Joseph.

Just remember that Jerry is sixty-six.

This is a test taste. How do you like it. It's all right. Silly. Silly sassy.

Jerry went alone and no matter why he did it . . . no reason is necessary. You didn't care really. Fortisimo Alleggro. The notes are long overdue. Tell Mary so. She will want to know and it is important. Hannah.

My senses were still very acute — vision . . . and hearing. We decided that since I wasn't having much luck coming out of the trance, we might as well use it to do some experiments. Besides the handwriting, I tried the typewriter. This frightened me a bit further, since I couldn't exert enough pressure to use the keys. All this time I felt completely weightless, unable to function in the physical world. Because my motions were so strange, Rob had the impression that my limbs were heavy. To me they were as light as air. I felt completely relaxed and still my senses were sharp and clear as never before. I was able to talk to Rob without difficulty, also. When Rob felt my hand, it was wet and floppy, and my body seemed to have no physical resistance at all.

Rob asked me to read the small print on the inside of a match cover and a few lines from a book — all held out much farther than I could usually read — and I was able to do this quickly and without effort. My sight was much better than it is normally.

While experimenting, we found that I could make a rapid decisive motion if I exerted great mental force. Rob asked me to lift a coffee cup with a normal gesture. (Earlier, he had held the cup while I sipped the coffee.) I concentrated as hard as I could on what he wanted me to do — which seemed hilarious to me, and an impossible task — and then really made a supreme physical effort. As a result, my hand jerked up high, suddenly, and then just as suddenly swung back, banging the cup back on the counter.

Applied suggestion by Rob would have snapped me out of this state easily, but we didn't know that at the time. As it was, the condition lasted about three hours, ending only when we went to bed, past midnight. By then I was no longer frightened but merely curious and trying with one part of my consciousness to find out what the other part was up to — and how it went about its business. Finally, I fell asleep, expecting nothing but exhausted slumber for the rest of the night.

The next thing I knew, I was dreaming that two men stood by the bed, talking to me. They wore ordinary clothing, slacks and sports jackets. Just then a loud noise awakened me. I sprang to a sitting position, instantly alert.

Astonished, I saw the two men still standing there. Surely, I thought, this was some trick of perception! I was still dreaming and didn't realize it, perhaps. But I pinched myself and rubbed my eyes. Then, quickly, I closed my eyes and reopened them. The men were still there! As far as I could tell, they were perfectly solid and fully three-dimensional. There was nothing ghostly about them.

I was too amazed to speak. Seth had barely begun any discussion of the dream-state realities and I was at a complete loss. Both men were smiling as they stared at me. Obviously, they weren't intruders in the usual sense, and they were not at all threatening. Their presence was a complete impossibility, yet I couldn't deny the evidence of my senses.

Finally, I just pulled the bedcovers up to my chin and sat there, staring back at them. The next moment, they began to disappear before my startled eyes, from the outside edges as if the air was consuming them. If their appearance surprised me, this bit-by-bit disappearance was even more startling.

As they vanished, I felt the strangest sense of loss. I 'knew' that the men were as real as I was, and that I had glimpsed some other dimension of reality quite as valid as the one I knew. Through all of this, I hadn't thought to disturb Rob, who was sleeping soundly beside me. My attention was utterly focused on the events. Now, turning toward him, I remembered the noise that had awakened me. Hadn't it awakened him? Had there ever been a noise?

Quickly, I rushed out of bed and opened the door into the next room. There on the floor, broken beyond repair, was a heavy flowerpot, laying in a pile of dirt and knotted geranium roots. Willie, our cat, had knocked it off the windowsill."

PART TWO

Introduction to the Interior Universe

5

Excerpts from Sessions 15 and 16

The Personality: Dissociation and Possession
The Inner Senses and Mental Enzymes
Seth Looks out the Window

*I*n the next session the following night, Seth launched into the nature of my last trance experience and used it as a stepping stone for his first real discussion of the nature of human personality. As the session shows, Seth apparently decided that it was time to take me in hand. From here on, he would continue to comment on my trance experiments and teach me to regulate them.

Rob was intrigued not only by the material but by Seth himself as he began to manifest his own personality more clearly. My voice had been undergoing changes, becoming more similar to what we now call the Seth voice — deeper, lower, richer in tone than mine and more masculine. But on this particular night, Rob watched, amused, while Seth told him in no uncertain terms what he thought of my experiment — using my own lips to do it! (I'm also including Rob's notes, as they apply.)

This is the first of several key sessions included in this portion of the book as introductions to the interior universe. The material is

included because of its importance in understanding the later concepts on dream reality and the methods of perceiving inner data.

(Excerpts from Session 15, Monday, January 13, 1964, 9:00 P.M.)

*(We began, as usual, by sitting at the board. A foot of snow had fallen
since Sunday night. Although we took the first few answers through the
board, from the beginning Jane received them mentally also. We did not
ask a question to open the session.)*

Yes. Good evening. Have you recovered?

"Yes, I think we have, Seth."

That's good.

"We're having a storm here tonight."

Storms to the stormy.

(Jane said later that this smart remark referred to her.)

"Do you have storms where you are?"

I do not get your kind of storms.

(Here Jane shoved the board aside, got to her feet and began to dictate:)

*I'm not going into so-called weather on my plane tonight. I
came in halfway on an interesting little experiment that Ruburt
tried on his own, and you can thank me that he came out of it
so well. Really, Ruburt, I'm surprised at you. In your past life
[in Boston] you would have known better.*

*Consciously, you didn't know what you were up to;
unconsciously, you knew very well. This sort of dissociated state
can be dangerous, particularly when induced haphazardly, as
was certainly the case with you. If I had not happened to look
in, you would have been in a great state for the rest of the
evening. Or should I say morning?*

*(Here Jane's voice began to get louder and to deepen as she paced back
and forth. Although there was quite a change, her voice did not reach
either the depth or volume of the previous session.)*

And yet you had the nerve to suggest that I might have played a part. You need have no worries on that score. The state of dissociation that you reached can be used most effectively. You blundered into it all unaware and unprepared, however. For shame.

The fact that you slipped so easily into this frame should remind you of abilities that you had at one time in another life; then you misused them. But without their previous experience, you would not have entered such a state so quickly, with so little knowledge and preparation. When I mentioned homework, I was not thinking of anything so strenuous . . .

If you recall, part of your mind was conscious in usual terms. You were capable of normal conversation; another part of your psyche was completely dissociated and waiting for your command. It floundered like a wet rag in a foul wind. . . . Since you were unaware of causing the dissociation to begin with, you were unable to find your blundering way out.

As for the writing, it was by an unorganized, unformed, possible personality of Ruburt's that merely took the opportunity to show itself and supercede the strong hand that has always dominated it. . . . Joseph, your part in these sessions is extremely important. Without your participation they could not have begun, nor could they continue. Because of our past alliances, the three of us are closely bound together . . .

Ruburt, you should cease smoking. For one thing, it is harmful, and I will go into the reasons at another date. For another, I refuse to sound like a hoarse horse. It is not good for my morale. Your voice is too sensitive this evening for me to attempt any transformation of it into the more 'melodious' accents of my own. I suggest — only to give Rubert's much maligned vocal cords a rest — that you take a break for a few minutes.

(*With a laugh, Rob told me that as Seth, I'd been pacing up and down the room, giving "myself" the dickens about the trance experiment, then switching to the humorous comparison of his voice and mine. I still*

*haven't stopped smoking, incidentally. Back in those days, I wasn't about
to have a trance personality order me about, even for my own good. Now
the habit still lingers, partially as a sign of my independence from Seth
and partially as a sign of my dependence upon tobacco . . .*

*During break, my voice returned to normal. We sipped some wine.
Rob began talking about schizophrenia, and then the session resumed.)*

Schizophrenia is caused by a personality fragment that is
broken off, so to speak, from the primary acting personality,
operating often in direct opposition to it, but in any case,
operating as a secondary personality.

*(In an earlier session, Seth said that while on vacation in Maine, we both
unwittingly created two images — versions of ourselves — and then reacted to them. See* The Seth Material.*)*

In your York Beach experience, had you not been able to
form those images outside of yourselves, and so endow them
with some physical reality, you might very well have turned
yourself into schizophrenic personalities instead.

Many people are unable to endow fragments with such
physical reality, and thus shove them more or less harmlessly
away at arm's length, as you did. Instead, the dissociated part
of the personality dons another personality and battles with the
dominant one for control. Many cases of so-called 'possession'
can be laid to this alone.

Actually, the dominant personality, in your terms, can be
compared to the dominant entity. Please understand that I am
using an analogy here. As the personality on your plane actually
changes, expands and grows to its potentialities, as it presents at
various times varied images to the world (such as — if you'll
forgive me for using cliches — a smiling face, a sorrowful face),
but is still basically the same personality, so on another level
does the entity present at various times a varied appearance and
speak in a different voice. As the smiling and sorrowful faces
also express and expand the personality, so, too, do the various

reincarnated personalities express and expand the entity as a whole.

Without the stages of childhood, adulthood and old age, the personality could not expand to its fullest degree, and without various incarnations, the entity cannot expand . . .

In dreaming, such a dissociated state as Ruburt reached is, of course, the rule, only the ability is used to form dream images. But these dream images work for the entity as a whole and serve as a means for the various personalities to communicate; that is, in many cases, the previous personalities communicate with the present one. This is a means of acquainting the present personality with its 'past' and also of reminding it of its goals, without disturbing the blatant awake ego.

Joseph, when your hands grow tired of taking notes, I do wish you would volunteer to take a break and relieve me of an ever-growing compassionate concern for your physical condition. Surely after our pleasant chat the other evening, you should know that nothing of this sort would offend me. I would much prefer more broken-up sessions if they are necessary, than sessions in which I see myself as a torture master.

And please do not think of yourself as some sort of a male stenographer. Through means I cannot explain at this date, I could not speak through Ruburt without you, and a kink in your present personality would quite prevent me from communicating with you alone. . . .

(*We took a break here. Rob said that his fingers felt as if they were falling off. It was almost 10:00 P.M. and Seth had been speaking quite rapidly since the beginning of the session at nine o'clock. We started up again in ten minutes, and once more, my voice began to deepen.*)

As a special favor, I would like to make a request, Seth said. Would you for a moment turn off your main light and open your blinds and curtains so that I can look out into the snowy night?

While I am with you, I am, in a way that I will later

explain, attached to Jane, in that I can see what she sees, and so forth. I can dissociate myself [from her], but the effort involved is really not worth it. It is like putting on one sort of diving equipment, removing it for another and then redonning the first. Costumes are not always physical attire. They may also serve as a sort of vehicle . . . in the manner of diving equipment.

(Still in trance, I turned off the brightest of our two lights, then opened the blinds. Rob said that I stood at the window, looking out at the busy intersection. Fresh snow covered everything. I remembered none of this.)

The view is truly astounding. I'm glad you live on such a nice corner. . . .

Now, there are various types of dreams and dream fragments. I will follow this through later on, since in these beginning sessions I am giving you what may be considered as a broad outline to be filled in. These dissociated states often occur in sleep, when the ego is quieted. At such times it is very possible for your present personalities to be visited by others such as myself, but only on the bidding of the entity.

(For some reason, Rob began to think of Frank Withers. Almost immediately Seth continued,)

And as far as assimilating our old Frank Withers, don't let me lead you too far astray. The entity never dominates a previous personality. Sometimes these personalities also travel divergent ways for their own benefit and with the entity's full consent.

There is no such thing as division as far as the personality is concerned. Even a fragment can turn into an entity in certain cases. There are no rules that hold any living thing down to one form or one kind of existence. And now, dear patient friends, a fond good night.

"I really felt that someone else was here, that Seth was looking

out the window," Rob said, when the session was over. "It was
. . . nostalgic." He told me what had happened.

"Wow, and this stuff . . ." I was reading Rob's notes. " 'A fragment personality can become an entity.' What's the soul, then?"

"I thought you didn't believe that we had one?" Rob said, grinning. "How come all the concern all of a sudden? You want it in
black and white, defined? Is that it?"

"Don't be silly," I said, loftily. But I'd never read anything like
this before, and the idea of fragments and entities was oddly disquieting. "It makes things more complicated," I said.

"Does it?" Rob asked, turning the remark around at me, as he
often does. He seemed so sure of himself and of the material; I
envied him.

Part of Rob's confidence came from observation. He could see
the change that came over me while I was speaking for Seth, and
Seth inspires confidence. Rob *liked* Seth immediately. The two of
them set up an excellent rapport. Through me, Seth related to
Rob. Almost from the beginning he was an objectified personality
to Rob; a visitor regardless of the unconventional situation; someone in whose ideas Rob was tremendously interested. On the other
hand, I only knew what had been said when the trance (or the
fun) was over. It was a terrific change for me to suddenly have to
rely on someone else — even Rob — to tell me what "I" had been
saying for a period of two or three hours.

As Seth continued to explain the inner sense and the unseen reality beneath the objective world that all of us know, I began to
understand a little of my situation. And, of course, Rob and I both
began to experiment with the inner senses. These experiments
gave us first-hand information that was invaluable — especially to
me. The next session cleared up several points I had been wondering about and gave us several clues as to how the inner senses
could be used. It also includes a brief mention of flying saucers
that I didn't delete because of its obvious general interest. Again,
Rob's notes are inserted whenever they help explain the text.

(Excerpts from Session 16, Wednesday, January 15, 1964, 9:00 P.M.)

(This morning at breakfast I announced suddenly, to Jane's surprise and my own, that light was a mental enzyme . . . We started tonight's session sitting at the board as usual, without asking questions.)

Good evening.

"How are you this evening, Seth?" Rob asked.

Just fine.

"Is there anything particular you want to talk about?"

Light is a mental enzyme.

Rob grinned. "Credit my subconscious then. I didn't sit down and figure it out. The thought just came to me this morning. There was something I wanted to ask you, though. Why do Jane's eyes appear to be darker and more luminous when she's delivering your messages? Our cat's eyes had that same look in the last session."

(Here I put the board aside and began to speak as Seth.)

The cat focuses upon one thing at a time even though it has no strong ego. So Jane concentrates while I give her the messages, even though it is not the ego which is concentrating. You get a subconscious focus different in many ways from conscious concentration. In this state the attention is focused inward rather than outward, and it is the inner rather than the outer senses that are being exercised. The cat is doing the same thing, in his way, that Jane is. Its inner senses were focused in my direction.

As far as light being a mental enzyme, this is true. I'm pleased that you came forward with this yourself. Mental enzymes create senses on the physical plane in order that they may be recognized and appreciated by the physical being. The mental enzymes are the same, basically, throughout the universe, but their materializations on any particular plane are determined by the properties inherent in the plane itself.

The quality called light on this plane could just as well appear as sound in another; and for that matter, even on this plane, light can be changed into sound, and sound into light. It is always interaction which is important. Even the mental enzymes themselves are interchangeable, as far as the principle behind them is concerned, though for practical purposes they maintain separate and distinct qualities in their materializations in one plane.

That is why it is possible for some human beings to experience sound as color or to see color as sound. Granted, this is not a characteristic experience, but if the mental enzymes were not interchangeable in principle, then the experience would not be possible. Light would never be heard, for example, and sound would never be seen.

In practical terms, these mental enzymes must — and do — give a predictable, more or less dependable, result. The thing to remember, though, is that this interchangeability can occur, and is, therefore, a property of mental enzymes in general. . . . On your plane, the action of these mental enzymes appear to be more or less inflexible, static, irreversible and permanent. Of course, this is not the case. . . .

Because mental enzymes seem to give the same effects most of the time in your system, your scientists blithely label these as laws of nature; that is, the apparent laws of cause and effect. If you'll forgive a pun, because a certain cause will usually give a certain effect in your physical universe, you may be justified in saying that the apparent results are laws that operate within your system. But stay in your own back yard.

What I am trying to say, is that there are apparent rules of cause and effect, but the same causes do not always give the same effects. . . . There is much more I want to say along these

lines. Please consider again our wires and mazes. I have said, if
you'll forgive the brief reminder, that these are composed of
solidified vitality.

They are the living stuff of the universe, even as they form its
boundaries and seem to divide it into labyrinthian ways, like
the inside of a honeycomb. The planes within the tiny wires —
that is, the planes formed by the connections and
interconnections of our imaginary wires — come into the sphere
of each different plane and take on the form inherent in the
plane itself.

Therefore, these wires, continuing our analogy, will grow
thick or thin, or change color completely, like some
chameleon-like animal constantly camouflaging its true
appearance by taking on the outward manifestations of each
neighboring forest territory. Then too, the inhabitants of any
particular plane are themselves chameleon-like . . .

The inhabitants see only the camouflage. They then accept it
as a definite rule of nature, never realizing that just beyond
their eyesight and just beyond their outer senses, this familiar
tamed animal of a law changes appearance completely. So
complete, in fact, is this transformation as to be in some cases
unrecognizable. However, by seeing beneath the camouflage in
any one case, you can see beneath all camouflage.

What these wires are, then, that seem to divide our planes
and appear so differently in one plane than they do in another,
is solidified vitality, whose camouflaging action is determined
by mental enzymes. Now, perhaps, you will understand why I
said earlier that sound can be seen and color can be heard.
There are many diverse examples along this line.

If you'll forgive me, Joseph, I would like to repeat: Mental
enzymes allow the solidified vitality to change form. Your 'light
is a mental enzyme' tipped me off that you were ready for this
discussion. Needless to say, mental enzymes and solidified
vitality are dependent upon each other in many ways. The

enzyme part of our little equation permits vitality to operate
successfully under diverse mental and physical situations and
forms the basis for each particular system of existence.

The inner senses are actually the channels through which the
entire composition of any plane is appreciated and maintained.
The mental enzymes act upon the vitality, which is, as I told
you, the structure of the universe itself. The inner senses, then,
are the means. The mental enzymes are the tools, and the
vitality is the actual material that forms the universe as a
whole, the apparent divisions within it, the apparent boundaries
between the systems and the diverse materials within each
division. These diverse materials, again, are only camouflage
formed by the inner senses upon the 'material' itself.

*(Break at 9:45. Jane and I were both surprised at the amount of material
delivered in forty-five minutes; the time seemed to fly. During break, I
mentioned to Jane that I would like to ask Seth to say something about
flying saucers. Resume at 9:51 P.M.)*

The strange thing, incidentally, about your flying saucers is
not that they appear, but that you can see them. As science
advances on various planes, the inhabitants learn to travel
between planes occasionally, while carrying with them the
manifestations of their home station.

As I mentioned, they carry their own particular camouflage
with them. You recognize it as not your own. Taking off at right
angles involves another of your natural laws which are not
actual laws but only seem to be from where you are. . . . When
science progresses on various planes, then such visitations
become less accidental and more planned. However, since the
inhabitants of each plane are bound by the particular
materialized patterns of their 'home,' they bring this pattern of
camouflaged vitality with them. Certain kinds of science cannot
operate without it.

When the inhabitants of a plane have learned mental science

*patterns, then they are to a great degree freed from the more
regular camouflage patterns. . . . The flying saucer appearances
come from a system much more advanced in technological
sciences than yours. However, this is still not a mental science
plane. Therefore, the camouflage paraphernalia appears, more
or less visible, to your astonishment.*

*So strong is this tendency for vitality to change from one
apparent form to another, that what you have here in your
flying saucers is something that is actually not of your plane nor
of the plane of its origin.*

*What happens is this: When the 'flying saucer' starts out
toward its destination, the atoms and molecules that compose it
(and which are themselves formed by vitality) are more or less
aligned according to the pattern inflicted upon it by its own
territory. As it enters your plane, a distortion occurs. The actual
structure of the craft is caught in a dilemma of form.*

*It is caught between transforming itself completely into
earth's particular camouflage pattern, and retaining its original
pattern. The earthly viewer attempts to correlate what he sees
with what he supposedly knows or imagines possible, in the
little he understands of the universe.*

*What he sees is something between a horse and a dog and
resembles neither. The craft retains what it can of its original
structure and changes what it must. This accounts for much of
the conflicting reports as to shape, size and color. The few times
that the craft shoots off at right angles, it has managed to retain
functions ordinary to it in its particular habitat.*

*I do not believe you will have any saucer landings for quite
some while — not physical landings in the usual sense of the
word. These saucers cannot stay on your plane for any length of
time. The pressures that push against the vehicle itself are
tremendous. It is literally caught between two worlds. To
conform to the laws of a particular plane is a practical necessity,
and at this time, the 'saucers' cannot afford to stay betwixt and
between for any indefinite period.*

*What they do is take quick glimpses of your plane — and
hold in mind that the saucer or cigar shape seen within your
system is a bastard form having little relation to the structure at
it is at home base. . . .*

"In other words, people from other systems of reality do appear
in ours?" Rob asked.

*They do, sometimes on purpose and sometimes by accident.
In some cases, your people have blundered through the
apparent curtain between your past and present, and so have
others blundered into the apparent division between one plane
and another. Usually, they have been invisible to your plane, as
the few who fell into the apparent past were invisible to the
people of the past.*
  *This sort of experience involves a sudden psychic awareness
that all boundaries are for practical purposes only . . . There
are many kinds of science, however, besides your own. There
are many, for example, just dealing with locomotion. Had the
human race gone into certain mental disciplines as thoroughly
as it has explored technology, then its practical transportation
system would be vastly different and far more efficient.*

"Would you mind telling us exactly what a plane is?" Rob asked.
He expected a fairly brief answer. Instead he got the following:

*A plane is not necessarily a planet. A plane may be one
planet, but a plane may also exist where no planet is. One
planet may have several planes. Planes may also involve various
aspects of apparent time. Planes can and do intermix without
the knowledge of the inhabitants. A plane may be a time . . .
or only one iota of vitality that exists by itself. A plane may
cease to be. A plane is formed for entities as patterns for
fulfillment along various lines. It is a climate conducive to the
development of unique and particular capabilities and
achievements . . . an isolation of elements.*

*It is often practical that entities or their various personalities
visit one plane before another. This does not mean that one
plane must necessarily be visited before another. . . . You could
say also that an entity visits all planes simultaneously, as it is
possible for you to visit one particular state, county and city at
one time. Also, you might visit the state of sorrow and joy
almost simultaneously and experience both emotions in
heightened form because of the almost immediate contrast. In
fact, the analogy of a plane with an emotional state is much
more valid than the analogy between a plane and a
geographical state, particularly since emotional states take up
no room or space. . . .*

We didn't realize it at the time, but in these early sessions, Seth
was gently leading us down the "garden path" — it became more
difficult to think of the world in the usual terms, for example.
Even though I had come to no conclusions as to what Seth was or
wasn't, the Seth material itself fascinated me. Its source in Seth
made it only too clear that other channels of information and experience were open to us beside those we had known earlier.

As a result of the following sessions, for instance, we began
"testing" physical reality for its subjective yields. We no longer
took for granted the normal day with its succession of moments.
Instead, we tried looking at time itself in a new way, practically
speaking. We tried to experience it differently, particularly after
the nineteenth session and an experiment in self-hypnosis that Rob
tried on his own.

6

Some Advice from Seth

Animals and Trees in the Interior Universe
Excerpts from Sessions 17 and 18

On January 17th, Rob and I tried another experiment together. This time, we decided not to have any "format" or particular plans but to leave ourselves open to whatever might happen. Before long, I began to speak for a personality called Malba Bronson, who told Rob that she had died in South Dakota in 1946 at the age of forty-six. The session lasted for an hour and a half; my voice was halting, with many pauses. I sat there, in the darkened room, hearing the voice as if it came from a great distance, feeling a mild astonishment.

Malba insisted that she was the same girl I saw die in Levonshire, England, in my earlier trance, except that her death had taken place when she was fourteen, not seventeen as I had reported. She told Rob that our work with Seth was a life-time project, that we would publish his manuscripts, and help spread his ideas. She also informed Rob that I could contact the deceased for their living relatives if I wanted to, emphasizing that a good deal of trial and error would be involved as both of us learned to use our psychic abilities.

I was less than impressed with Malba and with the session. For one thing, I distrusted the "prediction" that the Seth Material would be published.

"It sounds too melodramatic," I said. "The Seth Material will be published, and you'll help the world — it's too much! We've only had sixteen sessions! I mean . . . well, I'm not some poor deluded idiot with the idea that I can solve the world's problems. And Malba didn't sound terribly bright; at least Seth is intelligent and knows what he's talking about. But what's the use in speaking for anyone else? This way I'm trying to figure out if Seth is independent or not . . . [and] worrying about a Malba, too."

"*You* wanted to experiment tonight," Rob said.

"I know, but I didn't particularly want to speak for someone else. I wanted something that I could observe, too. When I'm in trance . . . well, that's it."

"We've only been at this a little over a month," Rob said. "Aren't you rushing things a bit?"

"Well, I certainly don't want to contact anyone's dead relatives," I said angrily.

"Oh, that's what the sense of outrage is about," Rob said. He was really laughing now, and I sulked. I realized he was right the moment he spoke.

"She didn't say you *had* to. Only that you could if you wanted to. See what Seth has to say about Malba in our next session. I'll ask him to comment, if he doesn't on his own."

Actually Seth opened the seventeenth session with a brief mention of the affair, saying,

I'll go along with your little joke about Malba Toast of the Midplane. Malba of the Midplane was your apt description. [Rob had made a remark to this effect earlier.] The midplane is indeed an excellent description of the semi-plane which she now inhabits. It is a waiting plane for personalities at certain stages of development.

*The midplane contains a conglomeration of fragments . . .
who have not attained sufficient knowledge or manipulability to
progress further at this point. They may be at various stages of
development, but, usually, they have attained only a fair level
of achievement. They have not excelled, neither have they
'failed.' They are working out problems of their own. They are
not as yet committed to the next plane of their advancement.*

*They can be of benefit along certain lines. The validity of
their information may be excellent. On the other hand, it may
be less than trustworthy at times, simply because their
achievement level is not high. If they err, they do so through
ignorance.*

The entire session ran three hours, and most of it was devoted to
the ego and the subconscious and to their relationship to health
and illness. While Rob's back was vastly improved since Seth's
reincarnational sessions for him, he still had some bad days now
and then. We'd been in the habit of blaming difficulties on the
subconscious.

Here, however, Seth said to Rob,

*The ego is the tool by which the hidden self manipulates in
the physical universe. In your case, it enables you to focus your
artistic ability along lines necessary to make it effective on your
plane. However, when the ego becomes involved with fears, it
ceases to be an effective tool and becomes instead a hammer
hitting you incessantly over the head. . . .*

*When the ego becomes overly concerned, it becomes overly
conditioned to negative responses. The creative energies build
up their thickly-dimensioned pseudo-realities of pain. For a
certain amount of time, according to your condition, they
automatically create the patterns of fear that belong to the ego.*

*These fears do not belong to what you think of as the
subconscious. Then these materializations of panic and pain*

*play about the physical body, projected by the ego, and steal
the powers of the subconscious mind from their natural
constructive tasks. . . . In other words, the ego becomes a tool
to disrupt rather than to create.*

*Your own subconscious is the fountain of your individuality
and personality; from it springs your talent. When the ego
becomes too concerned with daily matters, with worry, then it
becomes far less effective. The freely working subconscious —
or the inner you — is completely capable of taking care of all
practical considerations and will use the ego as a tool to do so.*

*Dissociation puts the power back where it belongs. Daily
methods of dissociation are extremely practical. . . . You will
notice within a few weeks' time an added energy. So-called
impulses on your part are often blocked because you do not
consider them practical. But the subconscious knows its own
meat and its own sauce and the best means for its nourishment.*

*Begin the yoga exercises and follow them faithfully. Your few
experiments with auto-suggestion upon falling asleep have been
ego-bound. Think of this in terms of muscle-bound, and you
will see what I mean. Be in a drowsy state and suggest, Rubert,
suggest — suggest, Joseph. Do not attempt to bully or command
the subconscious. Joseph, if you are uncomfortable, I suggest
you move to your sturdy old rocker.*

"No, I'm O. K." Rob said. We'd purchased the rocker earlier
when Rob's back was bothering him badly. Rob told me later that
he was squirming some, as I paced back and forth, delivering this
material as Seth.

*My affection for you is strong. If I speak heavy-handedly, it is
because I want you to have a light touch. Dissociation brings
about a strong unity with the creative aspects of personality. It
puts you back, or it puts your creative talents back, in the
driver's seat.*

The largest segment of the session dealt with personal matters connected with Rob's earlier illness. This led Rob to wonder what had caused our three animals to die shortly before the sessions began.

Seth said:

The particular atmosphere surrounding your personalities just prior to the animals' deaths was short-circuited and filled with inner panics. I do not want to hurt your feelings. This is, I'm sorry to say, a natural occurence often on your plane. The fact is that the animals caught your emotional contagion and, according to their own abilities, translated it for themselves.

The viruses and infections were, of course, present. They always are. They are themselves fragments, struggling small fragments, without intention of harm. You have general immunity, believe it or not, to all such viruses. Ideally, you can inhabit a plane with them without fear. It is only when you give tacit agreement that harm is inflicted. To some degree, household pets are dependent upon your psychic strength. They have their own, it is true, but, unknowingly, you reinforce their energy and health.

When your own personalities are more or less in balance, you have no trouble at all looking out for these creatures and actually reinforcing their existence with residues of your creative and sympathetic powers. In times of psychological stress — or in periods of crises — quite unwittingly you often withhold this strong reinforcement. . . .

In the cats' deaths, both inherited the peculiar illness, which was a virus, that killed them. In the case of the first cat, you were able to reinforce its strength and maintain its health for some time. Then you needed your energies for yourselves. The second cat barely enjoyed such reinforcement at all and quickly succumbed." (*We'd obtained both kittens from the janitor at the art gallery. Both had the same mother.*)

Your dog's illness was incipient. You could not have maintained his health for many years in any case. I would like to make it clear that animals do have energy to maintain their own health, but this is reinforced as a rule by the vitality of the human beings to whom they may be emotionally attached. The fact is that you were unable to give your dog the added vitality at a time when he needed it most. There is no need to blame yourselves. It was beyond your control at your stage of development then.

I was crushed by this material when Rob read it to me after the session. We were both completely unacquainted with such ideas, yet, intuitively, we accepted them. Ever since, we've been very aware of the effect our behavior and moods have on our cats and have observed the same reinforcement or lack of it in other people's relationship with their animals.

The interior universe had its influence even as far as pets were concerned! The whole concept fascinated me. Seth showed us in the next session that not only animals but all living things had their primary existence in this inner world. He also carried on with his discussion of the ego and health, giving an excellent analysis of the ego's relationship to the personality as a whole. I took what he said to heart and found myself opening up, becoming more free and creative. In this session, he also spoke about the consciousness of trees in such a way that I was never able to look at the trees outside of my window with the same old detachment. Through the sessions, the whole world seemed to come alive.

Following Seth's suggestions, Rob began doing a few simple yoga exercises, and the night before the eighteenth session he used self-hypnosis to relax his muscles. The results were so immediate and excellent, and Rob was so limp when he finished, that both of us were amused. He looked so like a before-and-after advertisement. Before he began the exercises, he was very uptight, with sore muscles and a repressive body pose. Afterward, he was like some happy rag doll. Seth began to comment on this in the beginning of the next session. As usual, he used our personal experience as a basis for some excellent information with great general application.

(Excerpts from Session 18, Wednesday, January 22, 1964, 9:00 P.M.)

(To begin, we sat silently at the board, hands on the pointer. Almost at once, Jane began to hear Seth mentally. After taking a few words through the board, she set it aside, stood up and began to speak for Seth as she paced about the room. Her eyes darkened considerably. At times they seemed to contain no highlights. This was our longest session to date, and at its end we were both weary.)

"Good evening, Seth. What did you think of my performance last night?"

Very good, if you are referring to the hypnosis session. Your condition following this and your first exercise bout should show you how badly you were in need of the treatment. When I suggested that you dissociate, incidentally, I didn't mean that you should break up into pieces. . . .

At times, the ego can hold you in a tight vice, which the dissociation breaks. This is what happened after your exercises. You have been doing very well . . . in allowing yourself psychic freedom. However, conscious fears cause the ego to tighten its grasp, and some effects of this nature were starting up. This is why I suggested the exercises at this time.

The fact that the fearful ego was beginning to tighten explains your reaction to the exercises. The ego can build up around the inner self like a glacier, and the exercises help melt it away. Even the prickles in your neck are like tiny picks chipping away at icy fears. . . . You were released so quickly as a result of the exercises that you didn't know what had happened. . . .

Incidentally, while we are on the subject, often when you thought you were dealing with a matter or a person in a dissociated manner, you were instead exhibiting a cold, conscious detatchment. This is a pose of the ego and is not to be confused with the lithe subconscious detachment which is actually warm, flexible and expansive.

As to Jane's feeling about the tree having a certain consciousness, of course this is the case. What you have here is latent energy, vitality and capacity, with much of it withheld or suspended momentarily. The tree is dissociated in one manner. In some ways, its living forces and consciousness are kept to a minimum. It is in a state of drowsiness on the one hand; and on the other, it focuses the usable portion of its energy into being a tree.

The state of consciousness involved here is dull as compared to the highly differentiated human ability in many ways. However, in other ways, the experiences of the tree are extremely deep, dealing with the inner senses which are . . . also properties of treedom.

The inner senses of the tree have strong affinity with the properties of the earth itself. They feel their growing. They listen to their growing as you might listen to your own heartbeat. They experience this oneness with their own growth, and they also feel pain. The pain, while definite, unpleasant and sometimes agonizing, is not of an emotional nature in the same way that you experience pain. In some ways, it is even a deeper thing. The analogy may not be perfect, far from it, but it is as if your breath were to be suddenly cut off — in a manner, this somewhat approximates pain for a tree.

The tree makes adjustments just as you do. It listens to its growth up from the earth and to the murmer of the growth of its roots beneath. It adjusts each root ending according to what impediments might lie in its way. Without the conscious mind of man it nevertheless retains this inner consciousness of all its parts, above and below the ground, and manipulates them constantly.

The tree is also aware of its environment to an astonishing degree. It maintains constant awareness and the ability to adjust itself in two completely different worlds, so to speak — one in which it meets little resistance in growing upward and one composed of much heavier elements into which it must grow downward. Man needs artifical methods to operate effectively on land or in water, but the so-called unconscious tree manages nicely in two worlds as diverse, certainly, as land and water, and makes itself a part of each.

And as far as motion is concerned, the tree moves upward and downward. It is quite unfair to say that it cannot transport itself, since it does so to an amazing degree; the roots and limbs moving in all directions. The inner senses of all plant life are well attuned, alert and very vital. All of these fragments have consciousness to a rather high degree, considering that man holds them in such low repute.

If you remember what you know of the trance state — in a light trance, you are able to maintain awareness of self, your environment and your place in it. You simply behave somewhat differently, not bestirring yourself in any direction unless the suggestion to do so has been given. The awareness of plant life lies along these lines.

Now, in a deep trance the subject, though fully aware of what is happening in the trance, may remember nothing of it afterward. The awareness of plant life is also somewhat like that of the subject in deep trance. Except for the suggestion and stimulus received by regular natural forces on your plane, the plant life does not bestir itself in other directions. But like the trance subject, our plant is aware. Its other abilities lie unused for the time, and latent, but they are present.

The awareness is focused along certain lines. The tree lives through its inner senses, experiencing many sensations and reacting to many stimuli of which you are unaware. Minute earth tremors, even the motion of small ants about its lower

trunk — these are recognized and experienced. Such
invisibilities as humidity, radioactivity and all electrical values
are felt as quite real things to your tree.

A tree knows a human being also . . . by the weight of a boy
upon its branches . . . by the vibrations in the air as adults
pass, which hit the tree's trunk at varying distances, and even
by voices. You must remember what I said earlier about mental
enzymes and my remark that color can sometimes be heard . . .
The tree recognizes a human being, though it does not see the
human being in your terms. It does not build up the image of a
man, but it builds up a composite sensation which represents,
say, a given individual. And the tree will recognize the same
man who passes it by each day.

As your own body senses temperature changes, it also senses
the psychic charge, not only of other individuals, but of plant
and vegetative matter. Your tree builds up a composite of
sensations of this sort, sensing not the physical dimensions of a
material object, whatever it is, but the vital psychic formation
within and about it.

Size is sensed by a tree, however, perhaps because of its
inherent concern with height. The table around which Ruburt
walks senses Ruburt, even as he senses it. . . .

Man's ego causes him to interpret everything else in light of
himself. He loses much in this manner. The ego can be
compared to the bark of a tree. The bark is flexible, vibrant,
and grows with the growth beneath. It is a tree's contact with
the outer world, the tree's interpreter and, to some degree, the
tree's companion. So should man's ego be.

When man's ego turns instead into a shell — when instead of
interpreting outside conditions, it reacts too violently against
them, then it hardens and becomes an imprisoning form that
begins to snuff out important data and to keep enlarging
information from the inner self. The ego's purpose is protective.
The ego is also a device to enable the inner self to inhabit the
physical plane.

If, for example, our tree bark grew fearful of stormy weather
and began to harden itself against the elements, in a
well-meaning but distorted protective spirit, then the tree would
die. This is what the ego does when it reacts too violently to
purely physical data. As a result, it stiffens, and then you have,
my well-meaning friend, the cold detachment with which you
at one time faced the world.

Nevertheless, lest Ruburt thinks he is getting off scott free, let
me remind him that the tree's bark is quite necessary and
cannot be dispensed with. But I will get into that, and into
Ruburt, at a later time. Take a break, and then I will have
more to say about the bark that barks too loudly.

(*Break at 10:26. Jane said that she had stage fright this evening. She
didn't know why. She still wonders where the material comes from, especially when she doesn't know what she is saying from one word to the
next. She resumed dictating at 10:35.*)

The idea of dissociation could be likened to the slight distance
between the bark and the inside of the tree. Here we do not
have a rigid bark, as you should not have a rigid ego. We have
instead a flexible bark, changing with the elements, protecting
the inner tree (or inner self), but flexible, opening or closing in
rhythmic motion. . . .

The inner tree can continue to grow because the bark is
resilient. It bends with the wind. It does not bend when there is
no wind, nor does it stiffen, stopping the flow of sap to the
treetop for fear that the dumb tree, not knowing what it was
up to, would bump its head against the sky.

Neither should the ego react so violently that it remembers
and reacts to past storms in the midst of clear and sunny
weather. You can understand the analogy, Joseph. You know
that such a tree bark would be death to the tree. What you
must still understand is that the same applies to any individual
and the ego. It applies to you. And Ruburt must learn that it is
equally ridiculous to act as if it is a summer day in the middle

of wintertime. The tree has enough sense not to show blossoms in a blizzard.

At times, Joseph, you have not trusted your ego's ability to protect you. . . . You have forced it into anxiety so that it over-compensated, trying to protect you, and ended up half choking you to death. Do you want to sit in the rocker?

"No, I'm okay." Rob said.

Much of the session had been directed to him. He sat, taking notes, as Seth dictated, stopping now and then to stare at him as he made a point. The session continued until nearly 1:00 A.M. The rest of it went into an analysis of the previous ten years, and was directed at both of us. All of this was fascinating, incidentally, and full of psychological insight that greatly helped us both.

But when I read the session, I thought of Rob sitting there, listening to what I thought of as criticism, while his wife paced the room "telling him off" in another voice and supposedly for another, invisible personality. "I worry that it's just a psychological trick," I said. "I mean, suppose that's really what I think, subconsciously — the idea that your ego is too rigid at times and closes you off. So I simply adopt another personality to tell you so. Then I wouldn't be responsible and you couldn't talk back."

"Is that what you think it is?" Rob asked.

"Who knows? I *wouldn't* know, of course, if it were true. I'd be the last one to recognize it."

"Do you realize that the entire session contained more psychological insight into me and more hints into my behavior than I've ever received in any way whatsoever? And that Seth just used me as an example to make more general pertinent points about the personality?" Rob grinned. "If it didn't bother me, I don't know why it's bothering you."

And I was forced to smile back sheepishly. "As long as Seth talks about philosophical stuff, I don't mind, I guess. But when he starts going into us, into personal habits and behavior, it gets kind of close."

"I suppose that's natural enough," Rob said. "Does it bother you that much?"

"Uh-huh. Not really." I said. But in the beginning, at least, I wasn't used to probing psychological analysis directed at Rob or myself from an invisible personality — or anyone else. Now we wonder how we managed to function effectively without all the knowledge about ourselves that we've received from Seth through the years.

The material on trees fascinated me, though. Vegetation was not just alive, but *aware*. And yet, in a strange way, the world was also in a trance. The session inspired the following poem that I wrote a few days later.

The Trees in the Forest

The trees in the forest
Stand secret and silent,
Their voices suspended
In lungs of leaves
That only can whisper
Of dreams held dormant,
That breathe only once
In a thousand years.

Deep is the sleep
Of the moss and the pebble.
Long is the trance
Of the grass and the meadow.
Footfalls come and footfalls pass,
But no sounds can break
That green-eyed trance.

7

The Inner Senses

More on Mental Enzymes
Excerpts from Sessions 19 and 20

Now and then I brooded about the Malba
Bronson episode. Had this been a valid contact within the interior
universe or unconscious play acting? At this point, the Seth sessions themselves had only been going on for a month and a half.
We had had no instances of clairvoyance or any evidential material except for that provided in the early séance, and we had both
decided that we weren't ready to try anything like that again for
some time.

Had I been using Seth's "inner senses" in the Bronson experience? If we tried to renew the contract, could we get her to give us
some checkable dates? I decided to try once more. On January
25th, Rob and I sat in the living room with this in mind. After a
short time, I began to speak as Malba. I mentioned this experience
briefly in *How To Develop Your ESP Power*, but here I'm including Rob's notes which provide a fuller version of the event and our
attitude toward it at the time.

Here are the facts Malba gave us as best as we can recall them. I wrote the notes immediately after the session, then Jane and I went over them.

Her maiden name was Shilcock. She grew up with an aunt and older brother, married at eighteen and worked in a dress or textile plant in Decatur, South Dakota. She could not describe her duties. We had great trouble with the name 'Decatur.' This is my interpretation of what she said, and now I wonder if I made a mistake. Her pronounciation was something like Dek-a-tur, with the accent on the first syllable.

Supposedly it was here where she met her husband, who was a foreman in the plant. He died in 1962 in Marlboro, England. He was not English himself but was visiting relatives there. While her husband worked in the factory, he also owned a farm outside of Decatur, and after marriage the couple moved there. The ground was poor, and Malba mentioned the place several times in a rather derogatory way.

They were married twenty-eight years and had a son and daughter. The son is still alive, in California, around the Los Angeles area. Malba didn't know where the daughter was, but she did know that her son now had two boys of his own. She told us that she worked in the factory for only a few months. Although obviously not intelligent, she showed an awareness of her comparative ignorance, and she regarded education as important.

According to what she told us, she died in the farmhouse kitchen. She was standing at the sink washing dishes and looking out at the 'dreary' flat landscape and at their pickup truck parked there. She felt a sharp pain in her chest, and died of a heart attack. She fell to the floor, breaking a plate as she did so.

The next thing she knew she was running across a field, looking for help, not realizing that she was dead. When she returned to the house she saw her body upon the floor . . . Her husband remarried seven months later. Malba was bitter about this. After his death, the second wife went to California to live with the stepson and his family, a fact that further upset Malba.

Malba said that she is still a woman where she is; she isn't transparent, for instance. She was highly amused at the plight of the clergy men of different faiths, who had died, because the circumstances were so different than those they had expected.

She couldn't explain much about her own situation, however, though she insisted that she was happier where she was than she had been in this life. Sometimes she was with others; sometimes alone. She didn't know how she 'got about,' but knew that she could travel to other places on earth. 'I don't know how I do it,' she said. 'I'll just find myself somewhere.' Nor could she describe how she got through to us. 'I'm here, though, aren't I?' she said.

Actually she was fairly inarticulate. She did say that she had no particular sense of light and dark, or sense of time. She remarked quite spiritedly that I asked a lot of questions, but added that she liked us because we didn't make fun of her.

She couldn't explain what she did, except to say that she 'learned things.' I asked further questions about her background and was told that her husband had grown alfalfa and wheat and tried tobacco and corn. She said again that he was a poor farmer and that her life had been a lonely one, since she had few friends. She knew the clerks in the town, and that was all. She did tell me, when asked, that Decatur had a population of about twelve thousand.

"Our road map does not list a town called Decatur in either North or South Dakota, nor any town with that high a population in that area. I may have confused the two names . . .

"Everything that she said was of a piece," Rob told me later. "She sounded well-meaning, but not too bright. The impression that she was herself was definite . . . she didn't seem anything like you. Her laugh was completely different . . . as was her way of using words. Her vocabulary was very limited, for example, and her voice had a petulant tone. The description of her death really struck me. It was so stark and undramatic that it really rang a bell. Not only that, but she still seemed bewildered by it herself."

"But what's the point of it, providing it was legitimate, just for the sake of argument?" I said. "I guess I'll 'specialize' with Seth. I can't see just trying to pull people in, if that's an apt phrase, for nothing."

But I still couldn't quite believe in personal life after death. I preferred to think of our psychic experiences as emphasizing, instead, the unknown abilities of our present consciousness. "The Seth material could be coming from some deep inner source, an intuitive bank of inner knowledge available to everyone if they only look for it," I said. "And just maybe, with the Malba episode, I picked up knowledge of her life from the same source."

"What's wrong with that?" Rob said. "If that's all it is, whose quarrelling with that?"

"But you're sure that Seth is . . . an individual. I admit he seems to be."

"Both ideas could be part of the whole solution," Rob said. "Hopefully, as Seth explains more about the inner senses, we'll understand more about what's actually going on and learn some methods that will help us."

(And in the next (nineteenth) session on January 17, 1964, Seth did carry his discussion on the inner sense further, and he gave us additional clues as to how we could use them. As you'll see, we were shortly to put his methods to work. The session was a long one, and he began by emphasizing the fact that all physical sense data was camouflage.)

Seth said,

Your scientists are correct in supposing that the universe is composed of the same elements that can be found in your plane. However, the elements that they know are, of course, camouflage patterns, that may show themselves in a completely different form somewhere else.

The elements — those that you now know and those you will create — are camouflages of the basic stuff or vitality which you cannot discover with your outer senses. Your scientists will find that their tools are no longer adequate. Because man has such a sense of curiosity, scientists will be forced finally to use the inner senses. Otherwise they will be dealing with camouflage only and find themselves in a blind alley — not because their eyes are closed, but because they are not using the right set of eyes.

The camouflage is necessary at this stage of development — intricate, complicated, various and beyond the understanding of the outer senses, which are the perceptors of the camouflage itself, peculiarly adapted to see under particular circumstances . . . It is only the inner senses that will give you any evidence at all of the basic nature of life.

Since very often the vitality or stuff of the universe seems as innocuous as air . . . then look for what you do not see. Explore places that seem empty, for they are full. Look between events. What you see clearly with the outer senses is camouflage. I am not suggesting that you take all this on faith. I am saying that what seems vacant lacks camouflage, and, therefore, if this is explored, it will yield evidence.

Effects would seem to be evidence. . . . In concrete terms, if a tree branch moves, then you take it for granted that something blows it. You know wind by its effects. No one has seen wind, but since its effects are so observable, it would be idiocy to say that it did not exist. Therefore, you will come up against the basic stuff of the universe and feel its effects, though your physical senses will not necessarily perceive it.

Granted, camouflage is, in itself, an effect. If you look at the observable world you can learn something about the inner one, but only if you take into consideration the existence of camouflage distortion. . . . There is so much to be said here, and you have so much to learn, that sometimes I have to admit that I'm appalled.

Rob laughed, and Seth said,

Your own experience with creativity should help you out here.

When you paint a picture, my dear Joseph, you are dealing with a transformation of energy and transformation of camouflage pattern. There is a brief but vital moment when you are dealing with the underlying vitality of which I have spoken.

You are forced to transform this creative energy into another camouflage pattern because of your earthly situation. There is nothing else you can do. But for this moment, you pluck this vitality from the inner senses. Then you transform it into a somewhat different, more evocative, new camouflage pattern that is, nevertheless, more fluent, more fluid than the usual pattern, and gives greater freedom and mobility to the vitality itself. You approach a transmigration of plane.

A certain distortion must be expected. The painting, however, achieves a certain freedom from camouflage, although it cannot escape it, and actually hovers between realities in a way that no thoroughly camouflaged object could do. Music and poetry also can achieve this state. . . .

Seth went on to explain that the more camouflage (physical dimensions) an art object had, the less its validity to the inner senses.

Your scientists can count their elements, and while they are on the wrong track, they will discover more and more elements until they are ready to go out of their minds. And while they create instruments to deal with smaller and smaller particles, they will see smaller and smaller particles, seemingly without end. As their instruments reach further into the physical universe, they will see further and further, but they will automatically and unconsciously transform what they apparently see into the camouflage patterns with which they are familiar. They will be, and are, prisoners of their tools.

More galaxies will seemingly be discovered, more mysterious radio stars perceived, until . . . the scientists realize that something is wrong. Instruments designed to measure the vibrations with which scientists are familiar will be designed

and re-designed. *All kinds of seemingly impossible phenomena
will be discovered with these instruments.*

*The trouble is that the instruments will be designed to catch
certain camouflages, and they will perform their function. They
themselves transform data from terms you cannot understand
into terms that you can understand. This involves a watering
down of data, a simplification that distorts the original
information out of shape. The original is hardly discernible
when they are done. You are destroying the meaning in the
translation. . . . When you decipher one phenomena in terms of
another, you always lose sight of whatever glimmer of
understanding that may have reached you.*

*It is not a matter of inventing new instruments any longer,
but of using the 'invisible' ones you have. These may be known
and examined. This material itself is evidence. It is like the
branch that moves, so that you know the wind by its effects;
and a windbag like me by the billowing gale of my monologues.*

*Scientists realize that the atmosphere of the earth has a
distorting effect upon their instruments. What they do not
understand is that their instruments themselves are bound to be
distortive. Any material instrument will have built-in distortive
effects. The one instrument which is more important than any
other is the mind (not the brain) . . . the meeting place of the
inner and outer senses.*

*The mind is distributed throughout the entire physical body,
and builds up about it the physical camouflage necessary for
existence on the physical level. The mind receives data from the
inner senses and forms the necessary camouflage.*

*The brain deals exclusively with camouflage patterns, while
the mind deals with basic principles inherent on all planes. The
brain is, itself, part of the camouflage pattern and can be
interpreted and probed by physical instruments. The mind
cannot. The mind is the connective. It is here that the secrets of
the universe will be discovered, and the mind itself is the tool of
discovery.*

*You might say that the brain is the mind in camouflage.
Imagination belongs to the mind, not the brain. Instruments
may be used to force imagination to move along in terms of its
owner's personal memories, but it cannot be forced to move
along the lines of conceptual thoughts because the imagination
is a connective between the physical individual and the
nonphysical entity.*

*Mental enzymes, by the way, have a chemical effect or
reaction on your plane, but the effect itself is, of course,
distortion. On the other planes, the distortion effect may not be
chemical at all. . . . If you are tired, I will close the session.*

"No. No. I'm okay," Rob said. "Please continue."

*As I told you, mental enzymes transform vitality into the
particular camouflage patterns. A chemical imbalance in a
physical body will also show itself as a corresponding distortion
of sensual data. That is, when the chemical balance is
disturbed, the physical world will appear to have changed. For
the individual involved, the camouflage actually has changed.*

*The subconscious is a property of mind and is, to a large
degree, independent of camouflage. While part of the
subconscious must deal with camouflage, for example, the
deeper portions are in direct contact with the basic vitality of
the universe. When you or Ruburt wonder if this material
comes from your subconscious, you take it for granted that the
subconscious is personal, dealing exclusively with matters of
your past. You are sometimes willing to concede that perhaps
some element of racial memory might enter in.*

*The subconscious, however, also contains the undistorted
material of the mind, which is uncamouflaged and which
operates between planes, knowing no boundaries.*

"I wish he'd get more specific about the inner senses," I said
after I had read the session. "Like — what are they and how do
they work?"

"You have to admit one thing," Rob said. "He really has your interest."

"I know it." Suddenly I felt giddy and full of fun, struck again by the incongruity of the whole affair. "Two adults waiting for an invisible personality to tell them about an invisible world, waiting for instructions on how to use inner senses," I said. "Sometimes I feel like an explorer, mapping out paths to an ancient forgotten dimension of reality. I can even feel reverberations beneath everyday activities, like clues that I only sense but still can't really perceive. And then sometimes I'm beseiged by doubts."

And gain before the next session, I had that odd stage fright, a feeling of apprehension and wonder. My afternoon at the gallery had been very busy. It seemed I had to rush through dinner and the dishes and my normal chores in order to get through by session time. I didn't have an idea in my own head about anything. In a half hour or so how would I suddenly find myself delivering such off-beat material in a voice that didn't seem to be my own?

I was really quite tired, yet after the session, I was astonished to discover that Seth had dictated an excellent exposition on the physical senses and had begun a description of the inner ones. According to Rob, he behaved in a most energetic fashion, pacing the room as usual, stopping to joke with Rob, or pausing for a moment to look out the window. Whatever energy was being used, I decided, it was certainly more than I expected myself capable of that night. This was the twentieth session, January 29th. The session began as usual at 9:00 P.M. and ended at 11:40. Again, only excerpts are being given. Seth began by speaking about the physical senses.

The sense of sight, mostly concentrated in your eyes, remains fixed in a permanent position in your physical body. Without moving away from the body, the eyes see something that may be far in the distance. In the same manner, the ears hear sounds that are distant from the body. In fact, the ears ordinarily hear

sounds from outside the body more readily than sounds inside
the body itself. Since the ears are connected to the body and
part of it, it would be logical for an open-minded observor to
suppose that the ears would be well attuned to the inner sounds
to a high degree. This, you know, is not the case.

The ears can be trained to some degree into a
sound-awareness pertaining to the body itself. And breathing,
for example, can be magnified to an almost frightening degree
when one concentrates upon listening to his own breath. But, as
a rule, the ears neither listen to nor hear the inner sounds of the
body.

The sense of smell also seems to leap forward. A man can
smell quite a stink, even though it is not right under his nose.
The sense of touch does not seem to leap out in this manner.
Unless the hand itself presses upon a surface, then you do not
feel that you have touched it. Touch usually involves contact of
a direct sort. You can, of course, feel the invisible wind against
your cheek, but touch involves an immediacy different from the
distant perceptions of sight and smell. I am sure you realize
these points yourself.

The outer senses deal mainly with camouflage patterns. The
inner senses deal with realities beneath camouflage . . . and
deliver inner information. These inner senses, therefore, are
capable of seeing within the body, though the physical eyes
cannot. As the senses of sight, sound and smell appear to reach
outward, bringing data to the body from an outside observable
camouflage pattern, so the inside senses seem to extend far
inward, bringing inner reality data to the body. There is also a
transforming process involved, much like the moment that we
have spoken about in the creation of a painting.

The physical body is a camouflage pattern operating in a
larger camouflage pattern. But the body and all camouflage
patterns are also transformers of the vital inner stuff of the
universe, enabling it to operate under new and various
conditions.

The inner senses, then, deliver data from the inner world of
reality to the body. The outer senses deliver data from the
outside world of camouflage to the body. However, the inner
senses are aware of the body's own physical data at all times
while the outer senses are concerned with the body mainly in its
relationship to camouflage environment.

The inner senses have an immediate, constant knowledge of
the body in a way that the outer senses do not. The material is
delivered to the body from the inner world through the inner
senses. This inner data is received by the mind. The mind,
being uncamouflaged, then, is the receiving station for the data
brought to it by the inner senses. What you have here . . . are
inner nervous and communication systems, closely resembling
the outer systems with which you are familiar.

I am repeating myself, but I want this to be clear. This vital
data is sent to the mind by the inner senses. Any information
that is important to the body's contact with outer camouflage is
given to the brain.

The so-called subconscious is a connective between mind and
brain, between the inner and outer senses. Portions of it deal
with camouflage patterns, with the personal past of the present
personality, with racial memory. The greater portions of it are
concerned with the inner world, and as data reaches it from the
inner world, so can these portions of the subconscious reach far
into the inner world itself . . .

"Seth, what about time?" Rob asked.

Time and space are both camouflage patterns. The inner
senses conquer time and space, but this is hardly surprising
because time and space do not exist for them. There is no time
and space. Therefore, nothing is conquered. The camouflage
simply is not present. . . .

I want to give you more detailed information about inner
realities themselves. Actually, they do not parallel the outer
senses; and this will sound appalling to you, I'm afraid, simply

because there is nothing to be seen, heard or touched in the
manner in which you are accustomed. I don't want to give you
the idea that existence without your camouflage patterns is
bland and innocuous because this is not the case. The inner
senses have a strong immediacy, a delicious intensity that your
outer senses lack. There is no lapse of time in perception, since
there is no time.

Camouflage patterns do, of course, also belong to the inner
world, since they are formed from the stuff of the universe by
mental enzymes, which have a chemical reaction on your plane.
The reaction is necessarily a distortion. That is, any camouflage
is a distortion in the sense that vitality is forced into a particular
form. Mental enzymes are actually the property of the inner
world, representing the conversion of vitality into camouflage
data which is then interpreted by the physical senses. Do you
have any questions?

Rob was taking down the dictation so quickly he hardly looked
up. "No," he said.

Then Seth told Rob to imagine a man looking at a tree in the
near distance on an ordinary street, with intervening houses and
sidewalks.

Using the inner senses, it would be as if, instead of seeing the
various houses, our man felt them. He would be sensitive to
them, in other words, as you feel heat or cold without
necessarily touching ice or fire.

He would be using the first inner sense. It involves immediate
perception of a direct nature, whose intensity varies according
to what is being sensed. It involves instant cognition through
what I can only describe as inner vibrational touch.

This sense would permit our man to feel the basic sensations
felt by the tree, so that instead of looking at it, his consciousness
would expand to contain the experience of what it is to be a

tree. According to his proficiency, he would feel in like manner the experience of being the grass and so forth. He would in no way lose consciousness of who he was, and he would perceive these experiences again, somewhat in the same manner that you perceive heat and cold. . . .

The inner senses are capable of expansion and of focus in a way unknown to the outer ones, and the inner world, of course, is a part of all realities. It is not so much that it exists simultaneously with the outer world, as that it forms the outer world and exists in it also.

When you receive more information on the inner senses, you will begin using them to a much higher degree than you are now. Of course, the inner senses can be used to explore reality that does not yield to the physical senses.

This session impressed me quite a bit, since after it I felt much less tired than I had earlier. Where had the extra energy come from . . . after three hours of dictation as Seth? I wondered. Besides this, both of us began to experiment with the first inner sense on the basis of the information we received that night. As you will see, the resulting experiences began to add another dimension to our lives.

8

Some Experiences with the Inner Senses

A Spontaneous Session and Some Answers
Excerpts from Sessions 22 and 23

*R*ob spent the next Saturday afternoon in his studio, as usual, painting and doing other artwork. It was snowing slightly. I was in the front of the apartment doing the weekly housecleaning. Rob's mind was on some innocuous chore, now forgotten; he may have been applying gesso ground to a series of panels to be used for paintings. With no transition or advance notice, a vision appeared to him. Although it was not exteriorized, it was clear in detail and very vivid. Like other experiences of this nature, it was intrusive, in that it seemed to have no connection with what he was doing or thinking at the time.

With the vision came its explanation. Rob "knew" that he was seeing the bedroom in which his brother, Dick, had died in a past life in England. We had already been given some information about this previous existence of Dick's in an earlier Seth session. The vision was so clear that Rob instantly made a quick sketch of it. Later in the day he matted it and put it on the bookcase just before we began our twenty-first session.

It was a fascinating session. Seth told Rob that he'd seen only part of the room, described the rest of it and gave further details about Dick's English life. The session lasted until 11:15 when Rob, not Seth, got tired, and suggested that we stop for the night. Seth said, *Sleepy time is no crime. Now I am no poet, and you know it.* Rob laughed, because Seth likes to tease me about my poetry.

Rob's vision was spontaneous. When he typed up Seth's material on the first inner sense, though, he tried a simple deliberate experiment. It is one that I now use with my beginning students though then, of course, it was new to us. Here are Rob's notes:

> First I looked at various objects in the living room, such as a vase, a painting on the wall, a plant, and so forth, and tried to let my mind's eye travel around these objects so that I could clearly picture the far side of them.
>
> Then, last night, I stood at the window and looked out across the Walnut Street Bridge. I visualized myself walking across it and felt the wooden flooring beneath my feet. I felt myself walk beneath the signal light at the far end of the bridge and let myself continue on along the street. Finally I tried to reach out and envelop the feeling of the houses and trees on either side of me — to sense them as if by inner touch, as I passed each one by.

In the next session, Seth told Rob that he was doing well and should try the exercise often. The session, the twenty-second, was one of our first spontaneous sessions. (At times, I knew I could have a session, for example, but mentally refused. Two sessions a week were more than sufficient, I thought — I was afraid of going into trance at the drop of a hat.)

That day, I'd received a letter from the publisher-to-be of my first ESP book. While I was alone in the kitchen, doing the dishes, I found myself wondering if Seth might "come through" and comment on the letter. Then, beautifully clear, with rich humor, came the answering mental message: "Are you gluttons for punishment?"

I gently put down the dish I was washing. Was that Seth, or Jane-playing-Seth? How could I tell? I said, mentally, "I'm wondering how the book will do."

Again the mental words — surely not mine — responded. *I can't afford to give you any predictions at this time, for fear that you'll distort them, and then it would seem that I was to blame.*

He was right, of course. In those days, I'd put him on probation and myself as well. And I never tried to visualize him. I could reconcile a mental voice as a valid and quite safe mechanism of the creative subconscious, as I liked to call it — but an image next to me in the kitchen while I did the dishes? Never!

Still, I thought I'd better tell Rob, so I went back to the studio. "Uh, Seth's around," I said.

"No kidding," Rob said, as if he knew.

I always enjoyed the lively art of conversation, said Seth's mental voice to me.

"Uh, He says that he always enjoyed the lively art of conversation," I said. The dish towel was still in my hand. Rob looked at me and laughed.

"You better get your notebook," I said. I could feel a good-humored vitality, not mine, close and present.

I was in trance almost at once. *Well, the chickadees must be restless tonight,* Seth began. *Incidentally, I rarely attend your little apartment unless in one way or another you ask me to, and tonight you were yelling my name from the rooftops,* he said.

"Seth," Rob asked. "Why this method of communication? Why not, say, automatic writing on Jane's part?"

This method suits me tempermentally. It seems to me that automatic writing could become like an institution. It is so one-sided. I enjoy the questions that you do manage to get in.

Often they remind me of other things I would like to say . . . I have never trusted the written word half as much as I trust the spoken word, and on your plane it is difficult to trust either, but as I mentioned, I always enjoyed conversation, which is the liveliest of the arts.

(Seth's preference here, incidentally, is the direct opposite of my own feeling on the matter. He uses emotional inflections delivering the material that greatly add to the meaning of the words themselves, however, and he may have had this in mind. Words really come to life as he speaks them.)

"Seth," Rob said, "Jane had several confused dreams in which she seemed to be getting or giving instructions in life readings."

I was not trying to reach Ruburt in her sleep. Even I am not so bold as that. A woman's slumber is, after all, a private and sacred thing. Seth said this with a dry sense of humor, then added, See how prim that last sentence would sound without the lively inflection I managed to give to Ruburt's voice? In any case, the inner senses were wide open as she went to sleep. The material was coming through from her own entity.

During all this time the curtains were open. It was not yet quite dark. There were voices and footsteps in the hall, Rob told me later, but I was not bothered at all. In fact, quite without knowing it, I was pacing about, talking as Seth, carrying an unlit cigarette. Finally Seth said, *This is a very pleasant little session. For heaven's sake, Ruburt, get yourself a match. The suspension and suspense is killing me. Will she or won't she light that cigarette? Please find a match.*

Rob laughed and went into the studio for one.

I lit the cigarette, again with no memory of any of this, and Seth continued:

It is true that Joseph receives much more data through inner visions. In the past, he has more or less translated this data automatically, without realizing it, into paintings, with no memory of any vision at all. You can learn to use the other inner senses as well, Joseph, and I will tell you more about them.

Because Ruburt deals in words, it is easy for me to communicate in this way. He automatically translates inner data given by me into coherent, valid and faithful camouflage patterns. The data that I give is not actually sound on my part. Its transference is automatic and instantaneous on Ruburt's part, and is performed through the inner workings of the mind, the inner senses and the brain.

Since you are more sensitive to inner visual data, Joseph, the pictures that you would get in this manner would need interpretation. It just happens that Ruburt's ability lies along the easiest route for us. That is, both of you have pursued separate abilities because of the bent of your particular personalities.

The problem is not only to receive data through the inner senses in an undistorted, coherent manner, but also to translate this into the particular camouflage patterns with which you are familiar. . . .

Seth went on to say, jokingly, that I had been blocking information about my own family. Then he said to Rob,

Some night we'll have a party. You can dispense with the notes or use a recorder, and we'll have a good informal time of it.

"I can hardly wait," Rob said.
Seth was very jovial; he and Rob joked back and forth.

There is so much to say, Seth said once. *I could run on for hours, but you would probably catch me. . . . It is fun to tease you. I always did, and you taunted me back.*

"Both of us?" Rob asked, now trying to lead Seth on.

It wasn't safe to play around with Ruburt in such a manner, ever. When you weren't looking he was apt to hit you over the head with a rock for something you had said ten years ago, and completely forgotten. Not really a rock, but you get the idea. Some things about a personality never change!

I just snorted when Rob told me about this data after the session. Still, the session impressed me. For one thing, since it was spontaneous rather than planned, I hadn't been at all nervous. For another, afterwards I felt surrounded by a residue of Seth's good-humored affection. This feeling was directed *at* me as well as at Rob, which meant that it wasn't coming *from* me. After the session was over, it seemed to follow me out into the kitchen while I finished the dishes.

Our regular session was due the next night and lasted, as usual, from 9:00 until after 11:30. I always want to give this particular session a title: "The Breather and the Dreamer," because as a result of the session, I wrote a poem with that title — one of three poems inspired by Seth's discussion that night. The session had quite a different effect on Rob, however, as you'll see in the next chapter.

(Excerpts from Session 23, Wednesday, February 5, 1964, 9:00 P.M.)

(The first section of the session dealt with personal reincarnation material.)

Some part of the individual is aware of the most minute portions of breath; some part knows immediately of the most minute particle of oxygen and other components that enter the lungs. The thinking brain does not know. Your all-important 'I' does not know. In actuality, my dear friends, the all-important 'I' does know. You do not know the all-important 'I', and that is your difficulty.

It is fashionable in your time to consider man as the product of the brain and an isolated bit of the subconscious, with a few other odds and ends thrown in for good measure. Therefore, with such an unnatural division, it seems to man that he does not know himself.

He says, 'I breathe, but who breathes, since consciously I cannot tell myself to breathe or not to breathe?' He says, 'I dream. But who dreams? I cannot tell myself to dream or not to dream.' He cuts himself in half and then wonders why he is not whole. Man has admitted only those things he could see, smell, touch or hear; and in so doing, he could only appreciate half of himself. And when I say half, I exaggerate; he is aware of only a third of himself.

If man does not know who breathes within him, and if man does not know who dreams within him, it is not because there is one self who acts in the physical universe and another who dreams and breathes. It is because he has buried the part of himself which breathes and dreams. If these functions seem so automatic as to be performed by someone completely divorced from himself, it is because he has done the divorcing.

The part of you who dreams is the 'I' as much as the part of you who operates in any other manner. The part of you who dreams is the part of you who breathes. This part of you is certainly as legitimate and necessary to you as a whole unit is, as the part who plays bridge or Scrabble. It would seem ludicrous to suppose that such a vital matter as breathing would be left to a subordinate, almost completely divorced, poor-relative sort of a lesser personality.

As breathing is carried on in a manner that seems automatic to the conscious mind, so the important function of transforming the vitality of the universe into pattern units seems to be carried on automatically. But this transformation is not as apparent to the one part of yourself that you are pleased to recognize, and so it seems as if this transformation is carried on by someone even more distant than your breathing and dreaming selves.

Seth went on to emphasize again that we form the world of appearances as effortlessly and unconsciously as we breathe. Then he said,

Because you know that you breathe, without being consciously aware of the mechanics involved, you are forced to admit that you do your own breathing. When you cross a room, you are forced to admit that you have caused yourself to do so, though consciously you have no idea of willing the muscles to move, or of stimulating one tendon or another. Yet even though you admit these things, you do not really believe them.

In your quiet unguarded moments, you still say, 'Who breathes? Who dreams? Who moves?' How much easier it would be to admit freely and whole-heartedly the simple fact that you are not consciously aware of vital parts of yourself and that you are more than you think you are.

Man, for example, trusts himself much more when he says 'I will read,' and then he reads, than he does when he says, 'I will see,' and then he sees. He remembers having learned to read, but he does not remember having learned to see, and what he cannot consciously remember, he fears.

The fact is that although no one taught him to see, he sees. The part of himself that did 'teach' him to see still guides his movements, still moves the muscles of his eyes, still becomes conscious despite him when he sleeps, still breathes for him without thanks or recognition and still carries on his task of transforming energy from an inner reality into an outer one. Man becomes trapped by his own artifically divided self.

It is true that, as a rule, you are not aware of your whole entity. There is no reason, however, why you must be blind to the whole self of your present personality, which is part of the entity, and which can be glimpsed in terms of the breathing and dreaming 'self' of which I have spoken.

It is convenient not to be consciously aware of each breath you take, but it is sheer stupidity to ignore the inner self which

*does the breathing and is aware of the mechanics involved. I
have said that the mind is a part of the inner world, but you
have access to your own minds, which you ignore; and this
access would lead you inevitably to truths about the outer
world. Working inward, you could understand the outward
more clearly.*

Then, just as Rob was about to ask how we could really perceive
the inner realities, Seth began to discuss the second inner sense,
giving us a valuable tool for our subjective dissections. We later
discovered, of course, the "inner senses" and "psychological time"
had been discussed under different names in many ancient manuscripts. Rob was really impatient to get the session typed up so that
he could study the material and put it to use.

Seth began by saying that physical time was a camouflage.

*Psychological time belongs to the inner self, that is, to the
mind. It is, however, a connective, a portion of the inner senses
which we will call, for convenience, the second inner sense . . .
It is a natural pathway, meant to give easy access from the inner
to the outer world and back again.*

*Time to your dreaming self is much like 'time' to your waking
inner self. The time concept in dreams may seem far different
than your conception of time in the waking state when you
have your eyes on the clock and are concerned with getting to
some destination by, say, 12:15. But it is not so different from
time in the waking state when you are sitting alone with your
thoughts. Then, I am sure, you will see the similarity between
this alone sort of inner psychological time, experienced often in
waking hours, and the sense of time experienced often in a
dream. . . .*

*I cannot say this too often — you are far more than the
conscious mind, and the self which you do not admit is the
portion that not only insures your own physical survival in the*

*physical universe which it has made, but which is also the
connective between yourself and inner reality. . . . It is only
through the recognition of the inner self that the race of man
will ever use its potential.*

*The outer senses will not help man achieve the inner purpose
that drives him. Unless he uses the inner senses, he may lose
whatever he has gained. . . .*

When Rob typed up the session and I read it, I went around in a
daze of wonder. Like many other people, I'd distrusted the "inner"
self to a considerable degree, believing that it held only repressed
primitive emotions and buried, unsavory characteristics. But
without it, we couldn't even get out of bed in the morning or
breathe, much less walk across the floor. Now this seems so obvious that it is almost impossible to remember what a revelation it
seemed at the time. The next day, the session inspired me to write
the following poem.

> *Who do I share this image with?*
> *What ghost haunts this house?*
> *I smile and reach for a cup of tea*
> *And motions beyond my will begin.*
> *My fingers move smoothly out*
> *And lift the curving spoon.*
> *With just the proper touch*
> *They pick the china saucer up.*
> *Yet I have nothing to do with this.*
> *Who moves the cup? Who moves?*
>
> *And while I speak to you, my lungs*
> *Rise and fall behind breastbones,*
> *Fill their secret tissue mouths*
> *With the air that swirls in this bright room.*
> *They breathe for me the very breath*
> *Upon which all I am depends,*

Yet I do not know how this is done.
Who is this ghost,
This other one?
Who moves the lung? Who breathes?

While I sleep and lie stretched out,
Eyelids closed and pupils dark,
Who walks wide-eyed downstairs
Through the door in the cold night air,
And travels where I have never been?
Who leaves clear memories in my head
Of people I have never met?
Who takes these trips while I
Never lift one inch from bed?
Who dreams?

The mover, the breather, the dreamer
Shares with me this fond flesh.
He is a twin so like myself
That I cannot recognize his face.
He goes his way and I go mine.
We never meet head-on, and yet
I am aware of this ghost
Behind my every word or act.
Who moves? Who breathes?
Who dreams?

If the twenty-third session roused me to write the poem, it also impressed Rob deeply enough so that he tried a rather complicated experiment with the inner senses — without letting his conscious mind know what he was up to.

9

The Inner Senses — Rob's Turn

More About Psychological Time
and How to Use It

Excerpts From Sessions 24, 27 and 28

Miss Cummingham and a Missed Session

*I*t was a weekend that we had company. The friends present had no idea we were involved in any psychic work, and the subject never came up in our conversation. (No one knew what we were up to, for that matter, except for one close friend. We hadn't even told our families.) In the middle of that innocuous evening, Rob suddenly had three experiences that were quite startling at the time and rather frightening. Here is an account from his own notes:

On the evening of Saturday, February 8, 1964, I had three separate and very strange sensations. We had company. I had just finished my first small glass of wine when a wave of 'feeling' swept over me from foot to head. It was a magnified tingling, or thrilling, suffusing the whole body, flooding up my legs into the abdominal and chest cavities. I was left feeling as though I might be lifted up and swept away.

The first time, the sensation was not as strong as the next two times. When it first swept over me, I wondered if the wine could be responsible, though actually I had drunk little. I waited quietly, and in a moment or two the sensation was gone. I was balanced on the arm of our davenport, talking to our company. I had the odd feeling that the sensation was related both to the subject of conversation, and to some kind of message or communication I felt within me.

The next two sensations came later in the evening. The second same over me around 11:30 P.M. as we sat around the table eating. This sensation was so strong that I put down my sandwich and took off my glasses, because I literally didn't know what might happen next. The wave of feeling washed over me very strongly this time. Although everyone about me was talking quite loudly, I had the weird sensation of voices *within* me, of mouths open or crying in soundless rhythm.

I also sensed, or felt, a great chute or trough or pathway of some kind that reached down into me from above me, or at least from outside of me. At this point, I definitely was apprehensive. The sensation in my chest was very strong. I even thought that perhaps I was having some sort of physical attack, though I felt no pain.

Looking back now, the next morning, I think the possibility crossed my mind that some psychic effects were being felt, but, actually, I was so startled that I didn't think much of anything.

Later, after our company left, the sensation came back yet again as I stood in the kitchen talking to Jane. Even then, I was not quick-witted enough to capitalize on it, perhaps by asking myself questions. I was too involved in the feeling to be that objective on such short notice. Now, the next day, the memory still lingers. What was it? Maybe Seth will know.

While writing out this statement, I'm reminded that I experienced a milder version of the same sensation last month, while I was working at my part-time job in the art department of a local greeting card company. I was alone in the art room, eating lunch at my desk, when the feeling swept over me. There was no warning or pain, but the surprise doubled me over my desk. I was frightened, thinking it might be some kind of an attack then, but it passed quickly and did not return.

I didn't tell Jane about this at the time, but in a recent session, Seth referred to it and said that I'd been calling — psychically — for help because my back had been bothering me then badly. Also when I had these experiences last night, I wasn't feeling my best. I wonder now . . . *had* I again called for help? Was this an attempt at an answer?

The next night, Rob and I purchased a tape recorder, hoping that we might be able to lighten his work load. We didn't get back from the shopping center until nearly 8:30 and then we began fussing with the recorder. As was usual in those days, I began to get the jitters as 9:00 P.M. approached; we finally decided not to use the recorder that night but to wait until the next session and give ourselves time to become acquainted with the gadget.

Seth came through immediately.

"Seth," Rob said, "why does Jane still feel nervous before a session?"

She is always slightly dubious and doubtful before a session . . . since she is the one through whom I speak. The inner senses are not accustomed to operating so freely, and this sometimes upsets the all-present ego. Usually in our sessions, one inner sense is in strong operation. . . . Often, just beforehand Ruburt does not have a thought in his head . . . and then my 'excellent' dissertations begin, if you will forgive a touch of egoism on my part. He wants to know where the words are coming from and still wonders if I am a part of his subconscious; and I must admit that I find such an idea appalling. He wants his answers given to him in a way that his conscious mind can understand. This is our twenty-fourth session, and I am still trying to give you the answers.

This last was given with rich mock humor. Seth went on to explain that great dimension would be given to the sessions as we progressed. He began to go into the inner senses more thoroughly and Rob really pricked up his ears, hoping that Seth would mention his three recent experiences. Were they the results of his fumbling attempts to use the inner senses?

There is an inner sense, Joseph, that, in a vague manner, corresponds to your own inner images. That is, you use this inner sense quite inadvertently in your visions, except that because of your lack of consistent training, you see these only dimly.

The inner senses, however, give much stronger impressions than those given by the outer ones. You should, in the future, be able to achieve the counterparts of sight, sound, smell and touch, embellished by inner counterparts of width and existence, using the inner senses. You have trouble now with the duration of your inner visions because you are trying to transpose them according to physical time — and this is going about it in the wrong way. As I mentioned earlier, you have at your command, even now, an inroad, a relatively accessible one, in what is termed psychological time.

This is closely related to the second inner sense, and it is upon psychological time that you must try to transpose your inner visions. You can see how handicapped we both are because of the difficulties involved in trying to explain inner data in terms of outer data. For instance, when I tell you that the second inner sense is like your sense of time, this does give you some understanding of what psychological time is like, but you are apt to compare the two too closely.

Any communications coming through the inner senses will exist in your psychological time. Psychological time operates during sleep and quiet hours of consciousness. Now, in dreams you may have the feeling of experiencing many hours or even

*days. These days or hours of psychological experience are not
recorded by the physical body and are outside of the physical
time camouflage. If, in a dream, you experience a period of
three days, physically you do not age for these days. Do you
see?*

"Yes," Rob said.

*Psychological time is so a part of inner reality that even
though the inner self is still connected to the body, you are, in
the dream framework, free of some very important physical
effects. Now, as dreams seem to involve you in duration that is
independent of clock time, so can you achieve the actual
experience of duration as far as your inner visions are
concerned.*

*But the minute — the physical minute — you try to transpose
these visions upon the physical minute, then you lose them.
Many times, in so-called daydreaming, you have lost track of
clock time, and this experience of inner duration has entered in.*

"Why did we invent clock time to begin with?" Rob asked.

*It was invented by the ego to protect the ego, because of the
mistaken conception of dual existence; that is, because man felt
that a predictable, conscious self did the thinking and
manipulating, and an unpredictable self did the breathing and
dreaming. He set up boundaries to protect the 'predictable' self
from the 'unpredictable' self and ended up by cutting the whole
self in half.*

*Originally, psychological time allowed man to live in the
inner and outer worlds with relative ease . . . and man felt
much closer to his environment. In prehistoric times, mankind
evolved the ego to help him deal with camouflage patterns that
he had, himself, created. This is no contradiction, as will be
explained later. He did the job so well that even when he had
things well under control, he was not satisfied. He developed at
a lopsided level. The inner senses led him into a reality he could*

not manipulate as easily as he could physical camouflage, and he feared what he thought of as a loss of mastery.

Here, we took a break. "If Seth doesn't mention my experiences, I'm going to interrupt and ask him," Rob said. He was still having back trouble, and now a spasm seized him so that he grimaced. Suddenly, Seth said,

You had better stand up and move around. That is what you are supposed to do in these frequent breaks from the material. There is no reason why you cannot stand sometimes to write, if it is more comfortable. There are articles of furniture upon which to rest your pad. Surely, I should not have to remind you of the practicality of camouflage patterns with which I am no longer concerned. If I were as dependent upon them as you are, I would use them better. Do please get comfortable.

Rob took his pad over to the high old-fashioned TV set we had then. It made a good desk, and he stood up to take his notes for the rest of the session.

Hypnosis can be used to better your condition, Seth said. It is, after all, a method of acquainting the ego, through effects, with the abilities of the whole self of which it is a part.

"Jane hypnotized me several times lately, with very good results, as you know," Rob said.

Now if you're ready, I have a few words to say about your beautiful, if haphazard, experience with the inner senses the other evening.

"Okay."

The circumstances at your end were right for something like this to occur. It was like a sudden opening of a door. You didn't know how to open it further, and if I may say so, you didn't know how to close it. Yet, you would not have consciously admitted the experience not too long ago, as something like it happened at an earlier date and you forgot it consciously.

The first time this happened, you were calling for help. Like many others, you feared the inner world so strongly, even though you were somewhat acquainted with it through your art, that nothing but panic would force you to try that invisible knob. This time, there was a remembrance of panic but that was all. Actually you opened the door out of desire, stimulated by our sessions and out of curiosity, but you were still frightened.

What you experienced is rather difficult to explain until we have a thorough discussion of the inner senses, but I will give you a simple explanation for now. You felt an onrush — or should I say an onslaught? — of data in its pure form, rushing through the inner senses like a wind in a kaleidoscope because you did not know how to control or disentangle it.

For this reason, you attempted a rather hilarious feat. You tried to switch over and pick up inside data with the outer senses, and then project this inward. For a beginner, it was quite a performance. . . . It was a defect on the receiving end that caused fear on your part. You felt sound. But, because you did not hear sound with your ears, you panicked and formed the image of mouths that could not speak. This was a projection of your inability and should not be taken as any condition of helplessness existing in the inner world, as I am afraid you interpreted the image.

Your feeling of a door or funnel is quite legitimate, however, and if you felt attacked because of the onrush of data that seemed to crash down upon you, it was only because of your inability to control the volume, so to speak. You switched yourself off automatically because the experience frightened you, but the whole affair was beneficial since it gave you some first-hand experience with pure inner sensory data. It was unfortunate that it was so uncontrolled, but I'm afraid this can often be expected in the beginning. If possible, try to relax if the experience happens again, and the data will slow itself up.

"Is there anything I can do to encourage such a flow of data again?" Rob asked.

At this stage you will do what you can to encourage it, without my telling you, just as you initiated the event to begin with. Your own innate inner knowledge will aid you. I suggest a brief break, and this time my dear Joseph, do copy your strolling wife and move about.

When the session resumed, Rob asked, "Can you tell us more about psychological time?"

It is a natural connective to the inner world. As you can experience days or hours within its framework in the dream state and not age for the comparable amount of physical time, so as you develop, you will be able to rest and be refreshed within psychological time even when you are awake. This will aid your mental and physical state to an amazing degree. You will discover an added vitality and a decreased need to sleep. Within any given five minutes of clock time, for example, you may find an hour of resting which is independent of clock time.

You can look through psychological time at clock time and even use clock time then to your greater advantage; but without the initial recognition of psychological time, clock time becomes a prison. . . . A proper use of psychological time will not only lead you to inner reality but will prevent you from being rushed in the physical world. It provides quiet and peacefulness.

From its framework you will see that clock time is as dreamlike as you once thought inner time was. You will discover that 'inner time' is as much a reality as you once considered outer time to be. In other words, peeping inwards and outwards at the same 'time' you will find that all divisions are illusion and all time is one time. . . .

Since you are both tired, I will end the session. Don't say that I didn't lead you a merry chase tonight, for when you reread the material, you will see that it must be studied carefully. One point, however: conscious fear is usually the main hindrance as far as inner data is concerned. Therefore, a realization that these senses belong to you and that they are quite natural, will help you avoid the closing off of such data by the conscious mind.

If you remember this, inner data will come through much more easily, and you will be able to control it. It is never of itself overpowering. You can train yourself in the recognition of such data, its utilization and control. Within the framework of psychological time you can also lengthen such experiences.

By now, the sessions were running from seventeen to twenty typed, double-spaced pages and they lasted anywhere from two and a half to three hours. Only one experiement using the tape recorder showed us that our usual procedure was the best one. Rob really had a great time, though, for the twenty-fifth session he didn't have to take notes while we tried out the recorder. Seth also spoke much faster. He congratulated us on our "twenty-fifth anniversary," and said jokingly, *You will be much older by the time I am through with you.* Most of the session was a discussion of ordinary subjective states emphasizing the fact that these could not be pinpointed in a laboratory or understood simply by the use of the ordinary scientific method. Yet, they are vital elements in our lives.

The next day, though, Rob found himself "paying" for his freedom from notes. The session lasted three hours. But he discovered that it took him much longer than this to transcribe the tape, since he had to start and stop the recorder so often. It was much easier and quicker to work from his own handwritten notes.

Then, the next Friday, Rob had another experience with his "sensation." The following description is taken from his notes of February 14, 1964.

At around 9:15 P.M. I was in the living room talking to Jane about her ESP book. She had been interviewing people in the apartment house about their experiences. I got up to look out the window, to try my mental experiment of traveling across the bridge again. I wanted to feel myself doing it as before.

As I looked out, that strange sensation came again. It began in the left leg and left arm and then spread to my chest and head. The sensation then localized somewhat in back of my ears. It was like an internal tingling or thrilling — a rich, suffusing feeling. Seth called it 'feeling sound' in a recent session.

Unlike last time, I wasn't frightened. I held up my hand without speaking. Jane stopped talking and we waited quietly to see what might develop. I hoped the feeling would somehow turn into sound or images, but it didn't. At least I felt that I hadn't slammed any 'interior door' shut.

The sensation passed, and we resumed talking. Yet, it lingers. As I sit here writing these notes, I feel it nibbling away — a bit in my back, on my cheeks and mouth, in my torso. Maybe it will return later.

Through all of these early sessions, Rob was not feeling well. He is in such good health now that it's difficult to remember how badly he felt. The session notes show his condition quite clearly, though. Often Seth would give us a break so Rob could rest. Frequently he took notes on the old TV set, standing up, and sometimes he sat in the new rocker.

That weekend he didn't feel well. Monday morning he tried self-hypnosis with good, though temporary, results. He felt better the rest of that day and on Tuesday. On Wednesday evening an upsetting incident happened, throwing our household and a neighbor's into confusion, and aggravating Rob's symptoms.

Again, from Rob's notes, inserted before the next Seth session as background:

Our twenty-sixth session, due Monday, February 17, was not held for two reasons. This is the second time we have missed a session since they started in December. The first time we missed one was during the holidays. This time the reason was far different.

I hadn't felt well. My back was acting up, work was difficult, and by suppertime, I was drained. I did not really feel like taking fifteen to twenty pages of dictation from Seth; I was concerned lest I miss some of the material.

Also, after supper, it developed that Miss Cunningham, the retired school teacher in the front apartment, suffered an attack of some sort and was in urgent need of help. Another neighbor and tenant, Don Jacobs, called us. Jane went to see what was wrong and found that Miss C had fallen on the floor, was suffering from severe lapses of memory and was in very poor condition. She had evidently taken several falls earlier that day, and had not been eating.

There followed a very confusing and, to me, upsetting several hours during which Jane and Don tried to make arrangements with Miss C's doctor, relatives and a hospital. The relatives refused to help, seemingly out of fear of Miss C herself, who had always been quite independent with them. In the meantime, Miss C was hysterical, pulling at her hair and so forth. Miss C's family (nieces and nephews) finally said they would take the patient to the emergency room at the hospital; her doctor told Jane he would be waiting for her there. In the meantime, the relatives changed their minds; the doctor was furious and left. Jane finally contacted another doctor who arrived at midnight and authorized Miss C's hospitalization.

As the regular hour for our session came and went, Jane began to get 'nibbles' from Seth. At the same time, I felt worse. I had not been helping Jane and felt guilty about it and was angry at Miss C's relatives. Once I had such a severe attack of back cramps that I couldn't stand.

Coming in and out of Miss Cunningham's apartment, Jane would tell me the snatches of thought she received from Seth. I was in no condition to cooperate, so Jane wrote the words down. Several comments were directed to me, and one, in particular, was quite illuminating. 'You want to help but fear to move. If you had helped tonight, you would not have felt the need to turn your emotions inward against yourself in such a self-destructive manner.' "

Once Jane said to me, 'Boy, you were some help.' And later she was mentally taken to task for the remark by Seth.

The next night Mark Ragen, a friend, dropped by. We were somewhat tired, but glad to see him. For the first time, I felt that Seth was "around" while we were socially engaged. My feelings were confused. I thought sardonically, "A guest from another layer of reality is one thing, but do you really want your friends to meet him?" Finally my nervousness was so apparent that Rob asked me what was wrong. For a moment I just sat there. Should I introduce Seth to Mark or not? I remember thinking that no book of etiquette even written could give me an answer.

10

Seth Meets an Old Friend in Our Living Room

The Dream Universe

This was to be the first time Seth really spoke to anyone else. I was half reluctant to hold a session and half curious as to how Seth would handle other people. I was also quite nervous. The session was actually a breakthrough in many respects, as these excerpts will show. I'm also including some of Rob's preliminary notes.

(Excerpts from Session 26, February 18, 1964, 10:00 P.M.)

(As we sat speaking with Mark, Jane finally told me that Seth wanted to have a session since we had missed last night's regular one. Seth also wanted Mark to stay. But tonight, since it was getting late and I had doubts about being able to keep up with the dictation, I thought it better that we pass up the chance. I also thought Jane would be too tired, after the exhausting time she'd had last night. Mark offered to leave after I explained as best I could what was happening, but I said that we'd rather wait for the next regular scheduled session night.)

(This statement, Jane told me, made Seth angry. She insisted that I get

pen and paper, and, so, the session began. At its end will be found a copy of Mark's statement.)

You are excellent teachers, I must admit. However, Joseph, while I admit I came uninvited and while I understand the reason for last night's absence, I took it for granted that we would have our missed session this evening. I find it very impolite of you to restrain me in this fashion.

Our sessions are important and not to be put off at the mood of the moment. As Ruburt told you, I was here at the regular hour last night and aware of the happenings, and perfectly willing to let the session go, understanding the circumstances.

This evening was different. You were polite to your guest, and I recognize his presence. You were not, however, as polite with me. Ruburt was dubious about a session with company present but willing to go along. You know that I have no objections to your friend's presence. For that matter, I welcome a witness, and it is time you had one for your own edification, not mine, and it should do our nervous pigeon, Ruburt, some good.

Mark sat there, considerably startled. I was in trance, of course, but, knowing him, I can well imagine how he must have stared at me as I strode back and forth speaking in that deep Seth voice and talking to Rob in such a manner. When Rob explained briefly about Seth before the session, he'd asked Mark questions he'd like answered. Mark said that he was interested in the connection between consciousness and evolution. Now, almost immediately, Seth said:

I want to reply to your friend's question. . . . When he asked it, he was referring to the point at which self-consciousness entered into so-called inert form. You know, now, that all form has consciousness, and so there was no point at which self-consciousness entered with the sound of trumpets, so to speak. Consciousness was inherent in the first materialization upon your plane.

Self-consciousness entered in very shortly after but not what you are pleased to call human self-consciousness. I do not like to wound your egos in this manner, and I can hear you yell 'foul,' but there is no actual differentiation between the various kinds of consciousness.

You are either conscious of self or you are not. A tree is conscious of itself as a tree. It does not consider itself as a rock. A dog knows it is not a cat. What I am trying to point out here is this supreme egotistical presumption that self-consciousness must of necessity involve humanity per se. It does not.

So-called human consciousness did not suddenly appear. Our poor maligned friend, the ape, did not suddenly beat his hairy chest in exultation and cry, 'I am a man.' The beginnings of human consciousness, on the other hand, began as soon as multi-cellular groupings began to form in field patterns of a certain complexity.

While there was no specific entry point as far as human consciousness was concerned, there was a point (in your terms) where it did not seem to exist. The consciousness of being human was fully developed in the cave man, of course, but the human conception was alive in the fish.

We have spoken of mental genes. These are more or less psychic blueprints for physical matter, and in these mental genes existed the pattern for your human type of self-consciousness. It did not appear in constructed form for a long period. . . .

Human self-consciousness existed in psychological time, and in inner 'time' long before you, as a species, constructed it. For your friend's sake, I will say this as simply as possible: Human consciousness was inherent and latent from the beginning of your physical universe. I suggest a brief break, and do not crack up into pieces. I give you this slight evidence of my humor,

Joseph, simply to show you that I am not, after all, one to carry
grudges.

More material was given than the excerpt just included. Actually, Seth spoke steadily for an hour before our first break. When I
came out of trance, Mark was staring at me intently.

"Seth answered each question I had the minute it came to
mind," he said. "Rob gave me a piece of paper. I intended to write
questions down as I thought of them, but I never got the chance to
do it. He answered them *in order*." He shook his head. "Seth did.
Or you did. Somebody did. I've never heard or seen anything like
this!"

"The material was all on related subjects," Rob said. "Could
that explain it?"

"It would be the simplest explanation, and I'd be a lot less bewildered if I could think that was it," Mark said. "But the answers
were just too specific, too on time, too direct. I'll tell you, I'll
make out a statement to that effect."

Was Mark right? I wondered. "I'm quite willing to admit that
telepathy might exist," I said. "But if I have any part in it, I'd like
to know what's going on and how Seth did it — or how I did it."

"What will I call, uh, Seth, in my statement?" Mark asked and
Seth interrupted,

You may call me Seth, Mark. Although, in case you are
interested, your entity name is Phillip. And because you are
such a good witness, I must admit that I knew you in the past.
I consider you an old friend, and we shall, to some extent,
renew an old acquaintance.

I delight in astounding the present personalities of old
acquaintances by letting them know we have known each other
before. It is a failing of mine, but I enjoy it. . . . There are
many times that our paths have crossed, and that is why I
wanted you here and why you happened onto the art gallery

where Ruburt is employed. Not that free will is not involved, because it is. Only that old friends have a way of meeting. And I was not joking when I spoke earlier of your having a predisposition to gout; for you have also been lecherous in your way.

Rob laughed. "Like me, in the Denmark life you told me about?"

Indeed like you, my dear Joseph, Seth said. In your case, as I have told you, you overcompensate now for past fleshiness by a most unnecessary self-punishing attitude. Phillip, on the other hand, is performing no such compensations, except for one instance of choosing a good-looking wife and therefore permitting himself to treat her kindly.

Now it was Mark's turn to laugh. Rob and I had never met his wife. Nor was he a close friend, merely a good acquaintance who lived out of town and visited Elmira only when his business required it, about once every six weeks.

He was in a different position when he was a woman, Seth said with obvious humor. And if I may give away some secrets, he was beaten by one pigheaded husband who had a snout to match!

"When did this happen?" Rob asked. He was trying to lead Seth on again. Mark just looked from one of us to the other.

Belgium in 1632, and our Phillip, in a rather sensational case for the times, actually brought this husband to a village trial — a particularly unusual occurence at that time. Her name was Yolanda Schrav. . . .

"Wait. Let's get the spelling on that," Rob said, and Seth nicely spelled it out.

Schravansdatter. He was thirty-three at the time and had been caught in an act of, shall we say, indiscretion, for which he was severely and unjustly beaten. Unjustifiably because the pigheaded husband was, forgive my pun, a bore. . . . I must admit that this brings us far afield from our discussion of evolution.

It is important that you tie in this material with previous data on the inner senses. They are always paramount in evolutionary development, being the impetus behind the physical formations. . . . The inner senses themselves, through the use of mental enzymes, imprint the data contained in the mental genes onto the physical camouflage material.

I become impatient, though I shouldn't, with this continued implied insistence that evolution involves merely the human species — or, rather, that all evolution must be considered some gigantic tree with humanity as the supreme blossom.

Humanity's so-called supreme blossom seems to be the ego, which can be, at times, a poisoning blossom, indeed. There is nothing wrong with the ego. The point remains, however, that man became so fascinated with it that he has ignored the parts of himself that make the ego possible, and he ignores those portions of himself that give to the ego the very powers of which he is so consciously proud. . . .

The session continued. I had long forgotten that we had a visitor. My previous nervousness was like a dream. I was aware of nothing except of a great supporting energy and, someplace far off, the room in which my body walked. Mark sat there fascinated, Rob told me later, his salesman's smile replaced by bewilderment and determination. He was to attend many other sessions. Whether or not he and Seth were friends in a past life, they became good friends in this one. Some excellent evidential material was to be obtained through sessions with Mark several years later. He was to recall Seth's warning to cut down on drinking because of his predisposition to gout; he came down with gouty arthritis.

But that night, Mark insisted that Seth had read his mind and listened spellbound as Seth told him about the inner senses. None of us suspected that Seth would give Mark detailed information about the inner organization for which he worked, or help him understand personal problems, or delight in telling him what had gone on at sales conferences that Mark had already attended — or with a great rush of humor tell him the exact amount of a new raise he had just been given. All of that was in the future.

That night, Seth emphasized only the importance of inner reality and the validity of the inner senses that made nonphysical knowledge available whenever we were ready to admit it. Once Seth smiled broadly and said,

There is nothing like a witness to convince our darling Ruburt that I am I, and not her, [meaning Jane] or like a good evening of telepathy, as in the case of this evening.

Why then do you [mankind in general] *insist that an inner experience such as telepathy or premonition does not exist because you cannot hold it in both hands? And yet, in many instances, such cases can be corroborated by others in a way in which many psychological experiences cannot be.*

There is no way of measuring inner experience, or the psychological experience, rather, of someone who has lost a friend in death, but you do not deny that such an experience happens. Yet, if two people see the same 'apparition,' then instantly twice the evidence is required.

It was midnight before the session ended. After it was over, and our salesman friend left for his motel in a nearby town, Seth came through with a few personal remarks for Rob. We had already gone into the bedroom when I felt drawn to go out into the front room to my desk. Standing there, silently, I felt Seth near. My mind was a whirl. I knew that I felt that Seth was near, but, intellectually, I was full of questions. Had Seth really read Mark's mind, or had Mark just wanted that to happen and convinced himself that it had? Did I feel Seth, or was I indulging in fantasies of a highly dangerous nature?

Rob, wondering where I had gone, suddenly stood beside me.

Already in trance, I guestured to the paper and Seth began to speak:

My dear Joseph, one word only. I would not leave you with the impression that I was truly displeased or that I judge you unjustly. I do not want to hurt Ruburt's feelings, and I have avoided making this statement thus far, but I have been emotionally more involved with you in past existences [than with Ruburt]. I know your capabilities so well that when I seem severe, it is only because I wish so for your happiness and success.

I suppose we judge those we love most in a harsher manner, but I should know better, and for once you have my apology. I think very much of you. I did not mean to push you too hard, and I certainly do not mean to make you feel inadequate in any manner.

The emotional feeling of this brief statement was alive in the room when I came out of trance. We just stood there, staring at each other. Then, as if to break the mood, mentally I heard Seth make a joke to the effect that Joseph was not to get a big head just because Seth had apologized. Then all feelings of Seth vanished, and we went to bed.

I did a lot of thinking in the next few days. As I worked at the gallery or at my book or did my house chores, the last session kept coming to mind. If Seth *had* read Mark's mind, this was an excellent progression. If not, then Mark had deceived himself, and Seth had gone along and taken advantage of the deception. And if Seth was a personification of my subconscious, then this would be an excellent example of subconscious fraud.

"You're just running yourself down when you think thoughts like that," Rob said, when I told him.

"It's easy enough for you to talk," I retorted. "I don't particularly mind a mischievous subconscious, but a deceptive one is something else again."

"Do *you* think Seth is deceptive?" Rob asked. "If you do, you should quit the whole thing."

"No. But even though I think telepathy is possible . . . I can't quite believe that in a trance state, through me, another personality read someone else's mind — that's it!" I said. "I've put my finger on it. Besides, I didn't like Seth taking you to task in front of Mark. And that made me question if I was really far more disturbed than I think I was because you didn't help with Miss Cunningham the other night. What a beautiful and sneaky thing to do! Have a secondary personality give you the dickens over it — and in front of company — with me supposedly in the clear, taking no responsibility for it at all."

"But then, you'd hide it all from yourself," Rob objected. "You'd never suspect."

"Yes. Yes," I said, near tears. "But maybe I'm just too smart for my own good."

"Why can't you just take Mark's word for it?" Rob said.

I looked up. "I don't know. But if it's true, then we're really involved in something with fantastic potential . . . highly unique in a way . . . and that sounds too egotistical. . . .

In this particular period, we had Seth and the Seth Material only — twenty-six sessions — and thus far, no evidential material at all; there was nothing to go on except our experience and faith in ourselves. I'd always trusted myself as a writer. As a psychic, I felt on very shaky ground for a while. Yet Rob always managed to help me see things in perspective, and this time, he again helped me maintain faith in myself and my abilities.

During the next days, I regained my positive frame of mind. Several times, flashes of concepts came to me while I was housecleaning — sudden intrusive patterns of thought accompanied by a feeling of intellectual and emotional illumination. I felt at these times as if new information was being "popped into my head," or rather, into my whole being. And I knew that, mentally, I only retained a part of it. These experiences made me accept the telepathy episode in the last session, though I still wasn't sure of the agent involved.

Rob felt my attitude was rigid, and it was, of course. Yet, I'd made some progress. In the twenty-seventh session, February 19, 1964, Seth told us we could dispense with the Ouija board completely. Up to that time we'd used it to open sessions. He said,

There are many things I want to tell you tonight. For one thing, you may dispense with the board. It was important in the beginning, but after this it served to upset Ruburt. It was in the way, and he kept waiting for the most favorable moment to dispense with it and begin speaking for me, so that he became anxious. Do not let it go, however. That is, do not return it. It has sentimental value.

Rob smiled, amused by Seth's rather cavalier advice to keep the board. It belonged to our landlord.

When your training is much further advanced, we may be able to take certain shortcuts, Seth continued. It is difficult for me to have to string this material out in words and for you to record it. You see, it is possible, in theory, for you to directly experience a concept-essence of the material in any given session. This would involve the utilization of most, if not all inner senses, operating as a whole cognizance field. You cannot perform such an achievement yet.

And as for advancements as of now — these have to do with the 'flashes' that Ruburt has received between sessions. He has achieved a state in which he can receive inner data from me more readily. But beyond that, he is now able in some small way to contact me. That is, I have contacted you in the past, and now he is gaining the ability to contact me.

"Does this apply to both of us, or just to Jane?" Rob asked.

That ability is also growing on your part, Joseph, and with you, it will involve visionary data, as you call it. And another word about our material; Ruburt's mind is an excellent one and well given to serve our ends at this time. There is a reciprocal

agreement here, a give and take, quite different from your friend's idea of psychological invasion.

"Mark's idea?" Rob asked.

Indeed. One reason for the success of our communications is the peculiar abilities in both of you and the interaction between them — and the use you let me make of them. Ruburt's intellect had to be of high quality. His subconscious and conscious mind had to be acquainted with certain ideas to begin with, in order for the complexity of this material to come through.

In the beginning particularly, there is always a distortion of such material by the person who receives it. So a person whose personal prejudices are at a minimum is excellent. Ruburt's prejudices happen to lie along lines which do not contradict what I know to be true — so much the better — and there is less resistance.

There must, of necessity however, be some distortion. If our communication involved invasion, then there would be no distortion because the person so 'invaded' would be blotted — out and this is not possible.

When you are tired, Joseph, we will take a break, or you may move around the room. Are you comfortable?

"Yes," Rob said.

Now people who believe strongly in your organized religions are used to thinking in terms of an inner world. For that reason, many of them have been recipients of inner data from others like myself. They are often endowed with a readiness to listen, for one thing . . . there are disadvantages involved, however, which I do not like to encounter.

Material like this is sifted through many layers of subconscious conceptions and is subsequently colored to some degree. People believing strongly in your organized religions often color the material in highly disadvantageous ways. Ruburt's mind is much like my own, though if you'll forgive me, in a very limited fashion. Therefore the distortions are much less harmful, more easily discovered and cleared. I suggest you break.

Ruburt's "Idea Construction" let me know that we could work together. Neither of you are empty channels to be filled, willy-nilly by my communcations.

(Rob's notes: I had to ask Jane to repeat the last few words of the above paragraph. As soon as I did, a startling thing happened. Jane-Seth began to talk in a very loud and exceptionally vibrant voice, as if an extra charge of energy was suddenly made available. This strong voice persisted, though it did drop some in volume as the session continued.)

In my operations in your plane, I must use the materials at hand, but despite any ideas to the contrary, this involves a give and take . . . Ruburt's "Idea Construction" was rather amazing under the circumstances. The inner senses provided him with much, but the manuscript itself [as written up] also represented an achievement of the conscious mind. I was drawn by this to realize that you were ready for me.

The session went on as Seth gave Rob some excellent psychological insights into his own behavior, and tied this is with early experience in this life, and with relationships with his present family in past life existences. The strong voice continued, and once during a break, Rob asked me how I felt. "Like a full sail, filled with energy, carried on, full blast," I said.

Then, toward the end of the session, Seth made a suggestion about our living quarters. Our living room is very large — opens from the apartment house hallway and runs down to three large bay windows at the other end. I always worked at my table in front of the windows. Seth suggested that we shield the door to the hallway with a room divider.

You are so consciously aware of your own needs for privacy, Joseph, that Ruburt's strong but mostly unconscious needs in these directions sometimes go unsatisfied, since he is not aware

*of them. . . . You are both very much alike beneath the obvious
differences, but Ruburt's largely unrecognized needs along these
lines are important. . . . He holds and collects his psychic
energy, and without knowing it, he does not like it to 'bleed'
outward. The illusion of an entryway — an inner hall — would
serve these ends. This is merely a suggestion.*

Then, room by room, Seth commented on our physical arrangements. He suggested that the bed be placed with the head at the
north, for example, and made other comments. He said that many
of my needs were really based on fears which would have to be
faced as time went by, and he discussed several of them in the
session. Then he said,

*Arrangements you can think of that will satisfy some of these
needs are worth it. If Ruburt had his way, something would
shield you both from the door, also, when you are eating. He
does not like to eat in view of others. (As when someone comes
to the door at mealtime.) Any corner working place pleases him
because it provides for the collection of psychic energy and
serves as protection.*

*[Ruburt] is unpredictable in that he is tempermentally
good-natured, but you never know when the rocks will fly, and
neither does he. Added to this is his strong domestic feelings
now as a woman — and this, my dear Joseph, explains the
incredible amount of furniture movings in which you have been
involved.*

*Your own working room should not be disturbed — that is,
you should continue to have it. This is very important for you.
Ruburt will benefit from the same kind of arrangement
whenever it is possible, but he will get along well in the large
room with the suggestions offered.*

Later, closing the session, he added two afterthoughts. Once he
said,

A barricade in front of the door is not necessary. Afterwards,

as we sat discussing the suggestions, he said, *I do not want
Ruburt's energies soaked up in trying to fight these needs. We
need all of your energies for our work — and for your own.
Later you will learn to use these energies well and to draw
energy from the basic vitality of the universe.*

"Oh," I said, "a ghost telling me how to arrange the furniture. I
am off my rocker!"

"I though you didn't think he was a ghost?" Rob said, grinning.

"You knew I'd react this way!" I said. "You think it's funny!"

"Well it does have humorus aspects," Rob said. "I could hardly
keep a straight face, hearing Seth make the suggestions and knowing ahead of time what you'd say. He knew too — it *was* funny."

But we spent the weekend rearranging furniture. Rob stacked
some bookcases, bought vertical dowels for the top, and arranged
the whole affair in front of the door so that we had an inside entry
hall. We used the bookcases for the books on psychic phenomena
that we were beginning to collect and started some potted philo-
dendron vines between the dowels. The minute the bookcase was
in place, I felt more at ease. We've changed its location several
times but never removed it. Today the vines go to the ceiling. I
know now that if it hadn't been for this divider, we would have
moved long ago. Just the same, with the attitude I had at the time,
I'm glad I didn't know about the letter that was to arrive the next
day.

About three weeks previously, Rob had written to a psychologist
interested in reincarnation. He enclosed some session copies,
mostly dealing with reincarnational material. Two days after the
twenty-seventh session, we received a letter from him. He told us
that the very fluency of the material suggested that it might come
from my subconscious, though it was impossible to tell. (He mentioned the Patience Worth case, with which we were now familiar,
as a notable exception.) But he also cautioned that in some circumstances, amateur mediumship could lead to mental problems.

The letter upset me considerably, yet it also objectified some of my own doubts. They were out in the air where I could at least deal with them. As far as we could tell, for all of my stewing and hemming and hawing, there were no alarming changes in my personality. I was doing twice the creative work I had done earlier. I was satisfied with the quality of the Seth Material; it was far superior to anything I could do on my own. If nothing else, I thought the sessions presented a way of making deeply unconscious knowledge available on a consistent basis.

I was determined to go ahead. There was too much to learn for me to stop. Besides, I felt that this was "my thing;" something that came unannounced, suddenly, into my life; something that I could not ignore; that I had to see through or regret my lack of courage for the rest of my life. Rob saw, much more clearly than I did, the connection between psychic experience and my poetry and earlier subjective experience.

But the letter made me cautious, too. Quite unknowingly, I set one side of myself — the intellectual — as a watchdog against the intuitive portions of the self. The tendency had always been present, but now I determined to go ahead — often by double-checking my every step. Later, I would have to learn to relax with myself again.

In the meantime, we held our twenty-eighth session. In it, Seth assured us that the sessions were constructive and made many comments quoted in *The Seth Material* about the nature of the subconscious, repeating that he was an independent personality.

There is no danger of dissociation grabbing ahold of Ruburt like some black vague and furry monster, carrying him away to the netherlands of hysteria, schizophrenia or insanity. I have consistently advised contacts with the world at large and advised you both to use your abilities to meet outside challenges. Withdrawal into dissociation as a hiding place from the world could, of course, have dire consequences. Certain personalities could and have fallen prey here, but with you this is not the case. . . .

Also, Ruburt has experienced and used dissociation in his

*work, though to a lesser degree, before our communications and
knows how to handle it. . . . Our relationship will enable you
both to deal more adequately with the outside world. . . . The
development of the inner senses will not blot out physical reality
but allow you to see it more clearly for what it is, and,
therefore, you will be able to manipulate camouflage patterns
better. . . .*

"I trust him," Rob said, simply. "The psychological understanding he's given me, alone, is terrific."

"Well, okay, ever onward," I said, because despite it all, I felt it foolish to look a gift horse in the mouth. I also felt that in each of us there is a deep connection with "magical" elements of our nature—magical in that they rise like poetic inspiration, filling the mundane world with a special living, personal meaning. To refuse such "gifts" from the "gods" might be far more dangerous than accepting them. These thoughts were far beneath my conscious ones, though. Only now, writing this book, did I recall entertaining them.

Still, I didn't know what to make of the material Seth gave us on dreams and the personality that night. Was it symbolically true or practically true or both? When it was typed, we both read it over several times. We were to discover that the dream universe was far more valid than we had ever supposed, but what Seth said then sounded like nothing we had ever read or heard before.

It was Session 28, February 24, 1964 and our second session without the board. Seth was right; I had grown anxious wondering just when to dispense with it in a session and let him speak, yet it represented something solid and real that helped the transition take place. Now I just sat there until suddenly I fell into trance and Seth began to speak.

*In a dream, I have said, you can experience many days while
no corresponding amount of physical time passes. It seems as if*

you travel very far in the flicker of an eyelash. Now, condensed
time is the time felt by the entity, while any of its given
personalities live on a plane of physical materialization. To go
into this further, many have said that life was a dream. They
were true to the facts in one regard, yet far afield as far as the
main issue is concerned.

The life of any given individual could be legitimately
compared to the dream of an entity. While the individual suffers
and enjoys his given number of years, these years are but a flash
to the entity. The entity is concerned with them in the same
way that you are concerned with your dreams. As you give
inner purpose and organization to your dreams, and as you
obtain insight and satisfaction from them, though they involve
only a portion of your life, so the entity to some extent directs
and gives purpose and organization to his personalities. So does
the entity obtain insights and satisfactions from its existing
personalities, although no one of them takes up all of its
attention.

And as your dreams originate with you, rise from you, attain
a seeming independence and have their ending with you, so do
the entity's personalities arise from him, attain various degrees
of independence and return to him while never leaving him for
an instant.

You are familiar through your reading with so-called
secondary personalities. Now, this idea comes close to the
relationship between the entity and its personalities. They are
independent to various degrees, and they operate on various
planes of existence for purposes of overall fulfillment and
development.

To a lesser degree, you function along these lines in varying
roles when you exist simultaneously as a member of a family, a
community and a nation and as an artist or writer. As you
attempt to use your abilities, so does the entity use its abilities,
and he organizes his various personalities and, to some extent,

directs their activities while still allowing them what you could call free will. . . .

Your own dreams are fragments, even as you are fragments of your entity. An unrecognized unity and organization lies within all of your dreams, beneath their diversity. And your dreams, while part of you, also exist apart.

The dream world has its own reality, its own 'time' and its own inner organization. As the entity is only partially concerned with its personalities after setting them into motion, so you are unconcerned with this dream world after you have set it into motion. But it exists.

To a different degree, it is filled with conscious semi-personalities. They are not [as a rule] as developed as you are, as you are not as developed as your entity is. That dream world experiences its own continuity. It is not aware of any break, for example, when you are waking. It does not know if you sleep or wake. It merely exists to a fairly vivid degree while you dream or sleep, and it sleeps but does not 'die' when you waken. . . .

The entity itself does not have to keep constant track of its personalities because each one possesses an inner self-conscious part that knows its origin. This part, for now, I will call the self-conscious beyond the subconscious. . . . I mentioned that some part of you knows exactly how much oxygen the lungs breathe, and this is the part of which I spoke. It also receives all inner data.

This portion of the personality translates inner data and sifts it through the subconscious, which is a barrier and also a threshold to the present personality. I told you also that the topmost layers of the subconscious contain personal memories and beneath — racial memory. The personality is not actually layered, of course, but continuing with the necessary analogy, beneath the racial memories you look out upon another dimension of reality with the face of this other self-conscious part of you.

*This portion is 'turned toward' the entity. When such abilities
as telepathy are used, this function is carried on continually by
this other self-conscious part of you. But as a rule, you act upon
such data without the knowledge of the ordinary conscious self.*

*There is also a corresponding, but 'lesser' self-consciousness
that connects your present personalities with the dream world,
which is aware of its origin and communicates data from you to
dream reality. . . .*

It was in this session that Seth made the analogy of the "weird
creature with two faces," one turned to physical reality and one to
inner reality, both conscious and aware, each representing one
facet of our consciousness.

I was going to mention the furniture arrangements that we embarked upon during this time but find that a few excerpts from
this same session give a pretty fair picture. They are pertinent for
several reasons. Seth seemed to know how we could best utilize
our surroundings to serve conscious and unconscious needs. We'd
been in the apartment three years when the sessions began, yet in
a few session comments Seth managed to clear up several points
that we had had never settled.

*Now a small chat about your hilarious furniture changings
and rechangings and rechangings. The bookcases should stay as
they are, Ruburt. Enough is enough, and you have optimum
benefit from them. The bedroom arrangement is fine, and if no
one will blame Ruburt's subconscious, then I would venture one
further suggestion. It is not, however, to involve any more
complicated arrangements on Ruburt's part. Simply put: The
addition of a small desk and chair to the bedroom as a more or
less permanent fixture for a small private place, accessible when
he wants it, for our so-sensitive and sometimes pig-headed
Ruburt. . . .*

*Otherwise, Ruburt should be satisfied. I suggest the bookcases
as a permanent arrangement. These are, after all, only logical*

suggestions to make your daily lives more comfortable, and
therefore free your energies. Ruburt can calm down now. I
never saw such stirrings and slammings and carrying-ons. . . .

Rob laughed about all this after the session. "A terrific lot of
new material, really startling, on dream reality and some suggestions about your furniture, all in one night!"

I had to grin. "I've always moved furniture, even as a kid," I
said. "I used to move from a side bedroom to a front one whenever
the mood hit me. The front room was my work-mood room, with
all my poetry books predominating and no curtains, very spare.
The other room was my play-it-safe-be-like-everybody-else-mood-
curtains and conventional paraphernalia."

"And now?" Rob asked.

"And now . . . the objects represent inner things we don't recognize, and when we move them around, we rearrange the inner
feelings too; or vice versa. But suppose Seth starts really telling us
how to arrange stuff. I mean, whenever he wants to. . . ."

"I knew you'd think of that," Rob said. But I had nothing to
worry about. After "settling us down," making the few changes
that seemed to be of such great help, Seth left all housekeeping
problems to me.

11

Seth Keeps Track of Miss Cunningham

So Do I

An Out-of-Body Experience

A few nights following Miss Cunningham's hospitalization, we went to visit her. We had never been inside the hospital before. As we went inside, I stopped dead. There in front of me was the lobby I had seen in my July dream — complete with the glassed-in gift area. I told Rob on our way to Miss Cunningham's room.

This time we both stopped in dismay. There sat Miss Cunningham, tied in bed, her eyes wild, her hair tangled. She was incapable of any communication. As I stood there, suddenly I "heard" Seth tell me, mentally, that my dream had forseen her condition which would lead to her death.

I wasn't used to any messages from Seth when I was out of the house, and I'd been in the habit of discouraging any when I wasn't having a session. The whole affair was disturbing. I was glad to get back out in the spring night air. There was little need to stay, and again, it was a session night.

Our living room seemed twice as cozy that evening, with the

warm lights and Willie sleeping on the rug. But I said to Rob, "Look, Miss Cunningham was as rational and bright as either of us not too long ago. What happened? How do we know it won't happen to us?" And the comfortable room suddenly seemed a facade. In years to come, where would we be? What difference could it make that we ever sat in this room, or had sessions, or moved furniture, or stroked the cat? So I didn't feel like going into a trance.

Yet, at nine o'clock, as always, I "clicked out" and Seth began to speak. Immediately he began to discuss Miss Cunningham, and my dream.

Ruburt wove a dream about a legitimate telepathic communication. The information was correct in its bare essentials. Any such inner communications are basically the same in that they are picked up by the inner senses, whether the information seems telepathic or clairvoyant in your terms.

The actual communication is not in words or pictures. Material from the inner senses is seldom experienced in its true form. What you get is a hasty twisting of channels, a rather inept and sometimes rather disastrous attempt to pick up such information with the outer senses.

At the precise time of Ruburt's dream, Miss Cunningham was deciding to leave this plane of reality. Ruburt received the message directly. The unwillingness on Miss Cunningham's part represented her present personality's protest against the change that a deeper part of herself deemed necessary and proper.

It was Miss Cunningham's discovery that she needed operations on both eyes that caused this deeper decision. When Ruburt learned about the projected operations, he leapt to the conclusion that this was the meaning of the dream. Subconsciously, however, he knew that far more was involved. Part of the subconscious fantasy in the dream was valid, representing a watered-down version of the actual communication — for example, Miss Cunningham's dark apparel.

Miss Cunningham had been preparing herself for her own departure since she heard of the possible operations. Yet consciously, she was ignorant of her own inner decision.

"Where does Frank Withers fit in here?" Rob asked.

She did not remember him . . . as she taught his children. He admired her very much as his children, one in particular, found her an excellent teacher. Frank Withers considered her a friend, attaching more importance than she did to her influence upon his children. But beyond this, Miss Cunningham's present personality has been gently disentangling itself from this plane of reality — and she simply did not remember him.

Of course, the conscious mind cannot be aware of such critical inner decisions. . . . The disentanglement of her personality has been gentle and gradual. She is focusing less and less in this plane of reality, and again, gradually, she will begin to focus in another. There is a period of adjustment after leaving any plane, although yours involves the most difficulty since your camouflage pattern is unusually rigid.

All kinds of questions came into Rob's mind. When Seth paused for a moment, he asked, "You said once that the shock of birth was worse than the shock of death. Why?"

The shock of birth is worse. The new personality is not entirely focused, and it must make immediate critical adjustments of the strongest nature. Death in your terms is a termination but does not involve such immediately critical manipulations. There is 'time' to catch up, so to speak. Already Miss Cunningham's vital core of awareness is appearing on another plane, and she appears there as a wondering, but not frightened, young girl.

"Will she be . . . fully materialized on another plane before she dies in this one?" Rob asked. It was difficult for him to ask questions and take notes at the same time, but if possible, he wanted the questions answered before he forgot them.

Yes. This is the case in her particular type of withdrawal. In a sudden death, however, this can be more upsetting to the personality involved, and since the new materialization is simultaneous, it can lead to confusion. . . .

"It's a nice thought," I said later to Rob. "I mean, that Miss Cunningham just leaves this old body of hers behind and appears someplace else as a young girl."

"But you don't think it's true?" Rob asked.

"Who knows?" I said. Later I started a poem on the idea, but couldn't follow it through. "I can believe that almost anything is possible, theoretically or . . . philosophically," I said. "When I think of the same thing in practical terms, apply it to life, that's when I pull my horns in."

So the first spring of the sessions came, a cold bright March. Miss Cunningham's apartment door became a stimulus to my constant questions. Every time I passed it, I wondered again: Was she transferring her consciousness to another level of reality? Would she survive death when it came, in meaningful terms? And behind all these questions there was the big one: Was Seth really a personality who had survived death? And would I really ever know?

I wasn't about to close off the Seth material until I made up my mind, though. Another possibility was always in the back of my thoughts. Suppose I stopped having the sessions while I tried to figure things out, then decided that Seth was right on all counts — and found I just couldn't have sessions again? That, to me, would be the worst possibility of all — that I might close off knowledge out of uncertainity. So I kept on.

But the deeper questions were now implied in ordinary events as I went about my day. Springtime again — the release of energy, the flowering of a landscape that, by all appearances, had been dead and nearly lifeless only weeks before. The implied promise of recurring life contrasted drearily with the few things we knew about life while we were in the flesh — much less free of it.

A few days after the last session, I sat in my small office at the art gallery, looking out at the landscaped yard. That afternoon it was difficult to keep my mind on my work. People were coming and going in the hallways. Had they lived before? Was their consciousness born anew, and was it really something quite independent of the images they wore?

Then strange dull sounds; commotion. Startled, I went to the window, hardly able to believe my eyes. The police were shooting down the starlings that always nested in the treetops. Real fury rushed through me. My eyes brimmed over with tears. I stood at the window and dashed out this poem — far too emotionally unrestrained to be esthetically a good one but an excellent example of my feelings at the time.

Rah, Rah, Rah

If there's anything I like to see
It's a bunch of pudgy God-fearing grown men at it
   again,
Shooting down the starlings.
I mean, crazy man. Go, go, go.
Why not have a band play and give balloons away?
There's nothing like killing birds
To clean up the business section.
We could feature a Starling Day, for our centennial
   celebration,
Such elation as the city fathers
And other pot-bellied elders
Did their best to keep the city clean.
We could give ice cream away to the kids who killed
   the most,
The hosts of observers could yell the cheer:
"Oh, it takes such courage and it takes such brawn
To drop the blackbirds on the County House lawn."

I wrote four more poems of varying merit about that one event and behind the whole affair was defiant recognition of the value of any consciousness, whatever its form. And the deeper question: Why was it ever annihilated, at least in our terms? Why was life constructed to be destroyed? I knew, even then, that I had to find my own answers — that each of us does. And yet at that point, I felt duty-bound to question my own experiences, Seth and the sessions because I refused to hide in self-delusions.

Unknowingly, in my poetry I had barely begun to form some concepts that would help me. Just before the sessions began the idea of "The Idiot" came to me as a symbol of inner truth that appears to be complete nonsense to the reasoning mind at times; or at best, highly impractical in normal living. I'd written two poems on the idea, and the day after the starlings were killed, I did another:

The Idiot

The idiot cries.
The tears slosh inside his boots.
The people say he's bats
Because he weeps
When the police shoot down the starlings
Aiming at the tall-eyed trees.

The idiot swears
That the birds are holy.
He shouts as the starlings drop
And the police chuckle good-naturedly
"Stop. The spirits are displeased.
Look how the bare branches rustle."

"Do unto others, I tell you."
He wanted to say more
But they carted him off.
The good people laughed.

> *On the ground was a puddle*
> *Of the idiot's tears.*
>
> *One man bent to wash his hands in it*
> *And saw*
> *The skin peel off like dirt,*
> *But the lawn was full*
> *With the falling corpses of the birds,*
> *And when he cried out, no one heard.*

I'd identified all life with the birds, of course. Miss Cunningham, Rob, me and all the people that we knew were surely getting shot down; falling through time, we were dying in a descent that we couldn't understand or control. Either that, or Seth and the material — still so strange to me — were giving answers that I refused, so far, to accept in practical terms.

And while I persisted in my uncertainty, Seth continued to explain the nature of the interior universe, giving clues and hints that I would eventually follow, laying down the framework that would allow me to deal with precisely those questions that concerned me.

He kept emphasizing the inner senses. In the next session, the thirty-first, on March 2, 1964, he said,

If you will use psychological time as I have told you, you will get immediate first-hand experience with many facets of reality which take me pages to explain with the use of words. All entities are self-aware portions of the energy of All That Is. They are self-generating, and if you understand this, you will stop thinking in terms of beginnings and endings.

The inner senses operate on all planes and under all circumstances. The outer senses vary according to plane and circumstance. The outer senses are dependable only in terms of the definite system of reality for which they were constructed. Their purpose, of course, is to enable the conscious personality to recognize as valid, camouflage patterns that are only valid under certain conditions. . . .

Joseph was correct when he spoke of entities creating stages upon which to act out their problems. The point is that once the play begins, the actors are so completely engrossed in their roles that they forget that they themselves wrote the play, constructed the sets or are even acting.

The reason is rather apparent: If you know that a situation is 'imaginary,' you are not going to come to grips with it. This way, you have your actors taking the situation as it seems to be but looking about in amazement now and then to wonder how they got where they are, who constructed the sets and so forth. They do not realize that the whole thing is self-created, nor should they in the main, since the urgency to solve problems would dissolve.

Rob was all ready to ask, "Well, how come you're letting us in on the secret?" But he never had a chance to ask the question.

I'm not worried that I'm going to disturb the balance. Far from it. The fact is that the realization can, and often does, come after the play is well under way, and at this point, the camouflage action is so involved that the realization itself appears in the framework of the camouflage and is often indistinguishable from it. . . .

Remembering how upset I had been about the death of the starlings, Rob asked, "Could you say something about the birds that were killed at the gallery?"

Ruburt was upset, and with good reason. . . . It goes without saying that a bird's death is inevitable, but a cat killing a bird does not have to juggle the same sort of values with which a man must be concerned. For now, suffice it to say that to kill for self-protection or food on your plane does not involve you in what we may call for the first time, I believe, karmic consequences.

*To kill for convenience . . . or for the sake of killing involves
rather dire consequences, and the emotional value behind such
killing is often as important as what is killed. That is, the lust
[for] killing is also a matter that brings dire consequences,
regardless of the particular living thing that is killed. This
involves value judgments of a very important type, and I will
not go into them tonight.*

"All right. Could you say anything about Miss Cunningham's
condition?" Rob asked.

*Only that she will regain periods of lucidity, but overall, her
condition will not improve.*

"Would it help if we visited her?"

A visit might help you.

Actually we didn't get up to see her for some time. In the thirty-
third session, March 9, Seth told us that April 15 would be a critical date for Miss Cunningham, but that is all he said.

During these springtime sessions, my voice began to deepen
considerably. At times it was startlingly vibrant and powerful,
with the masculine tones quite noticeable. Rob was convinced
that it contained an additional energy, rather impossible for my
own vocal chords — the resonance in particular.

One night Rob asked Seth about it, and Seth said,

*It's one of my little tricks to add to Ruburt's faltering and
erratic confidence — and again, this is with his inner
permission.*

*It is not my voice, but a representation or approximation of
it. Furthermore, in your terms, I do not have a voice. . . .*

Both of us had been wondering about the crisis Seth had mentioned for Miss Cunningham on April 15. As it happened a regular
session night fell on that date, and, having heard nothing, Rob
asked Seth if there had been any distortion in the message.

*No. Today or rather late this evening, before 2:00 A.M. in
the morning, she will undergo a severe crisis, and rapid*

deterioration of brain tissue will result. The last struggles of the ego will take place. It will finally understand, however, that it will not be dumped aside but taken along as itself, independent as always, to stand beside other independent egos each of whom represents facets of the entire entity. . . .

On April 23, I met Miss Cunningham's niece in the hall and asked about her condition. "Oh, didn't you know?" she said. "We had to take her to a nursing home. She became so violent that the hospital called and told us we'd have to move her. She upset the whole floor, ran screaming up and down the halls, threw dishes at the nurses and was completely irrational."

For a moment I didn't know what to say. It was almost impossible to imagine Miss Cunningham indulging in such behavior. Then I remembered the date given by Seth, so I asked as casually as I could, "When did all this happen?"

"Right in the middle of the month — April 15, I think it was," she said, without hesitation. "The hospital refused to keep her for even one more day, and that night we had her transferred."

Miss Cunningham stayed in the nursing home for a short time when the family was notified again that she was unmanagable, and that other arrangements would have to be made. Once she ran out of the place in her nightgown, out into the busy street in the middle of evening traffic. Not wanting to commit her, the relatives returned her to the apartment, in care of a part-time housekeeper.

She stayed here several months, without ever showing any signs of violent behavior. But her mind deteriorated more and more. She thought she was getting threatening letters.

"Mrs. Butts, Mrs. Butts," she'd call, and when I answered my door, she'd say, "Come, see. Look." And she'd rush ahead of me down the hall, so agitated that she'd shake all over. "Here's one of those letters. Oh, where is it? It was here. Oh, I know I saved it."

She'd almost tear the apartment apart looking for the threatening letter that she was sure had come in the mail. She was so persuasive that the first two times this happened, I wondered if she *was* getting threatening mail, as unlikely as this seemed. I suggested that we open her mail together each day, but then she still insisted that the letters came — slid beneath the door — and, of course, she always misplaced them or lost them. So, for a while it was touch and go. I was very worried about her.

During this period I was trying the psychological time exercises suggested by Seth, and often, just when I got started, Miss Cunningham would interrupt me. One day I went into the bedroom where it was quiet, closed my eyes, lay down and began clearing my mind of thoughts for my psy-time exercise. Several times Miss Cunningham came to mind: I wanted to ask her doctor about her condition but hesitated because I wasn't a member of her family.

Suddenly I felt a strong jolt at the top of my skull; the next instant, I found myself standing on the front steps of an ordinary house. The bedroom was gone. Utterly bewildered, I looked about me, somehow "knowing" that I was still in Elmira. The neighborhood was middle-class, the house gray-framed, two-storied, with a front porch.

I blinked my eyes. Did I have amnesia? Had I actually walked here under my own power and forgotten? It didn't occur to me then that I was having an out-of-body experience. For one thing, Seth had only mentioned them briefly; and for another, everything was so real that I took it for granted that I was in my body and as physical as anything else was.

Then the screen door opened. Dr. Levine, Miss Cunningham's doctor, came out on the porch. He stood talking for a moment with a woman who remained inside. I thought: "I might as well ask him about Miss Cunningham anyway, regardless of what's going on." So I waited; in a moment, the doctor came down the steps. I walked over to him and said, "Hi Sam. Could I talk to you for a minute?"

He looked right through me, taking no notice of me at all. Since we were acquaintances, I was indignant. "Sam," I said again, but he walked briskly past. I looked at him fully in the face, running ahead of him, ready to confront him with "What's the matter with you?" But, instead, I realized that he didn't see me. He never saw me at all.

Now I was really frightened. Was I a ghost? The warm sunlight was everywhere on the lawns, and the shadows were real. There was no doubt that this was the physical world. Then why didn't I show up in it? Suddenly I remembered the jolt I'd felt at the base of my neck . . . had I had an attack of some sort? Maybe I was delirious? But I was thinking rationally.

In the meantime, the doctor got into his car and drove away. I stood there, yelling at him and wondering how I would get home. Then suddenly I thought: "Could I be out of my body?" But how, since I didn't remember leaving it? Quickly I looked at the house. The street number wasn't visible, and I was in the middle of the block, away from street signs. At that moment, I felt another sharp jolt at the back of my neck and instantly found myself back in my bedroom, fully alert and awake.

All kinds of thoughts flooded to my mind. Consciousness *was* independent of the body — Seth was right — and if that was true, then there was no reason why he couldn't be what he said he was: an independent personality, out of the flesh. But why hadn't I caught on sooner? And why hadn't I run up to see if the house mailbox had a name on it? I couldn't wait till Rob came home so I could tell him what happened.

He was envious. I was triumphant. This time, I didn't have to wait for him to report what I'd done while I was in a Seth trance. I'd been myself. "And I know it wasn't a hallucination," I said. "I was completely alert, and the whole thing brings up so many questions . . . and ideas for experiments."

"You should call Sam and ask him where he was when you saw him," Rob said.

Yet, as badly as I wanted to check this out, I just couldn't bring myself to call Dr. Levine. "He'll think I was out of my mind instead of out of my body," I said. "And what excuse could I use? If I knew what the street was, I could at least say, 'I thought I saw you on such-and-such a street.' "

"The impetus must have been your desire to ask Sam about Miss Cunningham," Rob said.

"Well, *I* know I was out of my body. That's what counts as far as I'm concerned," I said. "In that 'Idea Construction' thing I didn't seem to have a body — I seemed to just be my consciousness. So I never made any connection at first between the two experiences. . . .

We had no idea then that I would be involved in still more startling episodes with Miss Cunningham, but I grinned, looking out the window. I'd been on my first real "field trip." I didn't have to take everything Seth said on faith alone. The psychological time exercises suddenly took on greater significance. I was ready now to really use the inner senses. And almost immediately after this, Seth began his discussions on the nature of dream reality and the methods that would let us explore it for ourselves. If I could leave my body and go out into the physical world, then I didn't see why I couldn't leave it and explore the inner one.

PART THREE

Exploration of the
Interior Universe

Investigation of Dream Reality

12

Dream Recall: How to Remember Your Dreams

Dream Investigation

As the Seth sessions continued, our activities fell generally into three main divisions. First of all, the emphasis was on the delivery of the Seth Material itself, as in the twice-weekly sessions Seth continued to explain the nature of nonphysical reality. Second, we became involved in trying to obtain "evidential" material, some definite instances of extrasensory perception on Seth's part. Along these lines, we embarked on long-distance tests with a psychologist and a year's series of envelope tests in which Seth was asked to identify the contents of doubly-sealed envelopes. At the same time, Seth began to send me on out-of-body journeys during some sessions and to offer, on his own, other instances of "paranormal" activity.

In my book, *The Seth Material*, I explained some of these episodes. They convinced us that valid instances of ESP were being demonstrated. In the out-of-body experiences, Seth correctly described events that happened across the country and in Puerto Rico. Our own envelope tests not only demonstrated ESP but also offered evocative glimpses into the methods by which such information is received.

Third, we were involved in vigorous subjective activity as we began to experiment with Seth's psy-time regularly and to follow his suggestions concerning dream investigation, recall and utilization. When we began, neither Rob nor I really suspected that there was a separate dream dimension in which dreams happened. Though Seth told us that the experiments in dream recall would automatically make our consciousness more flexible, his real meaning didn't come through to me until I found myself manipulating dreams and later having out-of-body experiences from the dream state.

The interior universe is at least as rich, varied and complicated as the exterior one. Dream reality is only one aspect of this inner universe, in the same way that our planet is only one of many others in a physical sky. Before our experiments began, I used to think that dreams were relatively chaotic productions, with a few subconscious insights thrown in for good measure, now and then — a nightly retreat into idiocy for the tired brain. I considered sleep a small death in which all sense of continuity vanished. Most of the dreams I'd recalled until then had been nightmares — the self gone mad, I thought — so I wasn't prepared for Seth's emphasis on the importance of dreams.

Yet, even when we admit the inspirational and supportive nature of dreams, even when we learn to recall dreams and apply them to daily life, we still only begin to glimpse their multidimensional reality. Dream interpretation is important to our three-dimensional mentalities, for example. We believe in utilization; if dreams can't be useful, then what good are they? Dreams can give us consistent, valid information about our motives, needs and decisions. They can be utilized as very practical aids to daily life. But this is only a portion of any real exploration of dream reality.

Dream investigation or manipulation as an aesthetic pursuit —

as an art, embarked upon for its own sake — this is something else again and is sometimes suspect because of its solitary nature. Yet the fact remains that there is a dream reality with a "structure," "landscape" and images that appear to be made of matter — but matter that obeys different rules than those with which we are familiar.

Dreams are not *just* psychological events. There is a dimension of reality (an "objective" dimension, if you prefer) in which all dream events happen. There are rules; Seth calls them root-assumptions that operate in all realities, our own included. We have to learn what root-assumptions govern dream reality. I know that we can on occasion manipulate dream events; my students and I do this frequently. If we follow certain "rules" given to us by Seth, we will get more or less predictable results in the dream state — an indication that an "objective" dream dimension exists quite independently of us or our dreams, a dream dimension in which my dreams and yours have their being.

Just reading such ideas will never convince you of their validity. Seth has always emphasized that all true knowledge must be directly experienced; therefore, I will include throughout this book his instructions and suggestions for dream recall, investigation and manipulation.

If we ever hope to "map" the dreamscape, we need a million trained dreamers: a million individuals trained to use dreams as vehicles and then, courageously, to leave them to explore the environment in which they find themselves. We need people able to distinguish between the environment-within-the-dream and the far vaster environment (or atmosphere or medium) in which these dream-places exist.

Records of individual dreams are not enough, nor are studies of the physiological effect of dreaming. Most psychologists would not admit the existence of a definite structured universe in which dream acts, rather than physical acts, happen. Therefore, at this time, they will not consider dreams in this larger context. Seth maintains that we will understand ourselves as dreamers only if we are also aware of the larger environment in which dreams take place, that we interact in the dream state as we do in the waking one and that we form mass dream events as we form physical events on a mass basis.

Because we must start somewhere, however, we will begin with dream recall and those practical aspects of dream investigation that let us use our dreams in daily life. For one thing, Seth followed this procedure with us, and it is the method I use to lead my students into dream reality. This is a gradual process that gently leads the ego into largely unfamiliar territory and at the same time encourages flexibility of consciousness.

This section of the book will include excerpts from Seth's manuscripts on the general nature of dream reality, dream investigation and recall and will be followed by a series of chapters on various kinds of dreams captured by Rob, my students and me as we checked out Seth's theories, as far as we were able. Later, we will journey further into the inner dimension in which dreams take place.

Seth gave us our first instructions in 1964. The whole idea of deliberate dream recall was new to us. The methods are not new, though we had never heard of them at the time. I'll paraphrase them here: Simply buy a notebook to be used exclusively for dreams. Keep it with a pencil or pen by your bed. Before you fall to sleep at night, give yourself this suggestion: "I can remember my dreams and write them down in the morning."

You will find that your dreams actually are in your mind when you awaken. Write them down at once, before getting out of bed. If you have a tendency to scribble, then use loose sheets of paper and later transcribe them in the notebook. Don't worry about neatness, but concentrate on capturing as much of the dream content as possible. If you recall several dreams, jot down a quick sentence about each, then add the details. Leave space after each entry for future notes.

This method is really easy and workable — but it can be sabotaged. One of my students, Gloria, had great difficulty remembering her dreams until I discovered that she was using a clock radio to awaken her in the morning and the news happened to be on. The dreams must be recalled before you become mentally involved with the world's activities.

If you have remembered only unpleasant dreams in the past, you may have built up a block against recalling any dreams at all. Mrs. Taylor, another student, had this problem. She gave herself the proper suggestions each night but had the greatest difficulty in remembering even one dream. "Maybe you really don't want to remember any," I said.

At first she insisted that I was wrong. Then she added dubiously, "I only recalled nightmares in the past. I suppose I could be afraid."

But the problem ran deeper than this, as we discovered in class discussion. Like many people, Mrs. Taylor was brought up on a combined emotional porridge of orthodox religion and Freud. In her mind, Freud's ideas of repressed subconscious material merged with religious teachings of hell and the origin of sin. Actually, she was afraid that dreams would reveal her "lower" instincts. I personally think that these distorted ideas about the nature of the inner self represent the main impediments to dream recall or to any real study of the subjective personality.

The unseen self is not a dungeon of repressed ideas and feelings, dangerous to behold, but the fountainhead of individual existence, upon which our present physical survival is dependent. Beyond this, it is our pathway to creative expression, inspiration and wisdom — a doorway to our own greater identity. This does not mean that we do not repress fears and desires beneath consciousness. It means that we must allow ourselves greater flexibility, look into ourselves, admit the fears and release the energy used in repression. As you will see later in this book, dreams can often release such repressed material for your conscious examination.

The method of dream recall just given will allow many people to remember more dreams in a month than they previously did in their entire lives. Variations will occur, however. Periods of excellent recall are sometimes followed by poorer ones, and each individual seems to have his own cycle of significant activity.

A recorder may also be used, of course. You must still play back the tape and transfer the dreams into a notebook, however, so that the records are easily accessible. This actually takes more time, but many people prefer to speak their dream recollections into a recorder at once, rather than to write them down.

It wasn't until 1965 that Seth began to suggest variations of the early dream recall instructions and to add other techniques for more advanced dream investigation. Here are a few excerpts from that material.

"Seth on Dream Recall"
(Excerpts from Session 206, November 8, 1965)

Ruburt's dream notebook is coming along very well. In most cases, however, he writes only those dreams which he remembers upon awakening in the morning. Suggestion will allow you both to awaken yourself as soon as a dream is completed.

The dream will then be fresh. If your recorder is suitably situated with the microphone easily at hand, then you can speak your dream with less effort than is required to write it down. Of course records must be kept. The simplest part of this experiment will involve the use of suggestion to awaken yourself at the completion of each dream.

The number of remembered dreams should be much higher than your present system allows. . . . I also suggest that the first recalled dream for any given evening be compared with the first recalled dream from other evenings, and that the second recalled dream from any one evening be compared with the second dream from other evenings, and so forth.

This should prove highly interesting, and if such experiments are carried on consistently over a period of years, then the results could lead to excellent evidence for the various layers of the subconscious and inner self, of which I have spoken for so long.

Particular notice should also be taken of characters and settings and the approximate period of history in which the dream action occurs. If the dream seems to happen in no specific location and in no particular time, then these facts should also be noted.

Unknown characters within the dream action, persons unknown to you in daily life, should be given careful attention also, and the roles which they play within the dream drama. The primary colors should be noted. It goes without saying now that all dream events should be checked against physical reality so that any clairvoyant elements are clearly checked and recorded. . . .

There are many ways in which you can approach these newer dream experiments. You may, if you prefer, begin by suggesting that you will waken after each of the first five dreams . . . If possible, we want to get the dreams in order here. . . .

Now, there is something else to be considered. The very self-suggestions that will enable you to recall dreams will also change their nature to some extent. This is all right, and the effect will be minimized when the newness has worn off. Again, we want the dreams in the sequence in which they occur. If you do not want to wake up after each dream of the evening, then the suggestion should always include 'I will recall the first three dreams . . . or the first five dreams, or whatever.'

You may try two different wordings for a start, and now I am speaking of precise wording. The first: 'I will wake up after each of my first five dreams and record each one immediately.' The second alternative wording would be the same as the one I have just given, but the 'wake up' would be omitted. That is, it is possible for you to record the dreams, speaking into the microphone without awakening in your terms.

This is not only possible but by far the most convenient. You should try both methods and discover which one works the best for you. If at all possible, the recorder should be in the bedroom (not in another part of the house.) It is the immediate dream recall we are after. We want you to record the dream at the instant of awakening or at the instant that the dream is about to dissolve.

The time involved in going from one room to another could result in the loss of dream content and vividness. The very motor responses demanded on the part of the body and the extra arousal tendency would force you to lose a good deal of valid material. I would prefer that you work less, if necessary, using the recorder in the bedroom, than work more intensively leaving the recorder in another room.

It is the dream we are after, the dream experience in all the vividness that we can capture, and if you are going to get a watered-down version in any case, then you may as well continue with your present method (of writing them down in the morning) and save your sleep.

With the method I have just given you, you will be able to capture as much of the whole dream experience as any investigators manage to do (in dream-labs) when the awakening is done by a mechanical device or by another person. You will also be gaining excellent discipline and training over your own states of consciousness and this, in itself, will be an important yardstick of progress for you both. . . .

Now, mankind uses but a portion of its capabilities. When you are well along in these experiments, you will find that you handle them very well, with no draining of energies. Your sleeping hours are already productive. We shall also use them to give you training in the utilization of various stages of consciousness. Added to this, the training will give you valuable *insight into the nature of dreams in general, the stages of the subconscious and the inner life of the personality when it is dissociated from its physical environment to some considerable extent.*

Much later, there will be other suggestions for you in which you will direct your sleeping self to perform certain activities, visit certain locations and bring back information. This is obviously still very much in the future, but it is well within the abilities of the inner self.

Peg and Bill Gallagher, friends of ours, attended the next session in which Seth continued with his suggestions for our dream experiments. He started out in a jovial manner: *I am indeed glad to see that you are all in such high spirits. For a spirit, I am in a rather high mood myself. Of course, I welcome our Jesuit and cat-lover, as always.* (Seth always referred to Bill as "The Jesuit" because of his quick, inquiring mind and to Peg as "the cat-lover," humorously, because of her strong dislike for cats.) After a few more personal remarks, he launched into the discussion.

There are several kinds of time that will appear within your dreams, and you must sort these out carefully. While sleeping in your present time, you may have a dream that concerns your past, with events that you know to have occurred years ago. Nevertheless, you may experience these events [within the dream] as happening within the present.

The present within which you seem to experience the dream is not, however, the present in physical time — the present in which your body lies upon the bed. There is a fine distinction here and one that you will learn through experience as you go on, so I will not discuss it now.

It should be obvious also that within your dreams a special location that belongs to the present physical time can be experienced in the past or in the future within the dream framework, and again, there is much more here also than meets the eye; so watch out so that you can catch these developments.

I am particularly interested in these experiments, and as a preliminary for them, we will have you work with suggestion alone before you attempt to begin with your recordings. . . . We shall have you both working well in your sleep, for the dream will not be captured in a laboratory — by scientists who will not look into their own dreams.

The nature of reality can be approached only by an investigation of it as it is directly experienced in all levels of awareness: reality as it appears under dream conditons, under other conditions of dissociation and as it appears in the waking state. Even studies dealing with the conscious state are usually superficial, dealing only with 'upper' levels of egotistical awareness. . . .

All layers of the personality are 'conscious.' They simply operate like compartments, so that often one portion of the self is not aware of other portions. As a rule, when you are awake you do not know your sleeping self; you know your neighbor far better, so your sleeping self seems mysterious indeed. When you are awake, as Ruburt himself has written, you cannot find the dream locations that have been so familiar to you only the night before.

In your sleep, you may have greeted friends who are strangers to your waking self. But consider the other side of the coin. For when you are asleep, you usually cannot find the street upon which you live your waking hours, and when you are asleep, you do not know your waking self. The sleeping self is your identity.

There are connections between these two conditions, and there are definite realities that exist in both states, and these are what you are looking for. Only by finding these can you discover the nature of human personality and the nature of reality within which it operates.

We have also spoken of the dream as a drama, and you must

discover the various levels within which these dramas take place. You will also find that the various levels of the 'subconscious' will yield their own characteristics, and as your records grow, this will become apparent. It is necessary, then, that dreams are recorded in consecutive order whenever possible.

Bill Gallagher had been staring at me steadily as I spoke for Seth, and once Seth said,

My dear Jesuit, shall I turn my chair around the face you full?

"As you wish," Bill said, with a smile.

I do have a thought, my Jesuit friend,

Seth replied with a still bigger smile than Bill's.

Surely you can arrange a spotlight and we could set it here . . . so you could get a better look.

Bill laughed and said, "I notice that you seem to be left-handed while Jane is right-handed."

I use one hand, and he uses the other primarily.

"Why?" Bill asked.

I always used one hand, and he used the other.

Seth was smiling broadly again. "I've just been wondering why your basic gestures are different than Ruburt's," Bill said.

My dear Jesuit. Do I not try to explain things clearly, and am I not grossly misunderstood? (This was pure banter, between the two of them.) I have said all along that I am myself, and Ruburt is someone else. It follows that our gestures would be different. Wouldn't you say so?

"I've been wondering. The circumstances are strange."

If you are thinking in terms of secondary personalities, you

can prove nothing one way or another. A secondary personality would also use different gestures. Either way, this would be no proof of my independent nature, but I'm glad to see you've been thinking about it.

"I was just curious as to what you'd say," Bill said.

My answer is that I am an energy personality essence, momentarily in contact with your physical system, in that I am able to operate through Ruburt.

"Then you use Ruburt's voice, eyes, and so forth, to communicate?"

I do, and I use them in the manner that I have used mechanical faculties of my own when I had them.

"This includes the facial muscles?" Bill asked.

Of course, though the face does not fully adopt my own expression. First of all, as far as the hands are concerned, to be left-handed or right-handed has to do with inner mechanisms and brain patterns that come before the motion of the hands. Characteristically, I operated in ways that resulted often in the primary use of my left hand when I was focused in physical matter.

As to facial expression, this again works in the same way, for in this case, matter does matter! Physical expression is again the result of the personality's characteristic method of manipulating the physical organism. When I operated as such, I had my own way of doing so.

Now and then with Ruburt, to a greater or lesser degree, my own habits therefore show through, for I use his muscles in a different way than he does. But scientifically, this would not be proof of my existence as an independent personality who has survived death. Not that this concerns me, for it does not.

Bill laughed, and shortly later, the session ended. By now I sat down during sessions, and changes had taken place in my trance state so that the personality change was very marked. Rob was used to this, but Bill and Peg attended sessions only infrequently, and to Bill it was a constant source of amazement. Peg took it for granted.

Until we actually tried the dream experiments, we didn't really have too clear an idea of what to expect. This series of sessions in which Seth explained dream reality and gave us instructions about exploring it, always struck me as highly evocative, yet oddly ambiguous. In a way, Seth was as nebulous as dreams are, but we already had over two thousand pages of manuscript he had dictated through me in trance; and surely he had changed our lives. Now here he was, telling us how to travel through a territory more naturally his, I thought, than ours.

For this series of sessions, we had also moved into the quieter bedroom. Seth usually devoted the first hour or so to his discussion on dreams and the last part of the sessions were given over to the experiments mentioned earlier with the envelopes and the long-distance tests with the psychologist. Compared to the large living room, our bedroom was quite small, and it was quite warm during these summer months of 1965.

I was fascinated with Seth's material on the dream universe. "A fantastic theory," I said to Rob.

"I have the impression that it's a lot more than just theory," Rob said, and I had to agree with him. The material on dream locations particularly intrigued me. Seth had told us to leave room in our dream records to note the locations and advised us to examine them carefully. I was quite surprised at the different kinds of dream locations in my own dreams and made up the following list of them. Look for these when you examine your own dreams:

1. Dream locations that represent places familiar to you in your present daily life.
2. Dream locations that represent places (such as foreign countries) to which you have never really traveled.

3. Dream locations that represent definite places that appear as they were in the past. If you dream of your childhood home as it was, not as it is now, then the location would belong in this category.
4. Dream locations that represent places that no longer exist physically.
5. Strange, completely unfamiliar, dream locations.
6. Indistinct dream locations.
7. Strange dream locations to which you keep returning.

Once my interest was aroused, I was really determined to find out where I went and what I did in my dreams. In one study of eight hundred of my own dreams, I was really surprised to find that only seventy of them took place in my old hometown, and even here, as a rule, the action involved the present rather than the past. Previously I'd taken it for granted that a much larger percentage of my dreaming involved childhood places.

In fact, the bulk of my dream locations in this study was equally divided between completely unfamiliar places and locations too indistinct to recall. Only seven dreams found me abroad. Most interesting of all, however, I found that most of my precognitive dreams happened in locations that were unfamiliar at the time of the dream. For this reason, I suggest that you pay particular attention to unfamiliar dream places.

I was also interested in what I did in dreams — not just generally, but for any given night. During one period of four nights, I recorded twenty-one dreams. In these I was involved in four exciting episodes in which I ran from danger, used my wits to overcome it or faced it directly. I ran through radioactive rain (in a dream that, oddly enough, proved precognitive!), wandered through lovely gardens, explored several unfamiliar houses, and spoke with a well-known author whom I've never met. Not bad, I thought, for someone who hadn't left the bed all night!

People who have always remembered many of their dreams

may be less than impressed with the idea of recording dream activities, but others for whom sleep means oblivion will find dream recall a fascinating endeavor and the variety of dream acts almost astonishing. Even those with good dream-memories will find that persistant dream recall experiments are invaluable. As we discovered later, it is the effort required to remember dreams, and the resulting stretching of consciousness that finally opens up dream reality.

Chapters Fourteen to Twenty will show you the value of dream recall and illustrate how dreams may be used to promote health, solve problems and strengthen identity. Besides exploring our own dreams and our dreaming selves, there is also the adventure of discovering the greater dimension in which all dreams take place.

But if all this is so important, why can't we do it more easily and naturally? Why do we need experiments? According to Seth, the way we use the ego and its idea of reality stand in our way. When he was still outlining these experiments for us, Seth explained this in some detail.

"On the Ego and Dream Recall"
(Excerpt from Session 181, August 25, 1965)

The ego skims the topmost surface of reality and awareness. This is not the result of any inherent egotistical quality. It is true that the ego's responsibility is with the relationship between the self and the physical environment. It must necessarily focus within the confines of physical reality. Nevertheless, it is fully capable of perceiving far more than Western man allows it to perceive. Fear, ignorance, and superstition limit its potentials and, therefore, limit even its effectiveness within the physical universe.

The ego itself cannot directly experience certain intuitions and psychological experiences, but it can experience them insofar as it can become aware of them on an intellectual basis.

*When training forces the ego to become too rigid and to limit
its perceptions of other realities, then the intuitions will not be
accepted by the ego because intuitional experience will not fit
into the framework of reality that it accepts as valid.*

*The ego in that case will therefore fight against what it then
considers an unknown threat to survival. Struggles are initiated
then that are entirely unnecessary. We want to bring intuitional
comprehension to a point where the ego will accept it. In our
dream experiments, this is one of the purposes we hope to
achieve. The ego is not equipped to delve directly into
nonphysical realities, but if it is trained to be flexible, it will
accept such knowledge from other wider horizons of the self.*

*And the ego must have its feet upon solid earth. It is naked
and out of its element outside of the normal environment of
physical existence. To some extent, its distrust of the dream
experience is necessary for the overall balance of the personality.
Physical reality is, after all, a rock to which the ego must cling;
from it, the ego achieves its prestige and reason for
existence. . . . This provides necessary balance and control, and
results in the sturdy anchorage of the personality in the
environment in which is must presently survive. You have here
one of the main reasons why you must request the subconscious
to enable you to recall dreams. The ego would see no reason for
such a memory and on general principles attempts to repress
them.*

*Again, however, this excellent balance and these fine controls
exist. The ego will accept knowledge derived from the dream
state as a man might accept a message from a distant land in
which he does not care to dwell and whose environment would
both mystify and astonish him.*

*In our dream experiments, then, we will allow you to bring
such messages to the ego. We will attempt to map this exotic
country in such a way that the ego can understand what is there
in terms of resources that can be used for its own benefit.*

"What's the purpose of the whole study exactly?" Rob asked. And this was Seth's answer,

We will be involved with a study of the characteristics of the dream world in general and attempt to isolate it as a separate reality for the purposes of examination. Then we shall regard it in its relation to physical reality, using comparisons and dissimilarities.

This will then allow us to procede into the relationship between the waking and sleeping personality and discover the many ways in which the personality's aims and goals are not only reflected but sometimes achieved in and through the dream condition.

Usually the dream state is considered from a negative standpoint and compared unfavorably with the waking condition. Emphasis is laid upon those conditions present in the waking state but absent from the dreaming experience. We shall consider those aspects of consciousness which are present in the dream environment and absent in the physical one. No study of human personality can pretend to be thorough that does not take the importance of dream reality into consideration.

In some discussions we will state the ways in which conscious goals can be achieved with the help of the dreaming self. All of this material will be reinforced with experiments that, I hope, you will conduct yourselves.

It is amazing how man regrets the hours spent in sleep. He does not realize how hard he works when the ego is unaware. We hope to make this clear. We hope to let you catch yourselves in the act of doing so. You will realize how productive dream experiences are and the ways in which they are woven into the tapestry of your entire experience.

As mentioned previously, we will also deal with the nature of space, time and distance, as they appear in the dream environment. Some of our experiments along these lines will be most illuminating. Here the ego cannot go, but it can benefit

*from the information, and perhaps in time, even a shadow of
the ego may pass through that strange land and feel in some
small way at home.*

Seth had set us some task and fulfilling it will be a lifetime pro-
postion. There is a rhythm, even now, to my own experiments in
dream reality. Some methods, to be given later, allowed us to come
awake while dreaming, to take our conscious selves into the dream
state, manipulate it and have deliberate out-of-body experiences
while sleeping. (In some of these, what I saw later checked out
against physical reality.) Sometimes I do very well and feel that I
am learning to manipulate in two levels of reality at once, to be
aware both in waking and dream states. And then for months at a
time, I am plunked down in physical reality again, dumb and
blind to my dream experiences. My students have noticed the same
rhythms; so has Rob.

Before we go into the various kinds of dreams and our experiences with them, the following chapter will give some preliminary
material Seth gave us on the general nature of dream reality and
our place in it.

13

Some Preliminary Excerpts on the Dream World

Dream Locations, Dreams, and Creativity

Electric Reality of Dreams

Moment Points

"On the Dream World"
(*Excerpts from Session 95, October 7, 1964*)

As there is in actuality no beginning or end to a dream, so there is no beginning or end to any reality. A dream does not then begin or end; only your awareness of a dream begins and ends. You come into awareness of a dream, and you leave it, but in your terms of time, the dreams that you seem to dream tonight have been long in existence. They seem to begin tonight because you are aware of them tonight.

You do create your own dreams. Nevertheless, you do not create them during a specific point in time. The beginnings of dreams reach back into 'past' lives of which you are not aware and beyond even this; the origins are part of a heritage that was before your planet existed.

For every consciousness existed simultaneously and in essence, even before what you may call the beginnings of your world. And what you are yet to be existed then and still exists now — and not as some still unfulfilled possiblity but in actuality.

What you will be, you are now, not in some misty half-real form but in a most real sense. You simply are not aware of these selves on a conscious level any more than you are aware of 'past' lives. But each of you creates a dream world of validity, actuality, durability and self-determination, in the same way that the entity projects the reality of its various personalities. As there is usually no contact between the entity and the ordinary conscious ego, there is usually no contact on a conscious level between the self who dreams and the dream world which has its own independent existence.

And in the same way that the dream world has no beginning or end, neither does the physical universe with which you are familiar. No energy can be withdrawn, and this includes the energy used in the continuous subconscious construction of the dream world. You continually create it — have always created it. It is the product of your own existence, and yet you can neither consciously call it into existence nor destroy it.

"On the Nature of the Dream World and Animal Dreams"
(Excerpts from Session 97, October 1964)

The dream world is, then, a natural byproduct of the relationship between the inner self and the physical being — not a reflection, but a byproduct — involving not only a chemical reaction, but also the transformation of energy from one state to another.

In some respects, all planes or fields of existence are byproducts of others. For example, without the peculiar spark set off through the interrelationship between the inner self and the physical being, the dream world would not exist. But conversely, the dream world is a necessity for the continued survival of the physical individual.

This point is extremely important. As you know, animals dream. What you do not know is that all consciousness dreams.

Atoms and molecules have consciousness, and this minute consciousness forms its own dreams even as, on the other hand, it forms its own physical image. As in the material world, atoms combine for their own benefit into more complicated structures, so do they combine to form such gestalts in the dream world.

I've said that the dream world has its own sort of form and permanence. It is physically oriented, though not to the degree inherent in your ordinary universe. In the same way that the physical image is built up, so is the dream image. You can refer to our previous discussions on the nature of matter to help you understand, but the dream world is not a formless, haphazard semi-construction.

It does not exist in bulk, but it does exist in form. The true complexity and importance of the dream world as an independent field of existence has not yet been fully impressed upon you. Yet, while your world and the dream world are basically independent, they exert pressures and influences one upon the other.

The dream world, then, is a byproduct of your own existence [from your standpoint]. It is connected to you through chemical reactions and this leaves open the entryway of interactions. Since dreams are a byproduct of any consciousness involved with matter, then trees have their dreams. All physical matter, being formed about individualized units of consciousness of varying degrees, also participates in the involuntary construction of the dream world.

"Dreams and the Crucifixion, Creativity and Inspiration, Importance of Dream Recall"
(Excerpts from Session 115, December 16, 1964)

I mentioned the Crucifixion once, saying that it was an actuality and a reality, although it did not take place in your time. It took place where time is not as you know it . . . in the

same sort of time in which a dream takes place. Its reality was
felt by generations and was reacted to. Not being a physical
reality, it influenced the world of physical matter in a way that
no purely physical reality ever could.

The Crucifixion was one of the gigantic realities that
transformed and enriched both the universe of dreams and the
universe of matter, and it originated in the world of dreams. It
was a main contribution of that field to your own and could be
compared physically to an emergence of a new planet within
the physical universe. . . .

The Ascension of Christ is . . . also a contribution of the
world of dreams to your own universe, representing knowledge
within the dream system that man was independent of physical
matter. . . .

Many concepts, advancements and practical inventions simply
wait in abeyance in the world of dreams until some man accepts
them as possibilities within his frame of reality. Imagination is
waking man's connection with the world of dreams.
Imagination often restates dream data and applies it to
particular circumstances or problems within the physical
system. Its effects may appear within matter, but it is of itself
not physical. Often the dream world possesses concepts which
will one day completely transform the history of your field, but
a denial of such concepts as actualities or possibilities within
reality hold these back and put off breakthroughs that are sorely
needed.

Such developments would mean the releasing of added energy
into your field. Ideas and concepts are nonphysical actualities
that attract unaligned energy, direct and concentrate it. The
dream world exists more closely in that spacious present of
which the inner self is so aware. It is not as involved with
camouflage. . . .

It might be said, then, that in many ways the dream universe
depends upon you to give it expression, in the same manner that
you also depend upon it to find expression . . .

The impact of any dream has physical, chemical, electromagnetic, psychological and psychic repercussions that are actual and continuing. The type of dream or the types of dreams experienced by any given individual are determined by many different factors. I am speaking now of the dream experience as it occurs and not of the remnant of it that his ego allows him to recall.

As an individual creates his physical image and environment according to his abilities and defects, and in line with his expectations and inner needs, so does he create his dreams; and these interact with the outer environment.

However, with the ego at rest in sleep, the individual often allows communications and dream constructions through — past the ego barrier. For example, if his present expectations are faulty, when the ego rests, he may recreate a time when expectations were high. The resulting dream will partially break the circle of poor expectations with their shoddy physical constructions and start such an individual along a constructive path. In other words, a dream may begin to transform the physical environment through lifting inner expectation.

"The 'Electric Reality' of Dreams and Dream Locations"
(Excerpts from Session 131, February 10, 1965)

We have seen that all experience is retained in electrically coded data within the cells and that the material of the cells forms about this coded experience. We have seen that the ego begins, sparked into being by the inner self, greatly influenced by heredity and physical environment; and that this ego, as it continues to exist, builds up an electrical reality of its own and forms its experiences . . . into the coded data within the cells.

At any given 'point,' the ego is complete within electrical reality as it is psychologically complete within the physical universe. This includes the retention of its dreams as well as the retention of purely physical data. . . .

The electrical system is composed of electrcity that is far different from your idea of it. Electricity, as you perceive it, is merely an echo emanation or a sort of shadow image of these infinite varieties of pulsation which give actuality to many phenomena with which you are familiar, but which do not appear as tangible objects within the physical field. . . .

This electrical system is vastly dense. This is a denseness that does not take up space, a denseness caused by an infinity of electrical fields of varying ranges of intensity. Not only are no two of these electrical fields identical, but there are no identical impulses within them.

The gradations of intensities are so minute that it would be impossible to measure them, and yet each field contains in coded form the actual living reality of endless eons; contains what you would call the past, present, and future of unnumbered universes; contains the coded data of any and every consciousness that has been or will be, in any universe; those that have appeared to vanish, and those which, seemingly, do not yet exist. . . .

This density is extremely important, for it is a density of intensities. And it is the infinite variety and gradations of intensity that makes all identities possible and all gestalts, all identies in terms of personalities and fields and universes. It is this density, with this infinite variety of intensity, which allows for both identity and change. . . .

The electricity that is perceivable within your system is merely a projection of a vast electrical system that you cannot perceive. So far, scientists have been able to study electricity only by observing the projections of it that are perceivable within their terms of reference. As their physical instruments become more sophisticated, they will be able to glimpse more of this reality, but since they will not be able to explain it within their known system of references, many curious and distorted explanations of reported phenomena will be given.

Yet the inner self offers so many clues. . . . It operates outside of physical references. It is, of itself, free of the distorted effects peculiar to the physical system. A study of dreams, for example, would make many of these points clear, yet many scientists consider such work beneath them.

Why has no one suspected that dream locations have not only a psychological reality but a definite actuality? A study of dream locations is most important. Dream locations are composed of electrical mass, density and intensity. Here is another point: Definite work may be done in a dream, but the physical arms and legs are not tired. This would seem contrary to your known laws, but no one has looked into this. . . .

It is most difficult to even hint at the myriad complexity and dimension of the electrical actuality as it exists. When you consider that each of your own thoughts is composed of a unique intensity of impulse, shared by nothing else; that the same may be said for every dream you will have in your lifetime; and that all your experience is gathered together in particular ranges of intensity, again completely unique; and that the summation of all that you are exists in one minute range or band of intensities, then you will see how difficult this is to explain. . . .

This not only applies to your physical field but also to all others. Your field is contained within its own range of intensities, a tiny band of electrical impulses a million times smaller than one note picked at random from the entire mass of musical composition that has ever been written or ever will be written. I am not going too deeply into this now because you are not ready. But because of the infinite range of intensities available, each individual has limitless intensities within which he can move.

All motion is mental or psychological motion, and all mental or psychological motion has its electrical reality. The inner self moves by moving through intensities. Each new experience

opens up a new pulsation intensity. . . . To move through
intensities within the electrical system gives the result, in the
physical field, of moving through time. We will also discuss this
later, in connection with so-called astral travel.

"The Dream World, Dream Images and Actions, Dreams as Actions"
(Excerpts from Session 149, April 26, 1965)

I would like to discuss dreams in relation to action. We
mentioned earlier that all action does not necessarily involve
motion that is apparent as such to you. To one extent or
another, all actions are unfoldings. The action of dreaming itself
is partially a physical phenomena. There is, then, the outside
action that makes dreaming possible, the action that is
dreaming.

Then there are the endless varieties of actions within the
dream which is, in itself, a continuing act. The images within a
dream also act. They move, speak, walk, run. There is, at
times, a dream within a dream where the dreamer dreams that
he dreams. Here, of course, the dimensions of action are more
diverse.

Many of these actions performed by dream images are
muscular ones, physical manipulations. But many of these
actions are also mental manipulations or esthetic realizations
and even aesthetic performances. These dream images are not
one-dimensional cardboard figures by any means. Their
mobility, in terms of perspectives and within space, is far
greater than your own.

You perceive but a small portion of these images which you
have yourselves created. You cannot bring them back into the
limited perspectives of your present physical field and are left
with but glimpses and flimsy glimmerings of images that are as
actual, vivid and more mobile than normal physical ones.

I have said before that the dream world is composed of
molecular structure, and that it is a continuing reality, even
though your own awareness of it is usually limited to the hours
of your own sleep. There is a give-and-take here. For if you
give the dream world much of its energy, much of your own
energy is derived from it. . . .

Nor is the dream world a shadow image of your own. It
carries on according to the possibilities inherent within it, as
you carry on according to the possibilities in the physical
system. In sleeping, however, you focus your awareness in
altered form into another world that is every bit as valid as
your physical one. Only a small amount of energy is focused
into the physical system during sleep, enough simply to
maintain the body within the environment.

In many respects, actions within the dream world are more
direct than your own. It is because you remember only vague
glimmerings and disconnected episodes that dreams appear
often chaotic or meaningless, particularly to the ego which
censors much of the information that the subconscious retains.
For most people, this censoring process is valuable, since it
prevents the personality from being snowed under by data that
it is not equipped to handle. The ability to retain experience
gained within other fields is the trend of further developments.
. . . Nevertheless, every man intuitively knows his involvement
here. . . .

Some dream events are more vivid than waking ones. It is
only when the personality passes out of the dream experience
that it may seem unreal in retrospect. For [upon waking] again,
the focus of energy and attention is in the physical universe.
Reality, then, is a result of focus of energy and attention.

I used the term, pass out of the dream world purposely, for
here we see a mobility of action easily and often accomplished
— a passing in and out that involves an action without
movement in space. The dreamer has, at his fingertips, a

memory of his 'previous' dream experiences and carries within him the many inner purposes which are behind his dream actions. On leaving the dream state, he becomes more aware of the ego and creates, then, those activities that are meaningful to it. As mentioned earlier, however, dream symbols have meaning to all portions of the personality.

The dream world has a molecular construction, but this construction takes up no space as you know it. The dream world consists of depths and dimensions, expansions and contractions that are more clearly related, perhaps, to ideals that have no need for the particular kind of structure with which you are familiar. The intuitions and certain other inner abilities have so much more freedom here that it is unnecessary for molecules to be used in any imprisoning form. Action in the dream world is more fluid. The images appear and disappear much more quickly because value fulfillment is allowed greater reign.

The slower physical manifestation of growth that occurs within the physical system involves long-term patterns filled by atoms and molecules which are, to some extent, then imprisoned within the constructions. In the dream world, the slower physical growth process is replaced by psychic and mental value fulfillment which does not necessitate any long-range imprisonment of molecules within a pattern. This involves a quickening of experience and action that are relatively unhampered by the sort of time necessities inherent within the physical universe. Action is allowed greater freedom. . . .

This is not to say that structure does not exist within the dream world, for structures of a mental and psychic nature do exist. But structure is not dependent upon matter, and the motion of the molecules is more spontaneous. An almost unbelievable depth of experience is possible within what would seem to you a fraction of a moment.

One of the closest glimpses you can get of pure action is action as it is involved with the dream world and in this mobility as the personality passes into and out of the dream field. Within the physical world, you deal with the transformation of action into physical manipulations — but this involves only a small portion of the nature of action, and it is my purpose to familiarize you with action as it exists, more or less, in pure form. In this way, you will be able to perceive the ways in which it is translated into other fields of actuality that do not involve matter as you know it.

Within the reality of the dream world, fulfillment and dependence, then, are not dependent upon permanence in physical terms. Bursts of developments are possible that have matured in perspectives that are not bound up in time.

These developments are the result of actions that occur in many perspectives at once and not developments that happen as within the physical system through a seeming series of moments. Basically, even the physical universe itself is so constructed, but for all practical purposes, as far as perception and experience is concerned, time and physical growth apply. As a result, the ego portion of personality is, to a large extent, dependent for its maturity and development upon the amount of time that the physical image has spent within the system.

A certain portion of physical growth, in terms of a series of moments, is, therefore, necessary for value fulfillment to show itself within a physical organism. But in the dream world, 'growth' is a matter of value fulfillment which is achieved through perspectives of action — through traveling within any given action, and following it and changing with it.

Now, you experience action as if you were moving along a single line, each dot on it representing a moment of your time. But at any of these 'points,' action moves out in all directions. From the standpoint of that moment-point, you could imagine action forming an imaginary circle with the point as apex. But

*this happens at the point of every moment. There is no
particular boundary to the circle. It widens outward
indefinitely. Now, in the dream world, and in all such systems,
development is achieved not by traveling your single line, but
by delving into that point that you call a moment. . . .
Basically the physical universe is at the apex of such a system
itself. . . .*

"Dreams and REM (Rapid Eye Movement) Sleep, Dreams and Chemical Connections"
(Excerpts from Session 194, September 29, 1965)

(Rob and I had read an article on scientific dream investigation.)

The reality of dreams can be investigated only through direct
contact. . . . REM sleep or no REM sleep, your dreams exist
constantly beneath consciousness, even in the waking state. The
personality is constantly affected by them. It is impossible to
deprive a person of dreams even though you deprive him of
sleep [as in certain dream laboratory experiments]. This
function will be carried on subconsciously. . . .

The eye movements noted in the beginning of REM sleep are
only indications of dream activity that is closely connected with
the physical layers of the self. These periods mark not the onset
of dreams but the return of the personality from deeper layers
of dream awareness to more surface ones. The self is actually
returning to more surface levels to check upon physical
environment. There is a transference of main energy in deeper
dream states from physical to mental concentration.

Quite simply, the self travels to areas of reality that are far
divorced from the physical areas of mobility. The muscles are
lax then because physical activity is not required. The energy
that is not being expended physically is used to sustain mental
actions. The chemical excesses built up in the waking state are
automatically changed as they are drained off, into electrical

energy which also helps to form and sustain dream images.

Your scientists would learn more about the nature of dreams if they would train themselves in dream recall. Again, the very attempt to deprive an individual of sleep will automatically set into mechanism subconscious dream activity. The tampering will then change the conditions. The direct experience of the developing dream is what you should be concerned with.

This could be studied if proper suggestions were given to an individual that he would awaken at the exact point of a dream's end [as in our own experiments]. The dream state and conditions could also be studied legitimately using hypnosis. Here, you are working with the mind itself and merely suggesting that it operate in a certain fashion. You are not tampering with the mechanics of its operation and automatically altering the conditons.

Using hypnosis, you can get good dream recall with a good operator. You can suggest ordinary sleep and dreaming and then suggest that without awakening, the subject give a verbal description of his dreams as he experiences them. . . . Another alternative is to suggest that the subject under hypnosis repeat the dreams of the night before.

Using these methods, the dreams of the mentally ill could also be studied if the affliction was not too severe. The dreams of children could be investigated in this way and compared with those of adults. Children dream vividly and more often. They return more frequently, however, to periods of near wakefulness in order to check their physical environment, since they are not as sure of it as adults are. In deep periods of sleep, children range further away, as far as dream activities are concerned.

The ego allows them more freedom. For this reason, they also have more telepathic and clairvoyant dreams than adults. They also have greater psychic energy; that is, they are able to draw upon energy more easily. Because of the intenseness of their waking experience, the chemical excesses build up at a faster

*rate. Therefore, children have more of this 'chemical propellant'
to use in dream formation. They are also more conscious of
their dreams. . . .*

*I have said often that any action changes that which acts and
that which is acted upon; and so in the sort of experiments that
are currently being carried on to study dreams, the acts of the
investigators are changing the conditions in such a way that it is
easy for them to find what they are looking for. The investigator
himself, through his actions, inadvertantly brings about those
results for which he looks. The particular experiment may seem,
then, to suggest conditions which are by no means general, but
may appear to be. Under hypnosis a subject is not as much on
guard, as is the subject of an experiment who knows in advance
that he will be awakened by experimenters, that electrodes will
be attached to his skull and that laboratory conditions are
substituted for his nightly environment.*

*It is impossible to study dreams when an attempt is made to
isolate the dreamer from his own personality, to treat dreams as
if they were physical or mechanical. The only laboratory for a
study of dreams is the laboratory of the personality. . . .*

While Seth was delivering this material we had embarked upon
our own dream experiments. Later, in 1967, I started my ESP
classes, and my students began their own work in dream recall
and experimentation. As you will see, these led to dream manipulation and, in many instances to projection of consciousness from
the dream state.

Though each person progresses differently, generally speaking,
the more advanced dream work follows the earlier stages of simple
recall, to more frequent self-knowledge within the dream state
and from there to manipulation of dream images and projection.
The following chapters deal, then, with our experiences with different kinds of dreams and their effect on daily life. Later chapters
will be concerned with the expansion of consciousness that results
from the earlier experiments.

Our interest in dreams spilled over into my own creative work also. The following poems were all written in 1964, when Rob and I first began our own experiments in dream recall and when Seth first started his sessions on the dream world.

In Midnight Thickets
(October 20, 1964)

In midnight thickets
Dreamers plunge,
While the moon
Shines calmly on.
The town is sleeping,
Bodies lie
Neat and empty
Side by side.

But every self
Sneaks out alone,
In darkness with
No image on,
And travels freely,
All alert,
Roads unlisted
On a map.

No man can find
Where he has been,
Or follow in flesh
Where the self tread,
Or keep the self in
Though doors are closed,
For the self moves through
Wood and stone.

No man can find
The post or sign
That led the self
Through such strange land.
The way is gone,
The self returns
To slip its bony
Image on.

My Dreaming Self
(December 8, 1964)

My dreaming self
Looked in the window
And saw me on the bed.
Moonlight filled
My sleeping skull.
I lay nude and still.

My dreaming self
Came in
And walked about.
I felt as if doorknobs turned,
Opening rooms up
In my head.

My dreaming self
Had eyes like keys
That glinted in the dark.
There was no closet
Within my bones
They could not unlock.

My dreaming self
Walked through
The framework of my soul.
He switched lights on as he passed.
Outside the night
Was dark and cold.

My dreaming self
Lay on the bed.
I stood aside with awe.
"Why, both of us are one," I said.
He said, "I thought you knew."

Vision
(June 10, 1964, published in EPOS)

I saw myself stretched out among the stars.
My skin, an open mesh,
Was hung with seeds and moons and fish.
Birds flew through my flesh
Which rose in continental mass
From seas of space. One arm,
A universe, was flung
Akimbo. My third left fingernail
Was earth, pearl tipped and turning
With the measured motion of my wrist.

One eye looked out upon the form —
The thigh's spread galaxies — and saw
The burst of each cell-star that plunged
Into instant shape within the flesh.
The other eye, turned inward, glimpsed
New webworks and cocoons
Spun from thoughts and dreams that spread
Images outward with each breath.

Dreamers
(November 30, 1964)

Dreamers make their own sidewalks,
Webs stretched out from thought to thought,
Extensions of the restless skull,
Invisible and dark and still.

These night-time projections rise
Like insubstantial lines of chalk,
Yet travelers follow them,
Suspended dark to dark.

Appointments are made and kept,
And records scrawled in haste,
While bodies wait in crisp white beds,
All untouched and neat and safe.

14

Dreams and Health

Seth on Therapeutic Dreams
Seth Has a Dream Talk with a Friend
How to Use Dreams to Promote Health

*O*ne of my students, Sue Watkins, is very gifted psychically and quite expert in her use of dreams. She and her husband Carl were living in a nearby town when she sent me this note, along with a copy of a dream that beautifully illustrates the close connection between dreams and health. She titled the note, humorously, "A Short History of the Shoulder, or Carrie Nation was Right About Bad Joints."

Sometime after I came home from college in 1967, I first noticed that my right shoulder hurt when I lifted it up — classic bursitus symptoms, I've since learned. After a while, the conditon cleared up gradually. Then in April, 1968, the symptoms returned and lasted for about three months, disappeared slowly and came back for a while in December, 1968. In February, 1969, I had a real bout that lasted off and on until my son's birth in October. Since then, the condition got worse until for the last month or so I haven't been able to get my right hand in my jean pockets, or comb my hair, or anything without severe pain in my right shoulder blade and right hand to the fingers.

Yoga and psy-time helped reduce the symptoms temporarily, but by last week, the stiffness was so bad that my entire shoulder was grinding like jammed sandpaper. I even found myself yelling at the baby, which made me feel awful. Then, on April 25, 1970, I had the following dream:

I came into Rob and Jane's apartment and walked into a Seth session. I sat next to Rob, who was transcribing notes, as usual. Seth (as Jane) turned toward me at once. His voice was almost angry, but not without compassion. 'Now then, I will tell you what to do,' he said, 'but I won't be communicating with the part of you that uses words.'

He began a long lecture on the methods of handling aggression and expressing it in acceptable ways. At this point, my critical self separated from my dream self who was receiving the lecture. [In other words, Sue became aware of herself and the dream self.] My critical self instantly felt put off, since it could not understand or translate the lecture. It seemed to have a definite function, though, perhaps in connection with the physical body. Both selves were equally aware.

Seth then sat in front of my dream self, feeding it something that looked like cereal. My critical self became upset then, almost feeling that the dream was worthless. Then Seth said to the critical self, 'This is symbolism . . . food for thought . . . far more complicated than you know and beyond any part of you that you understand.' At once the dream self became soothed, almost hypnotically. The critical self kept thinking that this couldn't happen in a dream.

Seth began to lecture again, and my critical self began to fade out. As it did, I asked, 'Seth, will I ever understand this?' The answer was lost except that I felt that the 'new knowledge' received in the lecture I could not hear was healing me and that as a wife and mother I was freer than I ever was before.

When I awakened, my shoulder, arm and hand were completely

free and loose. The lumps — called calcium lumps by my doctor — were still there under the skin, but I could move my shoulder with no difficulty for the first time in months. I could reach into my jean pockets also. I'd had some trouble with my complexion and this cleared up, along with a three-week bout of cramps.

In closing, Sue added: "Of course, the dream itself was only the impetus. My inner self knew what to do all along. Maybe it had just forgotten how to keep a neat file!"

Whether or not Seth actually spoke to Sue in the dream is beside the point here. What is important is that symptoms disappeared as a result of a dream. She had worried about the condition and had requested help from her inner self; the dream was her answer. It's possible, of course, that Sue's unconscious adapted an authority figure to get the information about aggression through with greater impact, using Seth as a figurehead. (If you want to believe that Seth is an unconscious production of mine, then you must admit he lends himself rather well to the unconscious purposes of others and possesses a reality to them quite independent of his relationship to me. Later examples will make this clear.)

Seth would call Sue's dream a therapeutic one, and he has devoted many sessions to dreams and health and the relationship between them. Before we go into therapeutic dreams, however, it's necessary to understand the reasons why we adopt symptoms. Are there definite reasons for illnesses? According to Seth, the answer is "yes."

"On Illness and Action"
(Excerpt from Session 164, June 23, 1965)

Illnesses can be seen as impeding actions representing actual blockages of energy, action turned into channels that are not to the best interests of the personality. The energies appear concentrated and turned inward, affecting the whole system.

They represent offshoots; not necessarily detrimental in themselves, except when viewed from the standpoint of other actions that form the personality framework. . . .

A certain portion of the energy practically available to the personality is spent in the maintenance of this impeding action or illness. It is obvious, then, that less energy is available for actions more beneficial to the personality system as a whole.

The situation can be serious in varying degrees, according to the impetus and intensity of the original cause behind the illness. If the impetus is powerful, then the impeding action will be of more serious nature, blocking huge reserves of energy for its own purposes. It obviously becomes part of the personality's psychological structure, the physical, electrical and chemical structures, invading to some extent even the dream system.

(And here Seth explains something that many people often wonder about: If illness is detrimental and we know it, then why does poor health linger at times?)

At times, illness is momentarily accepted by the personality as a part of the self, and here lies its danger. It is not just symbolically accepted, and I am not speaking in symbolic terms. The illness is often quite literally accepted by the personality structure as a portion of the self. Once this occurs, a conflict instantly develops. The self does not want to give up a portion of itself, even if that part may be painful or disadvantageous. . . .

(This has serious implications. Obviously, the easiest time to cure an illness is before it is accepted as a part of the self-image. Seth goes on in this session to explain some of the other deeper reasons for the continuance of symptoms and our acceptance of them.)

For one thing, while pain is unpleasant, it is also a method of familiarizing the self against the edges of quickened consciousness. Any hightened sensation, pleasant or unpleasant, *has a stimulating effect upon consciousness to some degree. It is a strong awareness of activity and life. Even when the stimulus may be extremely annoying or humiliatingly unpleasant, certain portions of the psychological framework accept it undiscriminatingly because it is a vivid sensation. This acquiesence to even painful stimuli is a basic part of the nature of consciousness and a necessary one.*

Even a quick and automatic rejection or withdrawal from such a stimulus is, in itself, a way by which consciousness knows itself. The ego may attempt to escape such experiences, but the basic nature of action itself is the knowing of itself in all aspects. In a very deep manner, action does not differentiate between enjoyable and painful actions.

These differentiations come later, on another level of development. But because personality is composed of action, it contains within it all action's characteristics.

(Seth continues to describe the ways in which various kinds of consciousness react to painful stimuli, ending up with a statement that at deepest cellular levels, all sensations and stimuli are instantly, automatically and joyfully accepted, regardless of their nature. At this level, no knowledge of threat exists. The "I" differentiation is not definite enough to fear destruction.)

Here we have action knowing itself and realizing its basic indestructability. It has no fear of destruction, for it is also a part of the destruction from which new actions will evolve.

The complicated organism of human personality with its physical structure has evolved a highly differentiated 'I' consciousness, whose very nature is such that it attempts to preserve the apparent boundaries of identity. To do so it must choose between actions.

But beneath the sophisticated gestalt are the simpler foundations of its being and, indeed, the very acceptance of all stimuli without which identity would be impossible. Without this acquiesence, the physical structure would never maintain itself, for the atoms and molecules within it constantly accept painful stimuli and suffer even their own destruction. They are aware of their own separateness within action and of their reality within it.

Now you should understand why even an impeding action can be literally accepted by the personality as a part of itself and why efforts must be made to coax the personality to give up a portion of itself, if progress is to be made.

We are also helped, however, by several characteristics of the personality, in that it is ever-changing, and its flexibility will be of benefit. We merely want to change the direction in which some of its energy moves. It must be seen by the personality that an impeding action is a hardship on the whole structure and that this particular part of the self is not basic to the original personality. The longer the impeding action is accepted, the more serious the problem.

(But can an illness ever serve a good purpose? Yes, according to Seth:)

The whole focus of a personality can change from constructive areas to a concentration of main energies in the area of the illness. Now in such a case, often the illness represents a new unifying system. If the old unifying system of personality has broken down, the illness, serving as a makeshift, temporary emergency measure may hold the integrity of the personality intact until a new constructive, unifying principle replaces the original.

In this case, the illness could not be called an impeding action unless it persisted long after its purpose was served. . . . Even then, without knowing all the facts you could not make a judgment, for the illness could still serve by giving the personality a sense of security, being kept on hand as an ever-present emergency device in case the new unifying principle should fail.

Unifying principles are groups of actions about which the whole personality forms itself at any given time. These may change and do change in a relatively smooth fashion when action is allowed to flow unimpeded. When action is not allowed to follow the patterns or channels for its expression that have been evolved by the personality, then blockages of energy occur.

These must be understood not as something apart from the personality, but as a part of the changing personality. Often, they point out the existence of inner problems. Often, they serve temporary functions, leading the personality from other more severe areas of difficulty. I am not saying here that illness is good. I am saying that it is a part of the action of which any personality is composed, and, therefore, it is purposeful and cannot be considered as an alien force that attacks the individual from without.

In this particular session, Seth is describing illness as a part of action, but, as he makes clear, this is not meant to imply any negation of psychological or psychic values. The nature of action, however, is important, for Seth states,

The personality is simultaneous action; it is composed of actions within actions. Portions of it are conscious of its awareness as a part of action, and portions try to stand aside from action. This attempt forms the ego, which is itself action.

If illness were thrust upon action or upon the personality from the outside, then the individual would be at the mercy of outside agencies, but it is not. Personality is affected by outside agencies, but in a most basic manner, it chooses those actions which it will accept.

An illness can be rejected. The habit of illness can be rejected. When action is allowed to flow freely, then neurotic rejections of action will not occur. . . . An illness is almost

*always the result of another action that cannot be carried
through. When the lines to the repressed action are released and
the channels to it opened, such an illness will vanish. However,
the thwarted action may be one with disastrous consequences,
which the illness may prevent.*

Let's consider Sue's symptoms, caused by explosive and repressed agression, in relation to Seth's statements. Sue had been
taught as a child to repress emotions, but the time had come when
expression was imperative. She wanted to strike out but didn't feel
that she should, and the denied actions then inhibited the function
of the right arm that would ordinarily do the striking. According
to Seth, even the calcium deposits were accumulations of repressed energy stored up in the body.

In her dream, Sue was given information that told her how to
release and use this energy creatively. While she remembered the
dream clearly and saw its instant results, the information was not
given to the conscious self (not even in the dream drama) but to
other layers more intimately concerned with body-mind mechanisms. Complete mobility of the arm and shoulder resulted, but
there was still some soreness from the calcium deposits that remained.

A few weeks after the dream, on May 12, 1970, Sue had another
therapeutic experience that straddled dreaming and waking reality. She was reading a book on the life of Edgar Cayce when her
shoulder began to ache. Suddenly she had the urge to leaf through
the book to a paragraph she'd noticed earlier on yoga exercises for
bursitic shoulders. As she read this, she heard a loud voice say:
"Put wet tea bags on it."

Startled, Sue looked up. The voice almost sounded as if it came
from a radio. Again it said, *"Put wet tea bags on it."* Sue noted,

So I went and got some tea bags, feeling awfully silly. I wondered
if I should put them directly on the shoulder or through a towel, and

the voice said, *'Directly.'* I took off my blouse, lay down and put the tea bags on the top of the shoulder joint.

'Lower. Underneath is the problem. The top is only an outcropping,' the voice said. So I turned over, moved the bags down and suddenly tuned in to a dialogue going on in my head. There were two voices, one slightly louder than the other, discussing this.

'For how long?' asked the second voice.

'One half hour,' answered the first voice.

'How many days?'

'Every day. It should only take six days, but the condition must be understood more clearly. Sixty days.'

At this point, I began to feel sleepy. *'Relax,'* the loud voice said. *'Relax the forefingers. Relax the legs. Allow circulation. Breathe in life. Breathe out poison.'*

I dozed for ten minutes. When I woke up, the pain was gone. I've been doing the yoga exercise and using the tea bags and the pain hasn't returned.

Two weeks later, Sue was awakened in the middle of the night by the same two voices. *"How is the condition now?"* asked the first voice.

"Much better," the second voice replied. *"The yoga exercises are repairing the effects worked on the physical system. She is also learning not to channel aggressions onto the shoulder."*

After six days of the treatment, all soreness disappeared, as did the calcium lumps. Since then, Sue was bothered by the shoulder during a few stressful periods, but she learned that a simple reading of the original Seth dream immediately returned the shoulder to normal once again. These experiences were highly valuable and produced undeniable physical results which last as long as Sue allows for normal release and expression of emotional energy.

According to Seth, poor health is caused mainly by destructive mental and feeling patterns that directly affect the body because of the particular range within the electromagnetic system in which they fall. Bad health, for example, does not happen first, resulting in unhealthy thoughts. It is the other way around. Seth states,

Illness must be treated primarily by changing the basic mental habits. Unless this is done, the trouble will erupt again and again in different guises. The system has the ability to heal itself, however, and every opportunity should be given to allow it to do so.

In most cases the stimuli [toward healing] come from deeper levels of the self, where they may be translated into terms that the personal subconscious can use. In such cases, these perceptions may find their way to the ego, appearing as inspirations or intuitive thought.

Many such intuitions appear when the personality is dissociated or in a dream state. . . . The effect of any thought is quite precise and definite and set into motion because of the nature of its own electromagnetic identity. The physical body operates within certain electromagnetic patterns and is adversely affected by others. These effects change the actual molecular structure of the cells, for better or worse, and because of the laws of attraction, habitual patterns will operate. A destructive thought, then, is dangerous not only to the present state of the organism but is also dangerous in terms of the 'future.'

Again, it makes little difference whether Sue's voices belonged to definite incorporal spirits or whether they were therapeutic hallucinations adapted to impress her conscious mind. The directions and instructions that they gave her worked. We were discussing this in a recent class session when Seth came through and said that he *had* communicated with Sue during the dream episode.

Seth first spoke of therapeutic dreams in the 198th session for October 13, 1965 — though he insisted from the beginning that the inner self had the ability to cure the body. In this session, he explained exactly how such a dream acted upon the physical system.

We have not spoken about the inner senses in some time. By now, you should realize that they have an electromagnetic reality also and that the mental enzymes act as sparks, setting off inner reactions. In the dream state, these reactions are easily triggered. This is the result of the lowering of egotistical guards, for the ego sets up controls that act as resistances to various inner channels [during the waking state]. . . .

A destructive attitude of mind has been changed overnight in the dream state to a constructive situation in many instances, and the whole electromagetic balance has been changed. In such a case, negative ions form an electrical framework in which healing is possible. Such healing dreams come most often when the self feels a sense of desperation and automatically opens up channels to deeper layers of personality.

Often we find an almost instant regeneration, a seemingly instant cure, a point from which the organism almost miraculously begins to improve. The same happens in less startling cases where, for example, a merely annoying health condition suddenly disappears.

Through self-suggestion, these therapuetic dreams can be brought about with practice. The suggestion (being action) has its own electromagnetic effect and already begins to set certain healing processes into action, while sparking the formation of others.

Such inner therapeutics may occur at various other levels of consciousness, where they may be sparked by exterior stimuli of an aesthetic or pleasing nature. Other exterior conditions also have an effect. To involve oneself in large groups, for example, is often beneficial not simply to take attention away from the self for a change, but because of the larger range of electromagnetic ranges readily available.

The overall health of the individual is important, as is the delicate balance of electromagnetic properties. . . . When the organism is set deeply in destructive patterns, then this is

*sometimes felt in the dream state, so that destructive dreams
then add to the entire situation. . . . For this reason, the use of
self-suggestion in bringing about constructive dreams is of great
benefit.*

Seth also mentioned that dreams could completely reverse
moods of depression and that such mood-changing dreams could
also be manufactured through the use of suggestion. One rainy
March morning, I decided to follow his instructions. I realized I'd
been blue and depressed for a week or more — upset because I had
not heard from a publisher and also because I was encountering
difficulties at the art gallery.

The sky was very dark, a light rain fell and a storm threatened.
After sitting at my desk disconsolately for an hour, trying to get my
mind on my book, I decided to take a nap. I went into the bedroom. It was 10:30 A.M. by the clock. I set the alarm for 11:00
and lay down. Just before going to sleep, I gave myself the suggestion to have a dream that would raise my spirits and restore my
native enthusiasm.

I lay there, aware of a growing disquiet. Suddenly I realized
that I was hearing voices, but they seemed to come from inside my
head. They grew steadily louder and louder. I was certain that I
was still awake. The voices rose. I felt as if a radio was turned on
full volume in my head, but with stations scrambled — for I could
make no sense out of what was said. Instead, I seemed to hear
fragments of conversations. Really frightened, I shook my head
and looked about the room.

Everything was normal. The morning was still dark and dis-
mal, the gray light of outdoors visible through the blinds. But the
voices were definitely booming now. Desperately I tried to find
their source. Then I realized that a transistor radio was blaring
from the bedside table. I turned it off. It didn't occur to me that in
reality, we had no such radio in the house. To my complete bewilderment, the voice continued. Then I "remembered" that there
was another radio in Rob's studio. Surely the voices were coming

from there! I leaped out of bed and rushed to the studio. There was the radio. Quickly I reached to turn it off and received a bad electric shock. Not only that, but the voices had actually doubled in volume.

Now I was too frightened to touch the radio again or to pull the plug from the socket and disconnect it. (This radio again, had no physical existence.) Instead, I ran through the bedroom and bath, out into the living room.

Here I stopped, dead still. The storm had come. It was pouring outside. Everything inside was strangely silent. The voices suddenly ceased. The whole room seemed to be in a state of waiting — but for what? Completely puzzled, I looked around, trying to get my bearings. And it took some doing. There was no denying the fact that a door had replaced our middle bay window. Curious, I approached and finally threw it open.

Here I found a table and chair set of fine dark wood, and beyond, another spacious apartment. Again I paused: Where had the apartment come from? Then it seemed to me that I had known about it in some dim past and forgotten. Indeed, as I hurried down the hallway I seemed to remember other such apartments also.

The hall opened into a large center area that was used as a clothing store. Preparations were being made for a sale. I recalled that the people here were friends of mine from that same remembered past and that I had visited them before in this same manner. The people saw me, recognized me at once and welcomed me with great joy.

As we chatted, I was filled with warm satisfaction and wondered how I could ever have forgotten our previous visits. A delightful conversation followed. At one point I remember coming down a stairway, while a handsome dark-haired young man took my arm and swung me around in an arc. I also noticed a lovely warm green jacket and realized that I had stored it away with my friends at my last visit.

I mentioned the other apartments and looked forward to exploring them. My friends thought it would be great fun and offered to go with me. A sense of adventure filled me. I couldn't remember when I'd had such a good time! Then I remembered that I had to return by noon to get Rob's lunch. Though I was very tempted to stay, I left my friends, promising to return that afternoon.

Next, I found myself running out in the back yard, through the rain. I dropped my cigarettes on the wet ground, picked them up, and discovered to my astonishment that they weren't wet at all. At the same time I found another pack in my pocket. This really stopped me. I was so certain I only had one pack. As I stood there trying to figure this out, a newsboy came across the lawn and called out, "Hi."

I looked up, really confused this time. He definitely was not our present newspaper boy, but the one who had delivered papers to us in another town, several years earlier. He couldn't possibly be the same age and delivering papers in Elmira! Besides, we got only the evening paper, and it was still morning.

For the first time I wondered: Could this be some kind of dream? A rush of disappointment flooded through me. If I was dreaming then the apartments would disappear when I awakened. I would never get to explore them! I looked at the yard again. It was our yard. The environment was brilliantly clear. And then, out of nowhere it seemed, a sense of freedom and exhilaration flashed — I *could* explore the apartments if I wanted to! I was out of my body. My body was in bed.

With that realization, my senses became super-alert. The yard and everything within my vision was significant, alive, super-real — seemingly more real than at any other moment of my life. At the same time, it occured to me that I had lain down at 10:30, and, surely, it was past the half-hour I had given myself. For some reason the clock hadn't awakened me. I would have to return. All the while, I stood fully conscious and alert out in the yard. Only then did I remember the suggestions I had given myself before lying down. I decided to return to my body at once.

With no transition at all, I sprang up to a sitting position in bed. Immediately, I checked the clock. The alarm had not rung because I had not pushed the little button down far enough. It was not quite 11 A.M., in any case. Only half an hour of physical time had passed.

Though it was still raining when I got up, I felt great. All I remembered at first was the second part of the experience, and only when this was written down did I recall the frightening earlier episode. I felt so vibrantly alive that there was no doubt in my mind of the "dream's" therapeutic nature. But how could the first, unpleasant portion be therapeutic? What did it mean? As you'll see, Seth explained this in the next session and used the opportunity to explain more about health and dreams.

I won't go into the out-of-body implications of that experience until later in this book; here, I'd like to emphasize, instead, the mood-changing elements of the "dream" and what it meant to me. In the next session, Seth explained it and showed how reincarnational background, present problems and personal symbolism were all used in the dream drama. Portions of the experience *were* dreams. Others were valid subjective events of a different kind, and the entire production was in response to my suggestions for a mood-changing dream.

This is what Seth said in Session 199 for October 18, 1965:

I am happy to see that Ruburt tried out the material on therapeutic dreams. The basic action of the first dream involved his reception of several voices. Though he does not remember this, they spoke words of encouragement. They presented excellent evidence of his own abilities, for initially they were crystal-clear and without distortion. There were four in all — all male. They belonged to personalities no longer within the physical system, but who were closely allied with Ruburt in past lives. The fourth voice was mine. This was an attempt to build Ruburt's confidence — to show how clear reception can be if his abilities are fully utilized.

The above portions therefore were actually not dreams but

experiences happening while he was dissociated. They shocked
him; hence, the shock later on when he turned this into a
dream. When he heard the voices, instead of becoming
confident, he fell into a dream state. He did not want to accept
the responsibility that he felt his abilities put upon him, and so
in the dream, he looked for an outside source for the voices and
dreamed the radio sequences. In the dream, however, the voices
continue [after he switched the radio off] because he knows he
is picking them up from a channel that is not physical.

He tries again, discovering another radio on your bookcase,
Joseph, where our manuscripts are kept. The connection is
obvious, for he knows that the Seth Material comes from the
same system as the voices. Here he reaches out to turn the radio
off and gets a shock; the shock is his realization that the
Material itself would cease were he to shut off his abilities. The
connection with you is also obvious, since your room is
involved. Were he to shut off his abilities as one can turn off a
radio, then you would also be deprived.

In the dream, then, he goes into his own room. He has
consciously forgotten this part, covering it with a vague
reference to an electrical storm. In the dream itself, however,
he discovers that his ability is as much a part of him as breath
and can't be turned off and on at will. There is an electric
storm. He stands in the middle of the room, touched by
vibrating currents. Though he is afraid, he realizes that he is
part of the storm — it is not destructive but creative and, most
of all, a simple elemental part of reality. This second realization
makes the second dream possible, with its therapeutic elements.

The second dream is one of expansion. The most meaningful
level was one in which the many rooms and apartments
represented psychic areas of development, endless possibilities
that continually open, but possibilities that were based on
previous life experiences. There are many aspects of
reincarnational data in the dream, all reinforcing the healthy
elements of Ruburt's personality.

Seth's interpretation was continued in the next (200th) session. He said that the green jacket represented a new ability that had been mine in a past life but which I misused, this new ability was now waiting for me to claim. The people were all persons with who I'd had past life connections. This caused the feelings of rediscovery and joy. Seth said,

When he leaped from the bannister, I was the one who extended an arm to help him. I appeared as the young man with olive skin. All of us tried to instill confidence and joy, and the responses were emotional. The dream generated sufficient energy to lift Ruburt's spirits and allow his normal enthusiasm to return in full force. It cut short his poor mood by several weeks.

Dreams can not only eliminate symptoms (as in Sue's case) or completely alter moods (as in my dream) but they can give us warning of incipient health difficulties — as happened to me several years ago. One night, in the early days of our psychic experience, I dreamed I saw Rob standing by the kitchen sink. He buckled over and fell to the floor. The dream frightened me so much that as I awakened, I caught myself saying, "That dream scares me. I don't want to remember it." In other words, I found myself in the act of trying to censor the dream. This alone told me that it must be important, so I forced myself to write it down at once. I didn't even tell the dream to Rob.

Three days later, Rob walked into the bathroom, suddenly blacked out by the bathroom sink and fell unconscious to the floor. If I had heeded the dream and told Rob, could the incident have been prevented? Had I told Rob, I now think that through dream therapy or in a light trance state he could have discovered the reason behind the symptoms and saved himself a difficult time.

The inner self does know the state of our health. At one time, I had some symptoms for which I was using a combination of healing methods suggestion, self-analysis and dream therapy. I seemed to be improving but wanted an inner check. One night, I requested a dream that would let me know my state of progress.

That night, I dreamed that I was being examined by a doctor I know. He told me that the difficulty was just about cleared up. In this case, of course, I apparently used an authority figure to impress my conscious mind.

Not all dreams of ill health should be taken literally. Often they are symbolic interpretations of your state of mind. You can request another dream that will make clear to you the symbols in the first one. In Session 173, Seth said,

As the personality is changed by any action, so it is changed by its own dreams. As it is molded by the exterior environment, so it is molded by the dreams that it creates and which help form its interior world. To the whole self, there is little differentation made between exterior or interior actions. The ego makes such distinctions. The core of the personality does not. . . . As an individual changes his physical situation through reacting to it, so he changes his interior or psychic situation in the same way. . . .

In dreams, you give freedom to actions that cannot adequately be expressed within the confines of normal waking reality. If the personality handles his dream activities capably, then problem actions find release in dreams. When the ego is too rigid, it will even attempt to censor dreams, however . . . and freedom of action is not entirely permitted, even in the dream condition.

If this solution fails, the impeding action will then materialize as a physical illness or undesirable psychological condition. If an individual has strong feelings of dependency that cannot be expressed in daily life, he will express these in dreams. If he does not, then he may develop an illness that allows him to be dependent in physical life. If he is aware of difficulties, however, he may request dreams that will release this feeling.

The individual would not necessarily remember such a dream. Psychologically, however, such an experience would be

valid, and the dependency expressed. I cannot stress this too
strongly: To the inner self, the dream experience is as real as
any other experience.

It follows that [by] using suggestion, various problems can be
solved within the dream state. The inner ego of which we have
spoken is the director of such unifying activities. It is the 'I' of
your dreams, having somewhat the same position within the
inner self as the ego has to the outer physical body.

Upon proper suggestion, the personality then will work out
specific problems in the dream state, but if the solution is not
clear to the [conscious] ego, this does not necessarily mean that
the solution was not found. There will be cases where it is not
only unnecessary but undesirable that the ego be familiar with
the solution. The suggestions will be followed by the sleeping
self in its own fashion. The solutions may not appear to the
conscious self in the way it expects. The conscious self may not
even recognize it has been given a solution, and yet it may act
upon it. . . .

Both psychological and physical illnesses could largely be
avoided through dream therapy. Rather harmlessly, aggressive
tendencies could also be given freedom in the dream condition.
Through such therapy, actions would be allowed greater
spontaneity. In the case of the release of aggressiveness, the
individual involved would experience this within the dream
state and hurt no one. Suggestions could also be given so that he
learned to understand the aggressiveness through watching
himself while in the dream state.

This is not as far-fetched as it might seem. Much erratic
anti-social behavior could be avoided in this way. Crimes could
be prevented. The desired but feared actions would not build
up to explosive pressure. If I may indulge in a fantasy,
theoretically you could imagine a massive experiment in dream
therapy, where wars were fought by sleeping, and not waking,
nations.

*[In practice, however,] there are many considerations to be
understood. If aggressiveness is the problem, for example, then
the preliminary suggestion should include a statement that in
the dream, the aggression will be harmlessly acted out and not
directed against a particular individual. The subconscious is
quite capable of handling the situation in this manner. This
may seem like a double censor, but in all cases it is the
aggressiveness itself that is important and not the person or
persons against whom the individual may decide to vent his
aggressiveness.*

*When the aggressiveness is released through a dream, there
will be no need for a victim. We do not want an individual to
suggest a dream situation in which he is attacking another
person. There are several reasons for this, both telepathic
realities which you do not yet understand and guilt patterns
which would be unavoidable. . . .*

*We are not attempting to substitute dream action for physical
action, generally speaking. Here we are speaking of potentially
dangerous situations in which an individual shows signs of being
unable to cope with these psychological actions through
ordinary methods of adaption. No one can deny that a war
fought by dreaming men at specified times would be less
harmful than a physical war — to return to my flight of fancy.
There would be reprecussions, however, that would be
unavoidable, [for again, basically, the personality does not
differentiate between sleeping and waking events].*

*Again, if the personality is fairly well balanced, then his
existence in dream reality will reinforce his physical existence.
You are involved in a juggling of realities. It is necessary to see
the personality as it operates within both, if you are interested
in understanding its whole experience.*

15

Precognitive Dreams

In following Seth's dream recall instruc-
tions, we found ourselves collecting some excellent examples of
precognitive dreams. Some were clear-cut and almost exactly
matched the foreseen future event. Others were partially disguised
in symbolism. Still others were so interwoven with other dream
material that we just marked them as indicative of precognition
and let it go at that. Sometimes dreams that seemed nonsense contained one clear, important image that shortly — within a few
days — would appear in a different context entirely. In several
cases, two or more future events would be condensed into one
dream.

Over the last few years, we have spent many hours with our
dream records, though the daily time spent in keeping them up to
date is negligible. For our own benefit, we frequently kept simple
journals of daily events also, so that it was easier to check dreams
against daily and weekly happenings and to connect dreams with
past, present and future events.

What is the point of it all? For one thing, records of your own precognitive dreams will convince you that you can perceive segments of the future. This personal knowing is far more vital than a bland intellectual acceptance that precognition may exist or is generally possible.

You don't have to take precognition on faith. If you keep careful dream records, sooner or later you'll find your own evidence of it. Each of my own precognitive dreams made a significant impression on me at the time and represented proof that I was moving in the right direction. Now I am much more interested in how precognition works, what triggers it and what translates into dream experience.

Each recaptured dream is not only a highly personal document but a clue into the nature of dream existence. Precognitive dreams are most evocative from this standpoint. The dreamer is baffled at his own ability to forsee a future event, and this makes him more than ordinarily curious about the nature of dream life in particular.

Even this intense interest waxes and wanes, however, in the ordinary sequence of events. My students and I both go through periods when we forget to remember and wake up for weeks at a time with only a few dream fragments. Often, months go by without a precognitive dream, and then there is that odd sense of discovery — always fresh — of an event forseen. Then the excitement hits again — of spying out the dreaming self and charting the strange environment in which it has its experience. Once more, I'm up at all hours, scribbling down my latest dream notes, checking them eagerly against daily happenings.

In such dreams, the physical future event is often perceived opaquely, distorted in at least some aspects, just as dream events are when seen from the viewpoint of waking life. I'm including here a few of my favorite precognitive dreams, choosing those which exemplify various degrees of clearness and distortion. Some of my original notes will be included so you can see the method we use in comparing dreams and later events.

For those of you who want to conduct your own experiments, remember: A precognitive dream is one in which you receive future information that you could receive in no normal manner. The dream should be recorded and dated. Write everything down, no matter how trivial. If you remember only dreaming about a person or name, record that. When you awaken, do not make intellectual judgments concerning the relative importance of a dream or decide it is not pertinent enough to record. We often forsee very trivial events that seem to have no particular meaning to us. But as you'll see from a later Seth excerpt, association can be at work, relating such experience in an intuitive rather than logical manner.

If possible, read your dream records at night, checking them against the day's happenings. Once a week, check the whole series. Remember that symbolism is important. Often, you must learn your own way of handling dream symbolism to make sense of dream. Not every dream is precognitive, nor is there any reason to waste much time with interpretations that seem too nebulous. Some precognitive information *will* be in symbolic form. However, as a few of my own dreams will clearly show, if you do not know the meaning of a symbol, give yourself the suggestion that it will be made clear to you intuitively — thus trust your answer.

Dream One
January 4, 1966

First I seemed to be floating above a car. The male driver buckled over in pain.

Next, I floated above a car, which was driven by another me. (Actually, I do not drive because of poor eyesight.) The car approached our corner, at Walnut and Water Streets. Others were also in the car. As I watched from my floating position, the "driving me" made an error at the light, and suddenly we ended up in the middle of a line of traffic. Cars came from all directions. I was terrified — certain that an accident would result. But none occurred.

COMMENT: *The next day a friend, Peter James, visited us. He had been having back trouble. As he sat on the couch, he suddenly buckled over with a spasm. We gave him aspirin. When he recovered, he offered to drive us to the garage to pick up our car.*

On the way, Peter suddenly went through a traffic light. We ended up in the wrong line of traffic, with cars coming at us from all directions. Vehicles in both other lanes had the green light, and we were right in their path. There was a squeal of brakes as the first car stopped less than two feet away. Yet, miraculously enough, there was no accident. Peter told us later that he just hadn't seen the light.

I didn't even connect the dream and the physical event until I checked my dream records as usual that night. Then the connections were clear. Close examination shows that a significant number of details agreed. This was the first incident of this type that happened to us — and we rarely ride with anyone else.

Similarity of Dream One and Physical Events

Dream One (Jan. 4, 1965)	Physical Event (Jan. 5, 1965)
Male driver buckles over with pain in car.	Yes, but on the couch.
Due to driver's error, car ends up in wrong lane of traffic.	Yes.
I am in car with others.	Yes.
I think accident will happen, but none does.	Yes.
In Elmira.	Yes.

The differences between the dream and physical events — the distortions, in other words — are also obvious. I wasn't driving as in the dream, Peter was. The near-accident happened about three blocks away from the Water and Walnut dream location. The main elements involving the event were definitely given in the dream, however.

Dream Two
July 3, 1965

I dreamed that it had been raining. I saw a motorcycle on a wet road. The driver lost his balance, the vehicle veered, but the driver regained his balance just in time and continued on. I said to Rob, "Motorcycles are dangerous on a wet road."

COMMENT: On July 10, we visited Rob's parents. In the course of conversation, my father-in-law told us that on July 3, from his window, he had watched a near-accident involving a motorcycle. Then he proceeded to outline my dream precisely, ending up with the remark: "Motorcycles are dangerous on a wet road" — the exact words I had spoken in the dream.

There is no need here to diagram the similarities. In both the dream and physical events, the road is wet from rain. A motorcyclist momentarily loses control of his cycle, and the vehicle veers but goes on. The identical remark is made. Here, however, I think the precognitive event was actually the discussion with my father-in-law, rather than the incident itself.

I've mentioned both of these dreams because each was involved with a near-accident. They were the only such dreams I recorded that year and the only such incidents in waking life. For a while, I wondered why I would pick up such an unimportant episode as a man veering on a motorcycle. What connection could there be? No one we knew even owned a cycle, and neither my father-in-law or myself had the slightest idea who the driver was. I hadn't been on a cycle in years. Neither had he. We had never even talked about cycles together. Then, I remembered that when he was a young man, Rob's father did have motorcyles. There were family pictures in an old album showing him proudly standing next to one when he was courting Rob's mother. And years ago, I rode on a cycle from New York to California. So the connection became clear: There was a hidden association in Rob's father's mind and my own, an emotional shared experience that "predisposed" us toward an interest in cycles.

Dreaming or awake, we perceive only events that have meaning to us. If the meaning or connection is not clear, it is only because we hide so much from ourselves. This holds true for normal perception as well as for extrasensory perception. We operate emotionally. Beneath words and logic are emotional connections that largely direct how we use our words and logic. The study of dreams, particularly of precognitive ones, can show us these inner workings that condition us toward the experience of certain kinds of events.

The following two dreams bewildered, confused and intrigued me. Each of them contains subconscious distortion, and strong precognitive elements interwound with other dream material. This type of dream may tell us more about the ways we interpret and receive precognitive information than dreams in which the forseen events and the physical ones are identical.

Dream Three
October 15, 1966

This dream was actually a series of four short sequences. In the first, I saw a young, black woman and a young, white woman on the corner of Walnut and Water Streets. They were hanging out clothes, and I stood applauding.

Next, I was teaching school — not an unusual dream under the circumstances, since I was acting as a substitute teacher in the public schools that autumn.

In the third sequence, I was having a long discussion with the white woman of the first episode, and there were a group of other women present.

Then, the scene switched again. The white woman was speaking on the telephone. In an aside, she disclosed that the caller was her husband, who was out of town. He was telling her that they must move. She was very embarrassed because she would not have time to give proper notice to the school or landlord. Then she laughed into the phone and said, "What?" in tones of mock disbelief. At the same time I saw in my mind's eye a picture of the house into which she would move. It reminded me of Dr. C's home in the country.

COMMENT: I wrote the dream down the next morning, wondering what on earth it could mean. On October 17, two days later, I was called to teach. This was only my second time out as a substitute, and I never knew when I would be working until an hour or so before school began. Since I'd never been to this particular school, I left early.

In the hallway, I was surprised to run into Anna Taylor. She lived in an apartment right at the corner of Walnut and Water Streets, but she was not a close friend — barely an acquaintance — and we saw her rarely. I knew she was a teacher, but hadn't the foggiest idea in what school. When she saw me, she burst out laughing, and said, "What? What?" in tones of great mock disbelief — as the woman had used in the dream. She didn't know I was teaching and had just been transferred to this school.

Immediately she told me that her husband had called her two days previously to tell her that they must move. He was out of town and had just learned that he was to be transferred to another area. Anna said that she was terribly embarrassed since they had to move quickly, and she wouldn't have time to give the proper notice.

We met at lunch in the teachers' room where we ate with a group of women, including one lovely, black girl who was particularly intelligent. Here Anna told me that she and her husband were househunting around Albany, New York. Later, in a free period, she showed me her first-grade classroom, specifically pointing out the closet and mentioning the difficulty involved in helping the children hang up their clothes.

After school I went home and sat down for a cup of coffee when the phone rang. It was Anna, calling to tell me that her husband had just called to say he had definitely rented a house in Albany. This was the first time in four months I had seen Anna, and the only time we ever spoke together on the phone.

In a dream so confused with definite precognitive elements and episodes that seem not to fit in, a simple diagram usually helps me to see the situation more clearly. So here is the listing of similarities between the physical and dream events that I prepared that afternoon as I tried to check out the dream:

Dream Events (Oct. 15, 1966)	**Physical Events** (Oct. 17, 1966)
1. I meet a young black woman and a young white woman together.	1. Yes. They are together in the lunch group.
2. At the corner of Water and Walnut.	2. No. But Anna lives right at the corner.
3. I am teaching.	3. Yes.
4. The woman says she is moving.	4. Yes.
5. Her husband just told her.	5. Yes.
6. She is embarrassed because she can give little notice.	6. Yes.
7. She says, "What?" and laughs with disbelief on phone while I listen.	7. She says this to me in the hall, with identical manner and laughs.
8. She makes a phone call.	8. Yes.
9. She is moving into a large house.	9. Yes.
10. Her new house reminds me of Dr. C's in the country.	10. Her apartment is three doors from Dr. C's office.

I wrote the list down and stared at it. Why hadn't I known Anna in the dream? And why the episode in which I saw her hang out clothes in the yard? I'd never dreamed of Anna before. Why now? Then suddenly the answers came to me. Anna herself wasn't really important to me. The information was really that the apartment in the house next door, on the corner, would be vacant. The clothing sequence was wrong in that no one really hung out clothes. Yet it was valid, symbolically. In the dream the women hang out clothes in the yard . . . and Anna showed me the childrens' closet at school, commenting on clothes. Anna's last name was Taylor. A *tailor* is someone involved with clothes. I think I'd known the name all the while and in the dream translated it into action; the clothes episode would, then, really identify Anna and forsee the event in which she showed me the clothes closet.

I just sat there, laughing. Dreams could be like charades, then, in which we act out words rather than see or speak them. Since this dream, I've always watched out for such acting-out and in many cases discovered clues that helped me interpret dreams that otherwise remained closed to scrutiny.

The next dream was far more bizarre and rather frightening, but it taught me even more about the nature of dreaming and illustrated many points that Seth had made earlier. Here are my original dream notes:

Dream Four
January 4, 1966

I run across a fairly large open space that was either dirt or only partially paved. It is pouring rain — darts of it hit the ground so hard that they ping and spatter back. I run to the end of this area and come to a building. Then I hurry past the main part of it to an extension. I look through to a small room or alcove and see two men enter. Behind them other men wait their turn in line. They all wear coveralls of some kind, and their faces are hidden by masks.

I realize that this is a decontamination center, closed to the public, very dangerous, and I become highly frightened. The men are obviously doing something connected with their line of work and are protected from radiation by their clothes. Now I remember that earlier I had seen a sign that warned me of this. I run back through the open area, only now I realize that the rain is radioactive. I run as quickly as I can to minimize the contamination. The rain spatters on my legs. After this, I meet Rob and some friends and tell them that from now on I will be more cautious.

Next I am standing on spacious, landscaped grounds with gravel paths neatly laid out, divided by trees and shrubs. There are several buildings, rather separated from each other, and lovely green grass. The buildings are stately, such as those in a public park. One building looks something like a church, though I don't think it is. All the buildings are of white or gray stone. There is a sign that says we can go no further, as the area is closed to the public. I notice a few elderly women sitting on the park benches. They are residents or patients here.

There were also some other dream elements that are too involved to mention here. The last part of the dream as given above ended up, for example, with a sequence involving J. P. Priestley, author of *Man and Time*, an excellent book that I had just finished reading. I woke up at 3 A.M. and wrote the dreams down at once, using the small bedside table. The bedroom was so chilly that I finally finished my notes in the warmer living room. The dreams were still so vivid, particularly the first episode, that I also drew a quick sketch of the building with the decontamination center in it. I could still feel myself running through the radioactive rain, yet the whole thing was so unbelievable that I could hardly see how it could be precognitive. I had some cookies and milk and read my notes over. Even if it was symbolic, I didn't like it a bit.

COMMENTS: On January 10, six days after the dream, Rob and I made an unexpected visit to the Motor Vehicles Bureau to check on the renewal of our car license. It had been ordered by mail several weeks earlier but had not arrived, though the deadline was approaching. As we stood in line, I picked up one of the pamphlets that were piled on the counters.

The pamphlet was entitled: Highway Signs For Survival. *Pictures of various road signs were shown. One read:* DECONTAMINATION CEN-TER; *another,* MAINTAIN TOP SPEED. *This was followed by the legend:* "Used On Highways Where Radiological Contamination Is Such As To Limit Permissible Exposure Time." *Another sign read* AREA CLOSED, *and carried the legend:* "Used To Close Roadway Entering An Area From Which All Traffic Is Excluded Because Of Dangerous Radiological Or Biological Contamination."

I stuck the pamphlet in my pocket and thought no more about it. Then that night as usual I sat down to check my dream records. As soon as I reread the dream for January 3, I saw the obvious connection with the pamphlet and ran to retrieve it. I was so surprised that I called Rob, and together we compared the pamphlet with the dream notes.

"It's the same thing as that Taylor episode," I said. "I acted the whole damn pamphlet out — translated the information literally, into action — running through the radioactive rain, seeing the men in the decontamination center."

With growing excitement, we checked my records. "Almost every sign's message was carried out in action," Rob said. "You were running through the radioactive rain to avoid contamination, running for your life, really, and the pamphlet refers to survival several times and 'Maintain top speed.'"

"What about 'Uniform traffic control?'" I asked. "All my men in the decontamination center wore coveralls and masks — they're uniforms of a sort."

"I don't know if you can really count that," Rob said, "Though you're probably right. But the clear words 'decontamination center' in the dream records are terrific. You couldn't have hit it closer."

We went on to read the last portion of the dream and I called out excitedly, "But look! The county building that houses the License Office is gray white stone with a steeple that definitely makes it look like a church. And there are other buildings nearby with gravel walks and grass and benches."

Looking over my shoulder now, Rob pointed at the sketch I'd done with the dream. "That layout is identical to the one at the License Bureau!" And it was. The Motor Vehicles Bureau is an extension of the county building, as the decontamination center was an extension of another building in the dream. Incidentally, I'd been in the License Bureau only once several years earlier.

Right then and there I made up my list of similarities between dream and physical events and was astonished — precisely because the forseen event was apparently the reading of the pamphlet, which I'd then transformed into that strange dream drama. As I wrote out the list, I discovered points that I'd missed earlier — which is why it is a good idea to make such a list with any involved dream.

Dream Events Jan. 4, 1966	**Physical Events** Jan. 10, 1966
1. I am outside decontamination center.	1. DECONTAMINATION CENTER sign on pamphlet found in License Bureau.
2. This center is the extension of another building.	2. License Bureau is extension of county building. Sketch of dream location matches county building layout.
3. Men in uniforms wait in line.	3. Men wait in line as we do, for licenses. In dream, men wear uniforms of a kind. The word "uniform" appears on pamphlet.
4. Dream area is closed to public —	4. Existence of radiological contamination specified on pamphet.
5. Because of radioactive contamination.	5. Existence of radiological contamination specified on pamphlet.
6. I run as quickly as possible to avoid radioactive exposure from rain.	6. Sign on pamphlet warns motorist to maintain top speed to avoid contamination.
7. I'm running for my life.	7. Pamphlet titled: *Highway Signs for Survival.*

Dream Events	**Physical Events**
Jan. 4, 1966	*Jan. 10, 1966*
8. Then I stand on landscaped grounds, gravel paths, shrubs, grass and benches.	8. County building surrounded by same.
9. One building looks like a church but isn't.	9. County building has a steeple.
10. All the buildings are gray or white stone.	10. County building is gray-white stone.
11. I think this may be a space for patients.	11. Pamphlet mentions Medical Center.

"Why did you bother to pick up the information on that particular thing though? Do you have any idea?" Rob asked.

"No, but I'm sure there must be an emotional connection someplace." I shook my head, but then suddenly the answer came to me. "Bundu," I said. "My science fiction novel that came out in *Fantasy and Science Fiction* years ago. It was on events after a world destruction. And I did another story and some of my early poetry on the same theme."

I felt as triumphant figuring out that dream as if I'd climbed some new mountain. Then I told Rob about another idea I had about it, one that I couldn't possibly prove.

"Something else, though," I said. "Its been coming to me in bits and pieces. What I really think happened is this: I left my body, wandered in my dream body around the County House grounds, went inside, saw the pamphlet, and then made up that dream about it. I know you can dream out-of-body as well as in it. I've caught myself doing it."

To me, there is great excitement in learning how the unconscious works, not just generally but specifically — in personal instances. In the same way that I acted out the original forseen event — the pamphlet — I'm convinced that other extrasensory data is picked up and woven into our daydreams, fantasies and creative works.

In the next case, interpretation was simple — and amusing.

One night I had a confused dream about a celebration. Rob and I were with a group of people, all laughing and calling out shouts and responses. I had a megaphone. We shouted one word over and over again: "Kangaroo."

This seemed like a pointless nonsense dream. A few weeks later I received a letter from a friend in California. Something about it struck a familiar chord: The whole bottom of one page was given over to a sketch of a kangaroo. In the letter, my friend also wrote a page about a family celebration.

My notes contain many records of plain precognitive dreams which are relatively clear, and which often concern very mundane situations. Oddly enough, I don't find these as "meaty" as some others, in which the information seems to give hints of its source or is "caught" in the process of being formed into dream material.

In March of 1968, for example, I received a letter in which my mother told me that Mike Myers, an old friend, was dead, and that his widow was very upset. I hadn't seen Mike or Mary in more than a dozen years. They lived in a distant town. "Maybe you dreamed Mike died," Rob said.

"No. I'm sure I would have remembered," I replied. But I checked my dream records. Sure enough, on December 24, I dreamed that Mike was "gone" and Mary could not find him. This was the only reference to Mike in any of my records, but I'd forgotten the dream entirely.

But there are precognitive dreams that tell me precisely what I want to know when I want to know it — if I'm deeply motivated enough to request them through suggestion. These are fascinating, not only because they are practical, but because they suggest the awesome abilities of the inner self to solve problems for us and to obtain information that we consider vital.

16

More on Precognitive Dreams

*B*efore I speak about some of my students' dreams, I want to give some further samples of my own, showing how precognition in dreams can give us pertinent information about events in which we have deep emotional interest. This particular book is a case in point: even before it existed in its present form, I was kept informed of publisher's decisions toward it. In a long series of dreams, over a three-year period, I foresaw the answers to my letters and inquiries.

On February 12, 1966, I dreamed that I was on a bed, with Rob on one side of me and another man nearby. There was no pain but a movement in the pelvis, and I delivered a baby. But then a doctor held up two infants and I thought with a laugh, "Oh, no! Twins. Really, this is too much!" — meaning that after having no children, two at once was really something. Then the doctor reassured me that only one baby was involved. The hospital was in my own childhood neighborhood. I was pleased that the delivery was easy and painless.

Was I pregnant? I was in the middle of my monthly period. There was no physical way to tell. Was the dream symbolic? Rob made a note of the dream and planned to ask Seth about it in our next session. As it happened, Seth interpreted the dream at once, without waiting to be asked. It was Session 233, February 14, 1966 (Valentine's Day). Seth said,

Ruburt's dream represented several layers of information. On a superficial level, it represented his inner knowledge that he is not physically afraid of childbirth. On another layer, it represented the knowledge that a future endeavor would at first seem to be two separate ones — two accomplishments, but on later examination, it will be seen that they are unified. These have not yet come to pass and they represent a new birth — from the unconscious. This spring will be the time. I am one of those represented in the dream, as Joseph is the other. The affair will be beneficial from many viewpoints and represents a creative endeavor. Again, he will think that two are involved and will realize that one unified product has been achieved instead. He saw a female baby because the product will be intuitive and psychic rather than born from logic. It will begin about the time of his own birth date, another reason why birth symbolism was used.

The product will not come from pain, so he felt none. It will be the result of psychic motion. This simply represents another creative endeavor which he will deliver with our help. Now, my fondest regards to you both, from your own valentine.

"The same to you," Rob said, with a smile. He'd forgotten it was Valentine's Day.

And if we are not all hearts and flowers, let it be said that hearts and flowers as a steady diet could become quite boring.

At the time, I had just begun two books — an initial draft outlining the ideas in the Seth Material and a manuscript on dreams that I thought of as my "dream book." It didn't occur to me that these two manuscripts could have anything to do with the dream interpretation because they were in the present rather than in the future. They were definitely *two* books, each with its own identity, and covering different subjects.

In the meantime, my book, *How To Develop Your ESP Power* was released. In 1967, I finished the dream book manuscript, and did much more on the Seth Material. I wasn't pleased with how I was handling that book, however, so I filed it away to look at later. It wasn't until February 1, 1968 that I sent the dream manuscript out to a publisher. On February 17, I dreamed that it was returned and that the person to whom I had addressed it no longer worked there. On February 23, the manuscript was returned. The letter was dated the day before my dream and written by a different editor than the one to whom I'd written.

On February 27, I sent the manuscript out again to another publisher. On the same day, I sent out a book of poetry, *The Sky Will Send Down Ladders*. On March 12, I dreamed that both had been returned. On March 22, both manuscripts came back.

I was disappointed, naturally, but again I sent the dream manuscript out; this time to Prentice-Hall, on April 2, 1968. On April 12, as I did psy-time, I received a strong impression that Prentice would give me a contract if I revised the book rather drastically. On April 19, I received a letter from Assistant Editor Tam Mossman, stating that the house might be interested in a book on Seth, utilizing parts of the dream book manuscript. I wrote back to see exactly what they had in mind.

A few weeks went by, and I heard nothing. On April 29, I lay down, telling myself I would have a dream giving me some information, letting me know whether or not a contract would be signed. It was 8:00 A.M. and I set the alarm for 9:00. I fell asleep instantly.

First there was an extremely vivid dream in which Rob and I were in a little town in New York. Then I experienced a false awakening: I thought I was awake, and about to get up to write down the dream. The phone rang. I jumped out of bed, rushed

into the livingroom. But as I reached the phone, it stopped ring-
ing. At the same time, I felt an instant sense of strangeness. It had
been bright and cloudless before I went to bed; now the sky was
much too dark. A brooding quality filled the room, and outside
the windows, everything was dimly lit as if it were suddenly the
hour just before dawn.

Then I recalled my previous experiments with dream states and
knew that I wasn't normally awake as I thought, but was wandering out in the living room, in an out-of-body state and hallucinating. The phone had never rung. My body was still in bed. The
darkness was an effect caused by the state of my consciousness. So,
while I had the chance, I decided to do some more experimenting
and went out the hall door, downstairs and outside.

At this time, the alarm rang. I snapped awake, in my body in
bed. Angry at having the experience cut short, I dozed off again,
once more giving the suggestion that I would learn what was going on at Prentice-Hall.

There were several normal dreams. Then I saw a letter about
my book from Prentice. It was on normal typing paper and requested, first, some further work on the book — either an outline
of a projected book to include portions of the dream manuscript,
but stressing Seth, or some sample chapters — before a contract
would be signed. One sentence read, "Or better, send on some
notes from the original Seth material, and maybe we can consider
that as advance work for a contract."

On May 5, I received a letter asking for a prospectus stating
Seth's views on various topics and strongly suggesting that this
would be considered a basis for contract. From the letter I took it
for granted that I'd have to go through the forty or so notebooks of
Seth Material that we had then, and find sections dealing with
various topics. This involved work that I really didn't want to do,
until the proposed book was begun. The next day, though, I
started to work on it.

On May 14, I dreamed that I was doing something wrong about

the prospectus. The dream bothered me so much that I called Prentice and learned that I'd misinterpreted Tam's letter. All I needed was a simple prospectus and outline. Except for the dream, I would have spent considerable time gathering data long before it was needed. I felt much better and mailed the whole package off on May 17.

Ten days passed without word. Then I had another dream that upset me considerably. In it, Rob had gone downstairs to get the mail. There was a letter from Prentice. Rob opened it, and began to read.

"For heaven's sake," I said, "Hurry. I think this is a dream, and you have to tell me what the letter says before I wake up."

"It isn't a dream," Rob assured me. "You're in your normal state of consciousness."

"No, I'm dreaming. Don't tease! Give me the letter or read it," I said, growing frantic.

"It's all right," Rob said.

"You mean its a real letter? It's not a precognitive symbol? Even if I do wake up, I can still read it?"

Again Rob assured me that I wasn't dreaming, but now I was sure that I was and afraid that I was about to awaken. Rob handed me the letter. Hurriedly, I grabbed it. Later I forgot much of what I read, but I knew that a contract would not be given yet — there would be a lag. Some obstacle had arisen, but there was still hope. There was also something about my being fired from a job because I was notorious as a writer.

From this, I went into a long dream sequence that involved the death of a young Italian man who was somehow connected with our landlord and another about the death of someone close to a student, Lanna Crosby. When I awakened, and wrote the dreams down, I wasn't too happy. I'd hoped that my prospectus would be followed quickly by a contract; and the other portions of the dreams weren't too cheerful either.

The following day, we learned that a young Italian man had

died — a former neighbor who had lived in this apartment house some time before; hence, the connection with our landlord in the dream. From experience, I knew that if one element in a dream sequence is precognitive, then the others usually are, too — at least in my case. So I waited. The next day, I heard that a friend of Lanna's had died. But still I heard nothing from Prentice-Hall.

Each day I watched the mail. There were no letters, no calls. On May 30, I had a brief dream in which I was talking on the phone to a woman about the projected book. I had no idea what that meant. I had always dealth with Tam — who is a man.

Three weeks passed. Finally, I called and discovered that my dream had been correct. There was some resistence. Tam, with whom I had been corresponding, had to sell the idea to his boss — a woman. Tam asked me if I would consent to having a well-known psychic writer tell my story for me because of the built-in publicity his name would lend. Thinking of my dream, I refused. Now I understood the reference to losing my "job" and the connection with the "notorious" writer. Tam said he had great faith in the book and would continue to work on my behalf. And there it rested.

Then again, nothing. On June 23, I dreamed that the publisher of my first book called, giving me all kinds of information about sales. On June 29, Tam wrote me an encouraging letter asking me for the sales figures on my first book.

In the end, I combined portions of the dream book manuscript into a new book called *The Seth Material*, which was published by Prentice-Hall in September, 1970. That book was one project, then, that seemed to be two entirely different ones. I had begun it on May 9, one day after my birthday. Seth's interpretation of that first dream, some three years ago, had been correct. In a series of dreams, I also knew that the unused portions of the original dream manuscript would appear in another book — and they are — in this book you are now reading.

That series of dreams was important to me, for each of them gave me additional information about a project in which I had the highest emotional interest, and they cut down the waiting period involved in normal communication.

Apparently Rob, too, has his dream eye out for my writing interests. Back in 1964, a national magazine accepted my short story, "Big Freeze." Payment was to be on publication. As time went on, I heard nothing from them, and the magazine was not one that we regularly purchase. I made a mental note to write them but kept putting it off. Then, on October 21, 1965, Rob dreamed that my story, "Big Freeze," had already been published. Rob told me about the dream and recorded it in the morning.

That day, in the art department where Rob works mornings, a co-worker told Rob that he had just read my story and liked it. It had appeared in the current issue of the magazine, then on the stands. The magazine had just come out and Rob had not seen it. I wrote them and received payment and their apology for the "oversight." In mentioning the dream during a session, Seth told Rob that he had also translated the title into the sensation of feeling chilly upon awakening — a fact that Rob had forgotten.

A friend, Jim Lord, realizes how helpful dreams can be, because one literally saved his life. Jim had only just begun dream recall experiments when he was sent to Vietnam. Just as I started working on this chapter, I received a letter from him:

> I'm making good progress with the suggestions for dream recall. Now I can remember at least one dream every two days. [Previously, he'd recalled dreams very seldomly.] It's unfortunate that I can't keep a notebook in the service, but I do make a quick note of dreams when I can.
>
> Recently, I had one of very great interest. Let me give you a few details first, though. I usually spend every Sunday afternoon walking on the beach. It just so happened that I worked late Saturday night, January 17, 1970 and had the whole Sunday off, instead of just half the day. As a result I looked forward to spending the whole day on the beach.
>
> That night, though, I dreamed that I was walking along the beach in the usual direction I take. As I did so, I wondered what would

happen if we had an incoming rocket attack in camp while I was out walking. I could see myself strolling along, even as I wondered. Just then I could also see a rocket hitting the water and heard the siren go off at base. In the dream, I ran all the way back.

The next morning, I was all ready to go for a walk when I remembered my dream. Was it a warning of a future event? I decided that I'd better take the side of caution, so I stayed at the hutch. At 10:00 A.M., we had an incoming rocket attack. The place of impact was the exact area where I usually go for my walk.

I couldn't have known about the attack through any normal information, of course, and there was no talk around the base about rockets or anything in the past to suggest the dream — except that such a possibility existed. We've only had two such attacks in the nine months I've been here, though, so they are hardly everyday occurrences.

According to the rest of Jim's letter, if he'd been on the beach as usual that morning, only a miracle could have saved him from death. In this case, he had been given information of the greatest value — and he acted on it.

Notice that his own death was not seen in the dream! But death dreams do not always foretell death, in any case. Some of them may simply allow us to release repressed wishes. Others may involve reincarnational data. Seth says that we use our inner perceptions as we use our outer ones — to discover more about things in which we are interested. If you are inclined to be pessimistic, most likely you will often have pessimistic dreams as well.

Sometimes we seem to tune into unfortunate events that do not even concern us. On June 20, for example, Virginia Mallery, one of my students, told our class the following dream: "I saw freight cars on the ground by the railroad viaduct. . . . I think the Gray Street viaduct in Elmira, though I'm not sure. They had fallen off the track. No one seemed hurt, and the cars weren't smashed badly. As I remember, two were lying down, and one was up on end. I don't recall seeing any automobiles."

On January 25, there was a train wreck in Elmira. Two freight cars fell off the same viaduct that Virginia had seen in her dream but a few blocks south of Gray Street. No one was hurt, the cars were not badly smashed and no automobiles were involved. Two, rather than three, freight cars had turned over, one on its side and one flat.

In our next class, Virginia wondered why she'd perceived this particular event. She had no idea why it would be pertinent to her. Actually, her husband came up with the clue. Virginia's father had worked for the railroad's business office, and it is likely that this emotional connection conditioned her to be interested generally in the railroad.

Clair McClure, a friend, had the following dream several times from June 26 through June 29. She saw herself having an automobile accident at an intersection. Two other cars were involved, though only one hit Claire's car. On the corner was a Mobil gas station. The dream upset her, since she was planning a trip to New York on June 30. During the trip, she was very careful, and she told her dream to her family, to me and to a friend in New York. Three days after her return, she was in an accident just outside of town. Everything, including the Mobil gas station, followed the dream events.

In a strict sense, Claire's dreams may or may not have been precognitive. She may have been accident-prone at that time in her life, and the dreams themselves may have acted as suggestion — as a sort of post-hypnotic suggestion that she could fight off for only so long. Or the dreams may have been legitimate glimpses into the future. If so, even though she used extra care in driving, she didn't change the events.

But is the future predetermined? Seth says no — that time is being changed at each point. It's impossible to speak of time and precognition without considering probabilities. The following two chapters on probabilities and dreams contain some of the most intriguing material Seth has given us — and precognition must be seen against this larger perspective. First, however, here are some excerpts dealing more specifically with dreams and precognition.

In telepathic, clairvoyant or precognitive dreams, exactly what is transmitted? I looked to my own dream records for some answers, but Seth discussed this point in Session 197 for October 11, 1965:

I have mentioned that any action has an electromagnetic reality. In telepathic and clairvoyant experiences, the electromagnetic pattern is transmitted. It must then be transformed into a pattern that can be distinguished by the ego, if the individual is to be consciously aware of the data.

Often the information is picked up translated by the subconscious and acted upon without conscious approval or recognition. In almost all cases, however, there must be an emotional attraction, for this is what allows for the initial transmission, and makes it possible.

The ego chooses channels of reception with great discrimination, and again, it censors anything which it feels is a threat to its dominance. In sleep, however, many dreams are of a telepathic nature, with strong clairvoyant overtones. [It is the ego's persistent discrimination in choosing the stimuli to which it will react that determines the nature of physical time as it appears to the personality.] The ego, because of its function and characteristics, cannot make swift decisions as can the intuitive self. Therefore, it perceives events almost in slow motion.

"What's the job of the intellect, then?" Rob asked.

In the future, Seth said, *the ego and intellect will expand to contain, use and appreciate all the other portions of the self which they now mistrust. Individual identity will expand to include a greater variety of impulses and stimuli. . . . The ego will become more of an organizer, in general, letting in, literally, a barrage of experiences and forming them into meaninful patterns. Now it fears such experiences because it is not certain of its strength or of its ability to organize them. . . .*

I mentioned in your last session that your scientists do not

*realize that man has, indeed, evolved since the development of
the brain. For it has learned to form millions of new
connections, meanings and concepts, new gestalts that have
made man something different than he was. All of these are
new electromagnetic patterns which are now indelibly a part of
the race. . . .*

*The size of the brain has little to do with this beyond a
certain point. The number of electrical connections are
important, however, and even the old portions of the brain are
affected by them. The old portions are not the same as they
were. Physical examination only discloses their condition in the
present.*

"Subconscious Layers and Precognitive Dreams"
(Excerpts from Session 212)

*You will discover definite correlations that exist between the
incidence of precognitive dreams and data having to do with
the temperature and weather. I don't believe it is possible for
you to carry your dream experiments far enough to discover
certain other factors that exist between various layers of the
subconscious and falling temperature rates in the body;
therefore, I mention it here.*

*It would be necessary to take your temperature many times
during the night and to correlate the findings with the levels of
the subconscious as they showed themselves within the dream
series. . . . It should be noted, however, that with the exception
of several other circumstances, these various subconscious levels
fall within definite temperature ranges. To some extent, this can
be ascertained through hypnosis. However, suggestion to the
effect that the subject's temperature rise or fall would tend to
obscure the effect. . . .*

*This correlation . . . is observable only when the personality
is in an inactive state. Suggestions of motion or excitement*

would change and affect the temperature reading, so that this characteristic temperature range would go unnoticed. Illness can also obscure the effect.

If we can see future events in dreams, does this mean that the theory of free will is a myth? Not at all. But in order to answer this question, Seth considers it along with the nature of time and probable events.

(Excerpts From Session 234, February 16, 1966)

Sometimes precognitive information will appear to be wrong. In some cases, this is because a different probable event has been chosen by the self for physical materialization. I have access to the field of probabilities, and, egotistically at least, you do not. To me, your past, present and future merge into one.

On the other hand, as I have told you, your past itself continually changes. It does not appear to change to you, for you change with it. The question of precognition, however, is not at issue with information concerning the past. Your future changes as the past does. Since precognition deals with future events, it is here that the issue [of changing time] shows itself.

In such cases, it is necessary that the correct channel of probable events be perceived; 'correct' meaning the channel which will ultimately be chosen in your terms. The choice is dependent upon your choices in both past and present. These choices, however, are based upon your changing perceptions of past and present. Because I have a greater scope of perception than you, I can predict what may happen with better facility. But this is still dependent upon my prediction of a choice you will make.

Predictions, per se, do not contradict the theory of free will, though free will is dependent upon much more than the freedom of the ego alone. If the ego were allowed to make all the choices, with no veto power from other layers of the self, you would all be in a sad position, indeed.

(The term "probable universe" was fairly new to us then, so Rob asked, "Will you tell us more about the probable system and its connections here?" Seth replied,)

The field of probabilities is quite as real as your physical universe. The experiences encountered there by other portions of the self are used by the whole self. The knowledge gained there is invaluable, not only in terms of overall experience, but as a means of training the ego and subconscious to choose between various activities.

All of this data is instantly available; only the ego is unaware of this field of reality. It would be snowed under. From this field of probabilities you choose patterns of thought which you will weave into the physical matter of your universe. The dreaming self sees both fields and operates in each. It should be realized that the probable self also has its own dreams.

This probable field seeds many other systems beside your own. It is composed of thought images, not physically materialized in your terms, but vivid storehouses of energy. Here is the material from which all pasts, presents and futures are made. It is far from a closed system. Not only does it feed the physical universe, but in it, many aspects of your own dreams become actual. Do you dream of an apple? The apple appears in the field of probability.

"On Precognition and Association"
(Excerpts from Session 239, March 7, 1966)

Association is not clearly understood, because psychologists, at present, believe that it works only in connection with past events. They also underestimate dream events, for many associations are the result of events that happen in the dream state . . . where the mind continues its associative processes.

Any given personal association may originate from a dream event, as well as from a past waking one. Psychologists, generally speaking, have not yet accepted the theories of your own physicists, and they continue to consider time as a series of moments. The inverted time system recognizes the actual nature of time. There is room in it for a rather complete explanation of the mind's associative processes. The mind, as opposed to the brain, perceives in terms of a spacious present. Therefore, it draws its associations not only from your present and past but also from your future.

Take an example: Frederick Y. becomes ill whenever he smells a certain perfume. He does not know the reason. A psychologist might explain the reaction by presuming that some unpleasant event from the past was connected with his perception of the perfume. The explanation is a good possible one; however, it is often the only one that would be considered.

Frederick may be reacting to an unpleasant event experienced in the dream state in which the upsetting situation was accompanied by the particular odor. [But] he could also be reacting to a future event of the same nature, for again, the mind does not break time into a series of moments. This is done by the physical brain.

The ego, as a rule, is not aware of this broader time experience, but the subconscious often is; and associative processes of the mind can and do react to the future. Therefore, it is possible for our Frederick to become ill this year at the smell of a particular perfume because, say, subconsciously he knows that in 1980 his mother will be wearing it when she dies. The associative processes work both forward and backward.

"On Precognition and Clairvoyance"
(Excerpts from Session 240, March 9, 1966)

I have told you that each individual creates physical matter, including objects and his own image. Coherence, illusion of permanency, placement in space, mass and color are all arrived at and agreed upon in the ways already explained. Telepathic communication is one of the methods by which such agreement is reached.

Long ago, primary and secondary constructions were explained. I emphasized that each individual perceives only his own physical constructions. Basically, there is no difference between telepathy and clairvoyance. The apparent difference is the result of an inadequate understanding of the nature of time. The important fact in both cases is that information is received that does not come through normal sense channels.

When an individual clairvoyantly 'sees' an event, this is what happens: First he forgets the concept of continual moments that usually hampers perception. His perception changes focus so that he is aware of an event that otherwise would seem to be in the future. Unconsciously, as always, he constructs material objects in line with the available data.

It goes without saying, then, that he helps to form the clairvoyantly perceived event, just as he helps construct any event in the present. The agreement as to physical dimensions is reached in the same manner as usual. . . .

Sense data is not basically dependent upon the physical body. The mind can bypass the senses and receive data in a more direct manner, translating what it perceives automatically, as it translates ordinary sense data.

Under ordinary circumstances, data is received through the physical senses and then interpreted by the brain. When a clairvoyant event is perceived, the data is received by the mind, then given to the brain which then interprets it. The physical body becomes aware of it, but the senses have actually been bypassed. The interpretation is made, however, in the same way as it usually is. Otherwise, the information would not register for the physical organism.

Actually, of course, much information perceived directly by the mind does bypass the physical organism completely. In some such cases, the subconscious does receive the data. In other cases, it is not recorded in any way within the physical system but is recorded at deeper layers of the self.

Even this data is available to the subconscious, however, if the need for it arises. Before it can be used by the physical organism, it must [first] be taken from the deeper layers to the brain for interpretation, as if it were new sense data. . . .

In the dream state, you smell odors that are not in the physical room. The memory of these is imprinted and registered by the body as faithfully and realistically as any 'real' odor. The experience becomes a part of [buried] memory and may be recovered through hypnosis. Sometimes it may arise spontaneously.

"Precognitive and Mass Dreams"
(Excerpts from Session 253)

There are many kinds of mass or shared dreams. For now, we will be concerned with mass dreams that have an almost universal nature; that is, dreams that are shared at one time or another by the majority of living persons on your planet.

This particular kind of dream is concerned with working out certain problems concerning physical reality. The dreams usually are not precognitive, although they might appear to be, since many of the dream events will later occur. They are not precognitive, however, because in a large measure they bring about or cause the later events.

They occur, comparatively speaking, just above that layer which Jung refers to as the collective unconscious. If you could tune into these dreams, you would have a good idea of the main events of the future because you would see them being born. They are concerned with significant events that affect many countries. They represent deep intents, wishes and purposes. At times they have immense power to bring about world-shaking changes of beneficial or destructive nature.

One individual is more important than you have ever dreamed, however, for the intensity and intent are important. One man passionately willing good or evil can overbalance literally a hundred men. And in the dream state, also, leaders can be born and make themselves known. The people already know them in mass dreams before they are recognized in physical reality.

17

Dreams and Probabilities

Sue Meets a Probable Rob and Jane

On Friday, October 9, 1970, I received a letter from a reader, Peg Boyles, about my book *The Seth Material*. With it she included an excerpt from *Living Time* by Maurice Nicoll, and another from a manuscript by Alice Bailey. We were expecting company that night. After dinner I watched "Mission Impossible" on television and began reading the Nicoll exerpts which were on probabilities. I did not even look at the Bailey material. The Nicoll pages intrigued me, and I thought of asking Seth about some of Nicoll's ideas.

After finishing my reading, I may have watched television for a few moments. Then I went out to the kitchen to wash a pan that I'd left soaking in the sink. As I did this, suddenly a concise clear stream of words came through my head: *"Great as these things are, there is a totality of experience and sensation that includes them all, a vortex that contains and transforms these infinite parts."*

The words were simply there, completely intrusive as far as I was concerned. I'd been scowling at the dirty pot and thinking of my company. "What?" I said.

Surprised, I went to my table and sat down with a paper and pen. The words returned exactly as before, and I wrote them down. I "knew" they were comments on what I had read — or additions. One page of written material followed, given in the same way. Groups of words were just popped into my mind. No more than a sentence came until that was written down.

I was totally alert and critical at the time, focused at a high point of concentration, though, in that all of my attention was pivoted expectantly. The experience was fascinating and increasingly enjoyable. Earlier, I'd sipped beer as I watched television. Now the half-full glass was beside me. I drank some now and then, and also smoked. A strong sense of exhilaration was present, as was the feeling of great energy. There was no feeling that any particular personality was giving me the information, yet there was the certainty that the words were being delivered from somewhere or someone outside my own reality. They didn't seem to well up from inside me, but to be dropped down into my head.

As I finished the first page, Rob came out, passed me and went into the kitchen. I was surprised that he didn't know without being told, as he usually does, that something was going on, and I didn't want to talk to anyone. Finally I managed to say, "Hon, don't bother me." It took great effort for me to withdraw that much energy away from what I was doing. But, instead of understanding, Rob began emptying the garbage into paper bags. The crinkley sound seemed magnified tremendously and had a new dimension as if it were ripping up space, crinkling the edges of space in the kitchen. Later, Rob said that he never heard me speak to him and questioned whether I'd really spoken. I thought I had, of course.

At the same time, the people in the apartment downstairs got company. They came tramping and laughing up the steps just beneath my open window. Suddenly, the sound of traffic also bothered me. I'd been unaware of it only a moment before. Now, the cars went rushing through the rain. All of these sounds merged together, intensified, while each retained its own unique quality.

I wanted to cry, and for a moment I almost did — to be so interrupted. Rob went on bagging the garbage. It seemed now that we were separated by a great distance that had nothing to do with space. I couldn't bridge it just then to explain what was happening or to ask him to stop. He went out and returned after emptying the garbage. The kids downstairs, full of fun, began yelling with great energy on the porch. Finally, the sounds quieted. I waited.

Nearly three more pages of dictation followed, coming in the same way as before. Because of the nature of the material, I thought I might be shown how to enter a probable moment from the present one. Initial instructions were given, though only preliminary, but I was ready to follow them. Now the speaker was addressing me, where the earlier monologue had been impersonal. At this point, unfortunately, our company arrived. I was really disappointed, but shook my consciousness to set it back to daily things, and with only a moment of reorientation attended to my guests.

Here is an exact copy of that material, delivered October 9, 1970 between 8:00 and 9:30 P.M., referring to *Living Time* by Nicoll.

Great as these things are, there is a totality of experience and sensation that includes them all, a vortex that contains and transforms these infinite parts. I know that of which I speak. Yet, each minute event immeasurably increases not only itself but all other events, bringing into birth by its own actualization an infinitude of novus actions and events, an unfolding or multi-dimensionalizing of itself, an initiation into dimensionalization. For all versions and possibilities of each event must be actualized in the limitless multiplication of creativity.

And warping outward from each act are a million openings,

*roads traveled and experienced by the soul, naturally and
spontaneously following its attributes.*

   *Any one moment in physical time then is a warp, opening
into these other dimensions of actuality, and any one moment
can be used as a passageway or bridge. The act of crossing will
be reflected in a million other worlds, but these reflections will
be themselves alive and the act of perceiving itself will create
still another vortex of actualization.*

   *Attention can be shifted from any physical moment to any
probable moment by a sideways parallel imaginative thrust — a
sideling off of —*

*(Here came the first interruption. . . . Rob came into the kitchen. The
dictation stops, or rather, it was still there, but I couldn't get it. It resumed after the interruption:)*

   *Each probable event is changed by each other probable
event. There is constant simultaneous interaction. These
'separate' probable systems do not operate isolated from each
other, then, but are intimately connected. All systems are open.
The physical moment is transparent, though you give it a
time-solidity. You see it as opaque.*

   Along with the last sentence, I saw an image that is difficult to
explain. It was a rectangular object that reminded me of a gadget
shown to us once by Jim Beal from NASA that reacted to light and
another that reacted to pressure. Both of those gadgets turned all
colors and achieved different stages of transparency and opaqueness. So did the object I saw now. It was supposed to represent the
moment as we perceive it. The center section of the rectangle was
most opaque and the ends most transparent. There were new
bursts of noise from downstairs at this point, and the image vanished.

   After a few minutes the dictation resumed, this time taking off
from the first point of interruption:

   Attention can be shifted from any physical moment to any

probable moment by a sideways parallel imaginative thrust, a sideling off of focus, if the mind can get over its fear of dying to itself.

In what other worlds, for example, do you sit writing these notes? Put down your glasses.

Startled by the question and the instruction, I paused, took my glasses off and put them on the table.

You have not put them down.

"I get it," I said mentally.

Slide imaginatively into a world where you do not perform the next small action you will perform in this world. Cough, smile, sneeze — in some other actuality your actions are non-actions and your non-acts are realized.

Greet the now-realization of all of your dreams, for they also participate in the probable system. As your dreams bleed into your normal conscious life, so do they bleed into other probabilities. A dream act is actualized by a waking you, as a waking you is actualized by a dreaming self.

The soul is too great to know itself, yet each individual portion of the soul seeks this knowledge and in the seeking creates new possibilities of development, new dimensions of actuality. The individual self at any given moment can connect with its soul. There is initially a sideral movement of consciousness, a dropping away sensation.

(End of script; company arrived.)

The next morning I typed up the material and went to check the title of the Nicoll book. Then I saw the Alice Bailey excerpt and read it. I was in for a surprise. It contained her description of the method used in scripts she received, and the description fitted my experience so closely that she could have been speaking for me as well.

I mentioned this and read my small script to class at our next meeting, adding that I thought further instructions would have been given if the session had not been cut short. Sue Watkins and I also discussed the episode. Both of us found it intriguing and wished we could get more practical experience with probable moments.

A few days later, on October 17, Sue had a dream in which Seth described probabilities in more personal terms. The following is from her notes:

> I 'come to,' realizing that my body is in bed sleeping. I walk in the bedroom where my father is standing, complaining about his problems. Immediately I get annoyed with him and begin telling him about *my* problems. He becomes very upset.
>
> Suddenly I am yanked away from this scene, and Carl [Sue's husband] and I are sitting in a large room with Jane as Seth. Seth turns to Carl and gives him a long lecture. Carl smiles at him, and Seth says, 'Now at the count of three, you will go into a deeper trance.' Carl begins to do so. I lie down on the couch and say, 'Wow, to be out at the count of three?' I close my eyes.
>
> Seth touches my shoulder, smiling. He tells me that I am to do something else and gives me a long, friendly lecture. The content is lost now, but I think it had to do with my own psychic development. Then Seth says, *'In the earlier dream demonstration tonight, your father had problems of his own, and you ignored them. The whole house was aware of your feelings and absorbed them. It will be aware of them for some time.'*
>
> On hearing this, I feel sorry and eerie, as I imagine the house actually absorbing my ill feelings. Seth then says that I can do the whole scene over by a simple method of stepping *sideways* into physical reality; he tells me that this is easier than I might suppose.
>
> Using a series of mental exercises explained to me by Seth, I *do* step sideways — it is as though I am squeezing between two bars, and I find myself back in the bedroom with my father there, again, complaining. This time I change the events from the way they happened the first time, realize how important his problems are to him, smile and send him good thoughts. At once I am propelled into another, similar scene.

In this experience, it is Thanksgiving Day. My mother's family is here also. I am in the sunroom watching my father take food from a buffet set in the dining room. My mother and her sister are in there, talking. Suddenly my father becomes angry, throws his plate onto the rug and grabs another. My mother begins to cry. I remember probabilities, however, and instead of becoming upset myself, I send my father thoughts of peace and health. I know that now the scene will not happen this Thanksgiving in physical reality — that I have helped choose another more positive one. The scene ends. I feel as though I have been both watching and participating. I hear Seth remark: 'You learn well, and manipulate equally well.'

I half waken and then drift into a recurring scene from an old childhood dream: There is a killer fog behind us, and we must get down a snowy path to home before the fog gets us. We are struggling past a large factory, when all at once I am sitting with Jane as Seth again, watching the snow dream as if it were a movie. I say, 'Of course,' and realize that I can relieve the people in the snow. Suddenly I feel the shell of my physical body for what it is — my own creation — and am aware of how much more I am. I go back into the snow scene. We all make the safety of the house, and I wish all the characters in the dream peace and safety from the killer fog. They will never have to fear it again. I wake up.

(NOTES CONNECTED WITH DREAM: I had the feeling that this was a demonstration of the many ramifications of probabilities in physical reality and in the dream state. Seth seemed to be an old friend there in a gentle, guiding way; almost as if he were a film projectionist, directing the film or experiences.)

Sue couldn't wait to tell me about the dream. We were both pleasantly astonished. Probable realities seemed like such an esoteric idea that we really hadn't hoped for much practical experience with it. But you'll see shortly, this was only the beginning.

In our next class, Seth commented on Sue's dream:

You did very well. Now, because you are interested in probabilities, you will have many more experiences along these

lines. We will hopscotch back and forth with our friend Ruburt,
for this is also one of his main lines of interest. Your own
experience can be used to benefit the class at large, for you must
be led to see that you can alter physical events in such a way.
You must be led to see that there are other dimensions of reality.

A few nights earlier, another student, Shirley, just missed having
an out-of-body experience. In the last class, Seth had told the students that he would help those who were ready to project. Shirley
felt Seth nearby a few nights later and was just about to leave her
body when she got frightened and held back.

When Seth finished speaking to Sue, he said to Shirley,

I have also been visiting our friend, here, but we have a very
scary soul indeed, for she ran the other way. You think of the
body as a warm house indeed, and you are loathe to leave it.

He spoke with such rich understanding humor that everyone
laughed, including Shirley. Through this entire period, Seth spoke
on probabilities in our own private sessions, as well as in class. He
was halfway through his own book, *Seth Speaks: The Eternal Va-*
lidity of the Soul which he is completing now and in which he
gives further methods that can be used to experience probable realities.

In the meantime, Sue began to have a series of dreams dealing
with probabilities, the first of them in August, 1970. She wrote the
dream down as usual, and called me on the phone to tell me about
it. I was astonished. As she read the dream, all kinds of images and
ideas came into my mind.

Projection-dream of Sue Watkins
(August 10, 1970 . . . evening)

After a long travel dream in which a friend and I pole a raft down a
long, lazy river and shot down a waterfall, I suddenly enter this
scene:

I walk down a street of a town not unlike Elmira and go into a small open-air restaurant which seems to have been made from one of those hexagonal pavillions. It is in a park-like place with grass and trees all around. The color and detail are vivid, even to salt and pepper shakers on the large common table in the middle.

There I see, to my surprise and joy, Jane and Rob Butts sitting talking to some other people. Or are they Jane and Rob? They are older-looking and both look very cynical about whatever they are discussing. I wonder if the town is Sayre, Pennsylvania and if we are all really there or if we have made this place up. The other people go away, and I go sit down next to Jane, and, to my surprise, they do not acknowledge or recognize me at all.

At this point, I am suddenly hit with the the knowledge that this is the dream state of another probability system involving Jane and Rob's probable selves here. I suddenly say to them, 'My name is Sue Watkins, and my husband's name is Carl.' They give me a rather nasty *'so-what'* look.

I look up and notice an older, short, stout man in a dark purple robe of some sort sitting across from us and realize with a jolt that it is *Seth!* I say, 'Do you know him?' and point. Jane laughs. 'You mean old Saint Nick over there?' I (whatever one it is) cringe.

I then observe how haggard they look. Jane is much heavier and is wearing a black long-sleeved turtleneck. Her hair is fuller but quite gray. Rob looks extremely tired and is sitting in a slouch; his face is not fat but *fleshy* — almost dissipated. He is smoking one cigarette after another. They both look bitter and not very happy.

I feel very protective of them. Somehow, I begin a discussion of the Seth Material with them and go into a talk on physical reality and such, and discover that a few years ago, they had received some strange messages through Jane from 'someone claiming to be a dead spirit.' 'But it was ridiculous,' Jane says, 'so we dropped it.'

'Look,' I say, 'You and I are in the dream state. I am from another probability system. You know me there. In mine, you kept on with the "messages" and found — I glance at Seth, who is smiling — 'they were from *him* and you went on to discover fantastic things about life.'

'You were somewhat younger-looking there, too — she is about forty and you, Rob, are fifty in that place, but age doesn't matter to you there. . . .'

'In that probability, you, Rob, painted constantly and Jane had published a bunch of short stories, a novel and poetry even before this got *started*. Do you do this now?'

Jane and Rob glance at each other and laugh — a nasty, bitter laugh. 'She still works all day at the taxi company' Rob says, "and I work too. Want to come home and see the paintings I've done?'

I nod and we walk out of the restaurant — Seth trailing along behind. We walk down a shaded, quiet street and turn in at a large white house with a screened lower porch. There is a large tree to the left of the porch, and a weedy driveway leads back to a large white barnish-looking building with double top-hinged doors. We go up a set of outside stairs and into an apartment which seems to have a large living room. Rob is about to haul out some paintings — they seem to be landscapes — when he groans in agony and nearly falls down in pain from his back, apparently. He manages to lie down on the floor and I try to show him some yoga exercises for it, but he brushes me off. I suddenly feel desperate to do something for them before it all ends.

At this point I hear a number of voices calling to me and I experience a false awakening, and know it, where I am lying in bed in a strange room but realize I must get up and write this experience down. I think then that this must be the astral system of my own probability system and that I have returned safely. I see Carl next to me, and I relax, fall asleep and wake up in my physical bed.

(Could these have been the York Beach couple? Or was it a simple learning method? I am filled with the conviction that this was legitimate.)

Nap at Home
(August 17, 1970)

Vague something about York Beach couple — are they happier now on an inner level? I think I sensed them re-assessing themselves.

After Sue read the dream to me, I didn't know what to say. The York Beach couple! With odd feelings of disquiet I let myself remember. The episode is included in *The Seth Material*, but it was one of the strangest events of our lives.

It happened some months before our first psychic experiences. Rob was ill, and we were vacationing in Maine. One night we went to a nightclub, hoping for a change of mood. Rob could hardly walk, his back hurt him so badly. The room was small and crowded, the tables were all full, and the band blared. Suddenly, I noticed an older couple sitting across from us. I couldn't take my eyes off them. As if hypnotized, I sat staring.

They looked like bloated, bitter copies of us, at a later age. The woman was much stouter than I but bore a striking resemblance to me. The man could have been Rob's twin, but older, with a face marked by disillusion. They frightened me badly. I kept thinking, "God, we could end up looking like that," and, in a strange way, I felt that they *were* us, in some terrible future.

I poked Rob, and told him what I thought. Then suddenly he just stood up, said, "Let's dance," and dragged me out onto the dance floor. A moment earlier I'd seen him grimace with pain. The band was playing a twist, and we didn't know the dance. For that matter, up to that point we hadn't gone out much and rarely danced. I resisted, but Rob wouldn't take no for an answer — very uncharacteristic of him.

Later the couple just disappeared as far as we were concerned. We thought they might have left while we weren't watching them. But from that night on, Rob began to improve. We danced all night, and now dancing is one of our favorite activities. We knew that something had happened very important to our lives, but we had no idea what was really involved.

After the Seth sessions began, Seth told us that we, ourselves, had created the images of the couple, projected all of our negative attitudes into them and then reacted. I didn't know what to think of this explanation at the time. Later as we explained the nature of personality and its creative potentials, I saw that this was precisely what we had done.

Seth told us that such images have a definite reality, but we certainly weren't prepared to hear that someone else encountered our York Beach selves in a dream! "To create them with all our negative feelings was bad enough," I said to Sue, "but then to cast them loose on their own!"

"Ask Seth about it," Sue said. It happened to be a session night night anyway, and without being asked, Seth suspended dictation on his own book to give us the following explanation:

Now, this is not dictation [on Seth's own book], *but it is some material that Ruburt can use in his dream book. I want to comment, therefore, on the experience of your friend, Sue Watkins, and its connection with the probable universe.*

The experience was quite legitimate, and it was meant as a lesson on many levels. First of all, it is apparent that there is communication between various systems of probabilities and that actions in one system can and do affect the other.

The couple do exist, probable selves of your own in a different system. Your friend, in developing her own abilities, has become involved with activities in probable fields and was drawn to the couple emotionally because of her emotional connection with you in this system.

The couple involved will recall portions of the experience, and it will serve to remind them forcibly of abilities that they are not using; acting, therefore, as a stimulus in that system, coming, however, from this one and through the agency of a friend.

The affair is also a lesson to you when you think negatively, showing you the results of such negative thoughts, followed without letup — and, in fact, followed in spite of redeeming actions that would change events. The other couple, for example, ignored the contact with me. The negative and bitter qualities of personality came fully to the fore, uncompromised

and unredeemed by the fulfilling and creative functions that
they had also smothered.

You see, they quite envy you. However, they were unable to
take advantage of your knowledge because of the condition of
their own psyches. The affair served to remind them once more
of my contact with them, to make them think twice, and it also
serves as a new stimulus for further contact.

*(Seth gestured humorously enough, but then quieted and leaned forward
in a mood of emphatic seriousness.)*

We attempt to save even the shadows of ourselves, and we
create light in even the darkest recesses of our own hidden
fragments. To that extent and in those terms, we are our own
redeemers.

To a large extent, you see, you and Ruburt were also
responsible for the contact, for were it not for your own present
experiences, your relationship with me and your friendship with
the girl [Sue], the help would not have been given to these
probable selves of yours. So one portion of the self lends a
helping hand to another, in the same way that I give you a
helping hand.

What I want you to see here is that the communications do
not just operate in a vertical, ascending or descending fashion,
but horizontally, in those terms.

At the same time, the experience was meant as a moral lesson
to your Sue Watkins. She sees you in a physical reality as people
she respects and admires. Through the probable experience, she
was able to see what could have happened to you in this system,
had you given in to negative thoughts and feelings and not been
persistent in your work and efforts.

By comparing the two couples, therefore, she receives an
object lesson both for herself and her husband. More than this,
however, through the experience all of you learned that help is
extended from one system to the other. The other couple, the

probable couple, have also helped you and your friend, though quite unknowingly at conscious levels, by serving as such object lessons.

Now, Ruburt has also done the same service for a probable Sue in another system of reality, though in an entirely different way. And you [Rob], incidentally, have helped a probable Carl [Sue's husband] in the same manner, using his creative abilities. The probable Carl, in other words, has strong creative abilities, and you have helped him understand this.

The experience brings up several points that have not been discussed in connection with probabilities. Because you are born physically into your system, you take it for granted without thinking of it that you are born in the same manner into other systems. This may or may not apply, but it is definitely not applicable to the system of probabilities as a whole.

The couple, the probable Robert and Jane Butts, came into being at York Beach, as given in the earlier material. They disappeared from your view, but energy created in such a fashion, as you know, cannot be negated and must continue along its own lines of development.

From this standpoint these are fragment personalities; therefore, they have your memories up to that point of their initiation, and they continued on from there. They were seen by you as far older, as you interpreted, created and then perceived bitterness and negative attitudes. To them, however, they were the age that you were at the point of their breakoff. Such personalities can be created and are created under varying conditions too many to enumerate.

In this case, however, you both sensed your lives at a period of crisis, and projected your fears outward into the formation of the images.

"You mean at York Beach, originally?" Rob asked.

At York Beach, originally. They contained, therefore, all of your fears, for you foresaw that in this system you could become such people — not that this was inevitable, but definitely probable and more than possible.

At the same time, however, you must understand that these probable selves were also created because of your own great hopes, hopes you felt you could fall far short of; so they were 'born' with the same hopes that you had at that time, but they were personalities that were overburdened with fears.

Having created them because of your abilities, you then perceived them as objectified apparitions in physical reality, when Ruburt immediately made the conscious comparison, and resolved that you should never end up looking like them . . . or filled with the bitterness that was written in their faces. The conscious notice, therefore, was all you knew of the deep unconscious creative endeavor and psychological mechanism that brought them into existence.

Even weighed down by fears and negative attitudes, they retained their own close relationship, but they were not able to help each other and were united by bitterness against the world, as much as by love for each other.

That Robert Butts did not continue his painting with any purpose, trying to be objective and sensible, lacking the understanding of his parents that you have achieved through sessions. He put security in financial terms above everything, took no chances at all along those lines, and despite this, of course, is not making much money because his heart was, with the painting, most largely abandoned.

Ruburt's creative ability quickly deteriorated, for bitter attitudes shrivelled up the source of the creativity. In that reality, you returned from York Beach, gave up your apartment in Elmira, returned to Sayre, lived for some time with your parents, [and] commuted to your Elmira job to save money.

You had planned for this as a temporary arrangement — six months, at most, to save money — then you were going to paint full time. Instead, however, you stayed, supposedly to aid your parents, but this was largely an excuse because you were afraid

to take the chance and paint full-time and also afraid to give up
the regular money, even though you had no rent to pay.

You felt the money might be needed for your parents, and as
you continued you became more bitter at the sacrifice you felt
you were making. Actually, the negative conditions were so
accepted that you simply followed them.

There is no need to go further into their history, but I assure
you that it was in keeping with the characteristics that you gave
them; and remember, these were your own strongest fears. With
all of this however latent, you see, they had your potential. I
was able to make an inadequate but definite contact, and their
existence can still be changed and altered, for they have free
will, as you do.

Unconsciously, you are aware of their progress, as
unconsciously they are aware of yours. You saw to it that they
would be helped. Remember that regardless of anything, you
gave them existence and consciousness, a gift of creativity, and
potentials that they will try in their own way to fulfill. Their
experiences have been different from yours. Their fulfillment,
when they achieve it, will, therefore, be of a different nature,
bringing out facets of activity that will not exist in your
circumstances — their meeting with your friend [Sue], for
example.

Now, in the life of each personality there are, of course,
moments of deep crisis and decision, where a personality decides
upon one of various possible choices. These moments are not
necessarily conscious at all, and the choices are not necessarily
conscious, though often they rise to consciousness. But by then,
the inner work and decision has been done.

The two of you were, therefore, freed largely of the most
volatile of your bitter attitudes and tendencies when you thrust
them out from you in such a way. You began your improvement
from that point. You got rid of a dangerous accumulation of
explosive negative energy and freed yourselves to that extent.

*You had not learned to change your attitudes, however, nor
learned how to prevent a new buildup, you see.*

*This was the next line of your development, however. You
cleared away debris. You gave yourselves psychic breathing
space so that your creative abilities could arise, and saw that
the way was open for our sessions to begin.*

It's one thing to accept the idea of probable systems and probable selves as an exciting intellectual concept, and quite another to
accept the practical considerations involved if you think of probabilities as plain facts of existence. Quite frankly, I didn't expect
any of us to have practical experience along these lines, thinking
that any probable realities were beyond our reach. But we weren't
finished yet, and I doubt that we are now. As you'll see, Sue kept
in touch with the probable Rob and Jane in her dreams. Through
our experiences, the concept became a reality with which we were
confronted.

18

Probable Selves

On January 22, 1971, a few months after the first dream about the York Beach couple, Sue had another. Here is the dream, from her notes:

I realize that I am dreaming, and tell myself to go to another probability system. I am standing by Chamberlain's Dairy outside Elmira, but the scenery doesn't change, so I will myself to Jane and Rob's apartment. The next thing I know, I'm there.

There is little furniture, and the walls are a dull beige. Artist supplies and papers are piled in disarray; someone is obviously moving into the place. Jane and Rob stand by the window. The plant room divider always in their apartment is gone. The room is very bare and barn-like.

Suddenly, I notice that Jane is slightly heavier, and her blouse which is partially unbuttoned, reveals two rather ample breasts. 'You're the York Beach couple again,' I cry, and this is the first time they notice me.

Jane's face is somehow softer than in the last encounter, and Rob seems more relaxed too. 'The what?' Rob asks.

'Look,' I say. 'Did you ever go to York Beach, Maine?' I sit down too.

'Yes, a few years ago.' Jane says.

'Well,' I say, 'Do you remember a younger couple staring at you in a night club? They couldn't take their eyes off you.

Rob and Jane look at each other. Jane says, 'No.' But somehow they both seem more like themselves, as I know them in daily life.

'They actually *were* you in a sense,' I say. 'At that moment they created you out of their fears and negative emotions, with all their talents but with all their aggressions and bitterness too. You had to go on from there.'

They change glances. Jane giggles.

'Look, do you recall anything about physical birth? About being a child?' I ask. It occurs to me that maybe they can't.

'Rob does,' Jane laughs. 'I don't like to.'

'You have their early memories.' They seem to believe me. I say, 'Do you remember the last time we met in the pavillion?'

At this point, I look up and see Seth sitting on some crates, very much heavier-looking than in the portrait Rob did of him — swarthier, in dark khaki clothes and boots.

The two of them don't answer me. They seem to be sharing a secret. 'Look,' I say again, to explain. 'This is a probable system of reality, one of many. In the one I come from, I also know Jane and Rob Butts. Do you remember that?'

Jane nods and answers, 'Yes.'

'In that probability, Jane is a lot thinner. She eats constantly to gain weight.'

We all laugh at that. I can't get over the change in them since our first dream encounter. Now their love for each other is much freer and more open than it was that first time, and they seem happier.

Here Seth turns to me and to some others who now appear in the room. Neither Jane or Rob see Seth or the others, although Seth is gesturing and his voice is audible, at least to me.

'Jane also has produced a lot of work,' I say. 'She has two books out and is now on a third.' I looked around at the disarray, and the unframed paintings that are stacked about. Rob nods at them, rather proudly, and we exchange looks of congratulations.

'The last books are on the Seth Material,' I continue, watching them. 'Do you know about Seth yet?'

Jane lights a cigarette and tries to be flippant. 'Isn't that funny!' she says. 'Just today Rob was on the phone, and had to hang up. He said, "Seth is coming, have to hang up." Then he didn't know what he meant. We figured that it was a slip of the tongue of some kind. But we wondered about it.'

'Has there been any contact with Seth?' I persist. They seem relectant to discuss it but finally Jane nods. Her eyes are very alert and bright.

'And you do remember the last time we met? And you must remember this meeting,' I say.

In the meantime, one of the other people with Seth speaks with him. One is a large, jolly-looking monk. I also notice that Rob's back seems much more comfortable than at our first meeting. 'You'll go on and develop your own way in this probability system,' I say. Affection seems to well up among us.

Jane then hands me a manuscript, a novel based on the August 11th dream encounter we had, from her perspective, but it includes this present dream experience also, the Seth breakthrough and someone named Michael J. Anthony. It seems to read well as I look it over, but I realize that the time sequence is confused here, in reference to me anyhow, and the story is mixing me up. 'I'm sorry. It's good, but I've got to go now,' I say quickly. With a last look at the two of them, sitting together on the edge of so much, I wake up fully and alert, sitting up in bed.

Apparently Rob and Jane were moving into the same apartment my Rob and Jane have lived in for years, but in another probability.

Sue has had several other short dream encounters with the York Beach couple and in each they seemed more confident and assured. Now, when she comes to our apartment, she senses this other Jane and Rob moving about just beyond the focus of our normal perceptions.

In one dream she seemed to meet a probable self of her own. This was the dream:

> I meet Carl [her real husband] in an underground tunnel complex near Fredonia. This is our first meeting. We talk for a minute, walking along. When we turn a corner there sits a huge Harley-Davidson motorcycle.
>
> 'Wow,' I say. 'Is this your bike?'
>
> Carl nods. At once I realize that somewhere — I don't understand where — Carl does not own a cycle and that the two of us are man and wife, and have a baby. It is as though I am remembering physical life as a dream, and yet I have the feeling that Carl and I have done this cycle bit before, that we are doing it still in another place and that we will do it even as we are doing it now. The all-at-oneness seems perfectly natural.
>
> We get on the bike and zoom through the countryside and while riding, I finally realize that this is a dream. I consider projecting but decide not to ruin the bike experience for Carl who would dearly love to own a motorcycle, even if he is only a dream Carl of mine.

The whole series of experiences concerning probabilities raised many questions. Seth answered several in a class session held several days after Sue's last dream. Speaking to her directly, Seth first mentioned the headache that had been plaguing her all day:

You are upset over the implication of probable selves, and that caused the headache. Simply tell yourself that you are doing well in this reality, using your abilities, helping your husband and caring for your child. You do not need to feel guilty over the creation of any probable selves. They come into reality with problems, but all of you come into reality with challenges that you have set 'ahead of time.' You have given them the gift of existence. They will learn how to use it and develop their own abilities in their own way. You have also

*given them individuality, which means that they are not
yourselves, but variations on yourselves.*

Sue said, "I was afraid that I'd created some pretty sorry probable selves of my own."

*Many do. You give probable selves a foundation and history
and identity, and without your creation of them they would not
exist. Would you, then, deny them reality in order to save them
from any pain? Now, your headache can vanish. All existence is
vulnerable . . . to the possibilities and probabilities of creation
that dwell deeply with it. Even when you thrust a pain apart
from yourself and give it as a heritage to a fragment personality,
you give it also your creative power and your hopes. You do not
set these personalities adrift without hope or potential.*

Another student asked, "Do we often project our fears and
guilts on to probable personalities?"

*You need not do so at all. Once you realize that your guilt is
groundless, then it can dissolve. It is only when you become
frightened that you project it in such a way.*

The following excerpts from the Seth Material will explain
probable systems more clearly, and relate probable selves with
dream experience.

"Dream Selves and Probable Selves"
(Session 232)

*We mentioned that the dreaming self has its own memories.
It has memory of all dream experience. To you, this might mean
that it has memory of its past, and, indeed, to you, memory
itself is dependent upon a past or the term seems meaningless.
To the dreaming self, however, past, present and future do not
exist. How can it be said to have memory?*

*All experience is basically simultaneous, as I have told you.
The dreaming self is aware of its experience in its entirety. You,*

obviously, are not. You are hardly familiar with your dream experience and barely aware of its significance.

The dreaming self is to some considerable degree aware of the probable self. There is give-and-take between the two, for much data is received by the dreaming self from the probable self — the self that experiences what the ego would call probable events.

This data is often wound by the dream self into a dream drama which informs the subconscious of dangers or of probable success of any given event which is being considered by the subconscious for physical actuality.

Were it not for the experience of this probable self, and for its information given via the dreaming self to the subconscious, then it would be most difficult for the ego to come to any clear decisions in daily life. The ego does not realize the data that is being constantly fed into it. It cannot afford to, generally, since its focused energy must be used in the manipulation of physical actuality.

This probable self has operated in each reincarnation, in each materialization of the personality, and has at its command literally millions of probable situations and conditions upon which to make value judgments. Of itself, however, it does not make the decision as to whether or not a particular event will be made physical. It merely passes on the information that it has received through experience.

This information is sifted often through the dreaming self to the subconscious which has intimate knowledge of the ego with which it is closely connected. The subconscious makes its own judgments and passes these on with the data. Then the ego makes its decision. In some cases, the ego refuses to make the decision, and it is done by the subconscious. On occasion, when an unwise decision is made by the ego, the subconscious will change it. . . .

The probable self can be reached through hypnosis but only

with excellent subjects and operators. Often it will not be recognized, however, for there will be no evidence of its experience in physical reality to back up its statements. Its data will agree when considered within its own framework. Reaching it in this manner would be highly difficult in any case. To my knowledge, it has not as yet been reached through hypnosis. It has been glimpsed but not recognized as a separate part of the self — in dream recordings and analytic sessions.

Again, these portions of the self exist in each reincarnation. In the materialization of personality through various reincarnations only the ego and layers of personal subconscious adapt new characteristics. Other portions retain their experience, identity, and knowledge. The ego, in fact, receives much of its stability because of this retention. Were it not for experiences in other lives on the part of deeper layers of the self, the ego would find it almost impossible to relate to other individuals, and the cohesive nature of society would not exist.

"Dreams and Probable Events"
(Excerpts from Session 235, February 23, 1966)

If you would have some idea of what the probable universe is like, then examine your own dreams, looking for those events which do not have any strong resemablance to the physical events of waking existence. Look for dream individuals with whom you are not acquainted in normally conscious life. Look for landscapes that appear bizarre or alien, for all of these exist somewhere. You have perceived them. They do not exist in the space that you know but neither are they non-existant, mere imaginative toys of the dreaming mind, without substance.

You may not be able to make sense from what appears to be a chaotic jungle of disconnected images and actions. The main reason for your confusion is the inability of an egotistical identity to perceive order that is not based upon continuity of moments. *The order within the probable system is based upon something that could be compared to subjective associations or intuitive flashes of insight — experiences that can combine ingredients that could appear to the ego as disconnected. Here they are combined into whole integrated patterns of action.*

The probable system does not achieve its order through subjective association, but the term is the nearest I can use to approximate the basic causes for this order. The events within it are, indeed, objective and concrete within their own field of reality, for example. Your own system is real and concrete only within its own field, remember.

In sleep, not only do you withdraw from the physical field of actuality but you also enter other systems.

So far, we've experienced two main types of dreams that seem to involve probabilities. Sue's, given earlier, represent the personally-oriented dream in which we seem to perceive probable events that could have happened or could happen in the future in our normal environment. Other kinds of dreams involve the "bizarre environments" Seth mentioned and show societies or civilizations quite alien to us, but built up around elements at least recognizable.

Several of us have had this type of dream. Again, two of Sue's come closest to being representative. Both also involve projections or out-of-body states, a matter that will be discussed in the next section of this book. The following is from Sue's notebook.

Dream One
(August 7, 1970 . . . nap)

I lie down on the porch couch and drift into a light sleep. I discover that I can do a peculiar thing to my brain by somehow tightening the muscles on my scalp and then doing something intense with a sound I can 'hear.' The sound holds, and I can feel my astral body shudder inside my physical one. It is as though I'm tearing loose from a Jell-O mold. I get out of my body this way, float above the couch and go back in. I try the same technique, tightening the scalp muscles and feel my astral body stir. This time I get out of my physical body and stand staring at it. The experience is so strange that for a moment I think I'm dead, though I know this isn't true. I know quite clearly that I am out of my body, experimenting and in no difficulty. So I turn, leave my body behind on the couch and walk out the door and down to the dock outside our house.

Here I find about twelve people in the water, in skin-diving outfits. They hand me some equipment, and there is a good deal of conversation about how difficult it is to get the suits on. When everyone is ready, they give me a mask. I've already put my suit on. We swim down the lake aways. We come to a particular cottage, find a space to swim through and find ourselves in an apartment that is completely underwater. During this time, I'm acutely aware of the noise of the diving equipment and the very cold water.

We swim about the apartment. An older woman comes into the kitchen. She is dressed normally except that her dress is of a strange metallic material. She looks surprised at our costumes, but I see a paper and pen on the kitchen counter and write a brief explanation. She glances at our flippers. I take one off and show her my foot. 'Just like ours,' she says, surprised. Her voice is clear but very high-pitched.

I write: 'Do you breathe water somehow?' She answers, 'Yes. They outlawed those suits a number of years ago, so we can't get to . . .' She stops suddenly and I get the idea that once again I'm in some kind of a warp of a probable dimension of submarine people, or people who live in a water-based atmosphere. My mask becomes uncomfortable and begins to fill with some water.

The others become frantic to get out too. We kick to the wall and push through up the fireplace, one by one, to surface. The instant I yank off my mask, I jolt awake. For some time I am disoriented. I find myself sitting on the dock and do not recall walking there. I'm in my physical body now, yet somehow the physical world around me is incomplete with enormous pieces missing. Finally, my head clears; it had been filled with a peculiar whine. It was as though the world outside of the immediate focus of my eyes was only half-formed; the rest, grayish and swirling.

Dream Two
(August 2, 1970)

A group of us are at my parents' house, in the cellar, projecting. I look into the furnace room and notice a formation of something like hot water heaters near the ceiling. It elongates and expands into a porcelain corridor. I step into it and meet several strange catlike people who explain that I have projected into a warp of dimensions and entered their reality. It is a probable system where consciousness decided to use the cat form as the most satisfactory and in which the cat walked upright, used tools and so forth.

The people have orange-ish faces, pointed ears and very long hair on their heads and hands. They are dressed in dark robes. One 'man' and I walk to a complex of offices. This particular room is done in dark wood and leather, with no windows. He tells me that this warp will only exist for a short time, connecting his reality and mine, before it disconnects and that the same situation probably will not happen again. He also tells me that it is difficult to get back.

I get upset at this, when the door opens and in walks my old fifth-grade teacher, confused and dazed. 'What are *you* doing here?' I exclaim, and the 'man' explains that the connection touched physical reality in several places. My old teacher does not realize what she is doing or where she is, he tells me. Now I become frantic to leave. I hear a bell tinkling and am pulled out the office door, down the corridor, through the cellar, up the stairs to my bed. I awaken.

According to Seth, children actually try out in dreams the various courses open to them. Speaking to Rob in Session 282, August 31, 1966, he said:

You may act out many probabilities within dream reality and try out alternatives, and not necessarily short-term ones. You would have made an excellent doctor, for example. In your terms, you worked out this possibility by weaving, over a period of three years, a dream framework in which you learned exactly what your life would have been, had you gone into medicine.

This was more than imaginative. You examined one probability and chose another. The individual, then, chooses which probabilities he desires to actualize physically. In one such episode, for example, you followed your present course through; therefore, you are subconsciously aware of your own 'future' — since you chose it. There are always new choices, however. You foresaw the future possibilities within the main choice system.

In your present life, the same process continues. Most of these dreams are very disconnected from the ego and will not be recalled. The self who pursues these divergent paths is actual, however. The doctor you might have been once dreamed of a probable universe in which he would be an artist. He continues to work out his own probabilities. He exists in fact. You call his system an alternate system of probability, but this is precisely what he would call yours.

Now you will have some experiences that are shared in the dream state. They will be involved with episodes familiar to you both before you went your separate ways. You are like two limbs from the same tree. You recognize the same mother. . . .

The dreams you will have and have had in shared experience are root dreams. They serve as a method of maintaining inner identity and communication. Projections can also occur from these — that is, you may, for example, project into the life of the doctor. (I am using you and the doctor as an example. Art, you see, is also closely connected with healing. The projections of which I spoke happen occasionally and spontaneously on both of your parts.)

Reincarnation is but a part of this probability system, the part that falls within your particular universe. There are also

*root dreams shared by the race as a whole. Most of these are
not as symbolic as Jung thought them to be but are literal
interpretations of the abilities used by the inner self. For that
matter, as you know, flying dreams need not be symbolic of
anything. They can be valid experiences, though often
intermixed with other dream elements. Falling dreams are also
simple experience in many instances, representing downward
motion, or a loss of form-control during projection.*

Seth told us that Rob's doctor probable self was a Doctor Pietra.
As mentioned in my earlier book, we tried to contact him — so
far, without success. Some years ago, Rob did do some medical
artwork and was astonished at his success. He has no conscious
knowledge of wanting to be a doctor as a child, but in painting he
always emphasized body structure and form.

But what is the point of all these probable selves? What do they
have to do with the development of personality as we think of it?
Seth is still discussing probabilities in his own book, so we don't
have all the answers, by any means. One night, Rob asked Seth
how our own egos had changed as a result of our sessions, however, and Seth used the question as an opportunity to give us more
information about personality and probable selves.

"Probable Selves and Multi-Dimensional Personality"
(*Excerpts from Session 309*)

*The ego structure remains, of course. The responsibility of
dealing with physical reality remains, but in some respects the
nature of this manipulation changes. It becomes more direct.
Physical properties are manipulated more and more at a mental
level. The ego becomes more like the inner ego and less like its
old self, comparatively speaking. It accepts large portions of
reality that it previously denied. Structurally, it remains intact,
yet it has changed chemically and electromagnetically. Now it is*

far more open to inner data. Once this freedom is achieved, the ego can never return to its old state.

I have told you that the ego is self-conscious action that attempts to set itself apart from action and to consider action as an object. Now this altered ego retains its highly specialized self-consciousness, and yet it can now experience itself as an identity within and as a part of action.

This is a cornerstone for consciousness and for personality. It is only a first step, however. Without it, no further development of consciousness can occur. It is not attained by all within your system. You are at that point now.

The next step is taken when identity is able to include within itself the intimate knowledge of all incarnations. Yet in this state, the independence of the various reincarnated selves is not diminished. Each of these steps of consciousness involve identity with the inner recognition of its unity with All That Is.

As each separate identity then seeks to know and experience its other portions, then All That Is learns Who and What It Is. Action never ceases its exploration of itself. All That Is can never know itself completely, since action must always act and each action creates a new unknown. Action must travel through itself from every conceivable point, and yet the journey, being itself action, will create new paths.

"Action and Probabilities"
(Excerpts from Session 309)

There are many you's in the probable systems, and each You is related psychologically in a personality structure. The You that you know is a part of this. In your system, all the other You's seem to exist in a probable reality.

To any of them, the others would seem to exist in a probable universe, yet all are connected. All of you did not have the same parents, for example, and there are portions of probable situations existing in your own parents' separate lives. [To Rob:]

In two probable realities, your mother did not have children.
You do not exist in these. In some, she married but not the man
you know as father. A psychological connection exists betwen
that first son in that other system and yourself.

Emotional charged feeling immediately sets up what you may
think of as a tangent. It is expressed in some reality system. This
is the inner nature of action. Those thoughts and desires and
impulses not made physically real in your terms will be made
real in other systems.

Now, the inner self is psychologically influenced by these
probable personalities, for they represent a whole personality
structure or gestalt with which you are utterly unfamiliar. Your
psychologists are dealing with a one-dimensional psychology, at
their best.

In the dream state, the portions of the larger 'structure'
sometimes communicate in highly codified symbols. It would be
highly improbable that you could decipher many of these now.
There is a feedback system that operates, and yet you must
understand that these other identities are fully independent and
individual. They exist in codified psychological structures within
your personality, as you do in theirs.

They remain latent within you, and unexpressed in your
system. You have their abilities, unused. You remain latent in
their personality structures, and your main abilities are unused
within their systems. Yet each of you is a part of one self in a
multi-dimensional psychological structure.

These do not necessarily represent more evolved selves.
Certain abilities will be more developed in them than in you,
and vice versa. I am not speaking of portions of your self that
exist in the 'future.' Each probable self, you see, has 'future'
selves.

This multi-dimensional personality or identity is the
psychological structure with which we will be concerned in
many sessions. The term includes probable selves, reincarnated

selves and selves more developed than the self that you know.
These make up the basic identity of the whole self. All portions
are independent.

"Probabilities and 'No Time' "
(Excerpts From Session 438)

You use probabilities like blocks to build events. This
presupposes inner knowledge and calculations, for you must be
aware of the probabilities in order to choose from them. The
inner self, therefore, has this knowledge. These probabilities
include webworks, probable actions and reactions involving not
only yourself but others. Computers are toys compared with
these inner workings.

The majority of events do not 'solidify' until the last moment,
in your terms. According to your understanding and
interpretation of the word events, none are predestined or
predetermined by sources outside of yourselves. Your childhood
environment, for example, was determined by you before
physical birth. Within this framework, you also give yourself
the freedom to manipulate and change. The main events of a
civilization are chosen by its people, but because a course is
begun, this does not mean that it cannot be changed at any
point.

Events, then, are materialized in your time from their origins
in 'no time.' There is no end to the source or supply of
probabilities, therefore 'no time' is not a static, completed
storehouse. Each event you form from any set of probabilities
automatically gives rise to new probabilities.

The nature of any given probable action does not lead to any
particular inevitable act. Probabilities expand in terms of value
fulfillment. One given act does not necessarily lead, then, to act
A, B and C, onward to some concluding action. Instead, it has
offshoots in infinite directions, and these have offshoots.

This is what I know of reality. There is far more to be known. Outside of the realities of which I am aware and others are aware, there are systems that we cannot describe. They are massive energy sources, cosmic energy banks, that make possible the whole reality of probabilities.

They have evolved beyond all probabilities as we understand them yet, outside of probabilities, they still have existence. This cannot be explained in words. Yet, none of this is meant to deny the individual, for it is the individual upon whom all else rests, and it is from the basis of the individual that all entities have their existence. Nor are the memories or emotions of an individual ever taken from him. They are always at his disposal.

All of these probable systems are open. In your system it seems as if you chose one course, one main line of probabilities, and that is the end of it. In your system, only one ego predominates and you think of yourself as that ego. In other systems, this is not necessarily the case. In some, the inner self is aware of having more than one ego, of playing more than one role at a time. As an analogy, this would be as if you lived, say, the life of a rich man of great talent, the life of a poor man and the life of a mother and career woman. You would be aware of each role and find abilities being developed in each. This is an analogy, and in several respects it could lead you astray if taken too literally. In such a system, there would be no breakup of time, you see. . . .

19

Out-of-Body Experiences from the Dream State

Flying Dreams

Dream Mobility of Consciousness

From 1963 until 1966, Rob and I worked alone, holding the twice-weekly sessions and following Seth's instructions. I had several spontaneous out-of-body experiences during Seth sessions and while doing the exercise Seth calls psy-time. These checked out in physical reality and are recorded in my book, *The Seth Material*. Some of these episodes concerned strangers who had written to me. In out-of-body states, I correctly described distant environments giving specific, checkable information. Such instances did much to convince me that projections were not just imaginative dramatizations.

In the meantime, the dream-recall experiments led first to spontaneous projections from the dream state, and then to deliberate experimentation. Rob and I were unacquainted with the information on projection to be found in esoteric literature. I was incredulous at the instructions and information given by Seth, yet I'd already had enough experience to know that Seth's "theoretical material" worked. As we followed it, our own results brought the material itself to life.

In the meantime, we joined a book club that dealt with psychic phenomena. Much to my amazement, their literature listed several books on projection. We ordered Oliver Fox's *Astral Projection*. Astonished, I discovered that my experiences followed his rather closely, even though most of my projections to that date had been spontaneous. I decided to do more deliberate experimentation from the dream state by napping during the day — something I hadn't thought of earlier.

Following Seth's instructions, I was learning to recognize when I was dreaming *while* I was dreaming, manipulate dream events if I wanted to, leave my body and separate halluncinations from reality.

But often, after doing all this, I would simply fall back to sleep again, dream normally until morning, and lose the clear memory of my experiences. I reasoned that if I just napped for an hour or so in the day, then I'd be less apt to forget. It became a great joke betwen Rob and myself, this "laying down on the job" or going to sleep in order to go to work. To some extent, it also upset my ordinary sleep schedule, so I usually experimented in this way for only a few weeks at a time.

We tried many experiments with various results, over the next three years. When I began my psychic classes, some of my students began experiments of their own. Before I give some examples from our records, here is some of the material on projection that Seth gave us during that time. It includes instructions, hints and the descriptions of the various realities in which the projectionist may find himself.

"Dream Bodies"
(Session 261, May 23, 1966)

For all practical purposes, of course, you will usually find yourself in some sort of body form in your out-of-body experiences. These are a necessary camouflage, for you cannot yet think of identity without some kind of body, so you project in such a form. It varies according to your abilities, and without it, you would feel lost indeed. The form itself is not important, but it can tell you something about the dimension in which you are having the experience.

The dream body is the one with which you are most familiar. It has been called the astral body. It strikes you as being physical when you are in it, but you can do things with it that can't be done ordinarily. You can levitate, for example. As a rule, however, you do not go through walls with this body. This is the body you use for ordinary dreams. Levitation is possible with it but on a limited basis.

When you enter a different dimension, the abilities of the body form change, and for all intents and purposes, it is a different body form — which we will now call a mind form. It still seems physical in shape, but you can walk through physical matter with it. You can levitate much more freely, traveling within the solar system. But you cannot go further with it.

In the first form, it is possible to perceive the past, present or future on a limited basis. In the second form, this perception is increased, the scope of consciousness widened. This is the form you will use if you meet by appointment with others in the dream state.

The third we may call the true projection form. In it, it is possible to travel beyond your solar system, and to perceive the past, present and futures of other systems as well as your own. The various forms that you use do not dictate your experience, however. You may begin in one form and change to another — or go from the first to the third. On such occasions you must pass through in reverse direction [on returning]. The forms merely represent stages of consciousness.

At physical death, after the last reincarnation, then the normal form is the dream body, and excursions are made from this point. It is possible, as mentioned, to suddenly switch from the third form to the dream body, but with a considerable jolt to consciousness.

There are, indeed, others who can help you in such experiences, and they can be of great assistance as guides. You will find projections much easier if your head is to the north. One small point here. Ruburt's waking projection upon first reading the Fox book was also legitimate, as he should know.

(Since Seth makes further reference to this incident, I'll describe it briefly, though waking projections will not generally be discussed in this book which is devoted to dreams and related material. I was so reassured by Fox's experiences that I instantly tried to project from a waking state. I lay down on the bed to support my body, closed my eyes and used all my will-power to eject myself out. Almost at once, and I must admit, much to my astonishment, I succeeded. There was a wrench, almost painful, a click at the back of my neck and I found myself flying through a window at seemingly incredible speed, out of the house at second floor level, gaining altitude and heading over Water Street toward the mountains in the distance. My head felt bursting with pressure. Fully alert and conscious, I was terrified of falling.

Here, as I told Rob later, the "brave experimenter" quite simply panicked. I was scared stiff; I'd bitten off quite a bit more than I could chew. At the moment I panicked, I was suddenly pulled backward through the air faster than I'd come, if that was possible. This frightened me more than the forward flight. This time, there was a strange, very loud noise, like the magnified twang of a rubber band or cable that seemed to be reeling me back in. I actually hit my physical body with a shock, my physical head and neck banging up and down on the pillow, so that my shoulders and neck were stiff for a week.

I realized only later that the cord or cable I'd felt was the astral cord. The experience put me off enough that for some time following I always used a light trance or dream framework for projections. Now Seth said:)

The actual physical window was behind his head. He felt impelled to have a window in front of him in order to get out

*of the physical house, and the window through which he went
was a fabrication of his own, a symbol. I found this amusing.
He did not have the confidence, you see, to see himself passing
through the physical walls, as he did in fact. Instead, he formed
the imaginary window and projected through it.*

*Now, when you project from the dream body, consciously you
are already outside of the physical one. You have already made
the initial change away from physical focus. The mass of valid
projections are made from the dreaming body. When the
excursion is over, the return to the dream body is made with no
strain, you see, for the ego is little concerned. In many such
cases, however, the knowledge is not available to the waking
self.*

*As you become more accustomed to the experience, the
waking self will recall more and more and not become
frightened. When you panicked this time, from the waking
condition, the experience ended. If the waking self had not
been taken along in this particular manner, the journey could
have continued.*

That particular experience was my most "shocking," and I'm
just as glad it happened in the beginning. Later, I always specified
that I wanted to get out of my body in my room or apartment or
go to another specific location. Very rarely do you go wide-awake,
speeding out of your body like a rocket. Dream projections are
quite different, in any case, and the ego is already protected, as
mentioned by Seth.

Everything was very new to us then, though. I was more than
satisfied with the experience, scare or no; and Rob was envious,
telling me that he wouldn't have panicked under the same con-
dtions. As it happened, he spoke too soon.

One weekend afternoon, Rob was napping, and I was doing the
dishes. He fell asleep and "awakened" to find himself hovering
about three feet out in the air outside his studio window, between
the house and the large pear tree that shades the room. For a mo-

ment he just couldn't understand what was happening. He knew that physically such a position was impossible, and he held his breath, waiting for the inevitable fall.

But nothing happened. He just hung there. Suddenly he realized that he was out of his body and didn't know what to do next. He yelled out for me, but I was in my physical body, humming merrily out in the kitchen, and I never heard a thing. Desperately, Rob wished for some support, and quite spontaneously he created a child's scooter that appeared beneath him. He could see the yard and garage clearly but the image of a grown-up man on a scooter up two stories from the ground was just too much — he snapped back to his body.

In the meantime, Seth continued with his sessions on projection.

"Hallucinations During Projections"
(Excerpt from Session 262, May 25, 1966)

I want to give you some idea of the conditions you may expect to meet in any successful projections, so that you will be prepared to some extent. For simplicity's sake, we will call the body forms discussed in our last session forms one, two and three.

Form one will spring out of an ordinary dream state. In spontaneous projections, you may become conscious in form one, project, return to the ordinary dream state and from there project again several times. You can expect these particular projections to be difficult to interpret now, though you may find the experience intact in the middle of any given dream record.

Your excursions with form one will be within your own system, largely connected to the earth, although past, present and future may be involved. You may, for example, visit New York in the year 2000.

The projections here are fairly short in duration, though

exceptionally clear. You may encounter phantoms from your own subconscious, however, and they will seem exceedingly real. If you realize that you are projecting, you may simply order any unpleasant phantoms to disappear, and they will do so. You may banish a nightmare also, if you realize that it is a product of your own subconscious. If you treat it as a reality, however, then you must deal with it as such until you realize its origin or return to the ordinary dream state.

In form two you will not, as a rule, encounter any subconscious phantoms. Ordinary dream elements will not be as frequent, nor will they intrude as much. A longer duration of projection is possible. The vividness is extraordinary. Here you will begin to perceive quite clearly constructions that are not your own, where earlier these are but dimly glimpsed. A certain period of orientation will be necessary, simply because these other constructions may seem bewildering. Some will exist in your future. Some may have existed in your past, and some were thought of, but never materialized.

But the reality of all of these constructions will be equally vivid, you see, for they are, indeed, equally real. I will give you a simple example. You may find yourself in a room with certain people. Later, upon awakening, you realize that both the people and setting belong to a particular sequence in a novel. You think then: 'This was no projection, then, but only a dream.'

It may, however, be a valid projection. The room and people exist but not in a way that you endorse as reality. They exist in another dimension, but as a rule you cannot perceive it. [To Rob:] The paintings that you will paint exist now. It is possible for you to project yourself into one of your own future landscapes. This would not be an imaginative projection. This is what I am trying to tell you.

You may find yourself, for example, in the middle of a battle that was once planned in some general's mind, a battle that never materialized in physical reality. In such a case, incidentally, you were not a part of the battle and could not be harmed. However, you might be attracted enough to project yourself spontaneously into the body of one of the soldiers, in which case you could experience pain until your own fear pulled you back. As you learn control, such mistakes vanish.

There are various situations you must learn to handle, attractions and repulsions which could pull you willy-nilly in any direction. Experience will teach you how to handle these. What is needed is a steady maintenance of identity under conditions which will be new as far as your conscious awareness is concerned. I cannot emphasize too strongly that projections into other dimensions do occur. Many such instances are often considered chaotic dreams because there is no way to check them against physical events since they did not occur in physical terms.

It is possible for you to project to a future event in which you will be involved and by an act that you make in the projection, alter the course that this future will take. Such an action would therefore appear to happen twice, once in your present and once in your future. But in the future, you would be the one whose course is altered from this traveling self from the past.

Let us take an example: While asleep, you project into 1982. There you see yourself considering various courses of action. For a moment you are aware of a sense of duality as you view this older self. You communicate with this other self; and we will go into this sort of thing more deeply in another session. In any case, your future self heeds what you say. Now in the actual future you are the self who hears the voice of a past self, perhaps in a dream, or perhaps in a projection into the past.

A few days after this session I tried my first deliberate "projection nap," as I called it. Instead of going to my typewriter at 8:00 A.M. as usual, I lay down and set the alarm for 9:30. I gave myself the suggestion that I would go to sleep, recognize my state when I began to dream and project my consciousness out of my body. Paper and pen were on the bedside table. I also closed the doors so I would not hear the doorbell or phone.

I fell asleep at once. The next thing I knew I seemed to be in a lovely garden that I had planted myself in some undisclosed past. Then I thought that I was wide awake, telling Rob about the dream. As I chatted with him, a nagging doubt bothered me. Was I really awake, or was this a "false awakening as described by both Seth and Fox, and which I had experienced in the past? I looked about the bedroom. Everything seemed perfectly normal. It was difficult to imagine that I might really be asleep and dreaming, and not awake. Yet I'd gone to bed to experiment, I knew, and to make sure I decided to take it for granted that I really was dreaming, despite the semblance of normality.

If so, I should be able to project. So I got out of bed and went into the bathroom where I sat on a chair to think things over. Again, everything seemed the way it should be, though the room did look exceptionally sharp, the details in brilliant focus. Could I be out of my body already, I wondered? If so, I should be able to levitate in this body which seemed physical enough to me. Feeling rather foolish, I willed to levitate.

At once, my feet and legs felt very strange, filled with a rustling sensation. There was a funny sense of inner shifting. Suddenly, I saw many mirrors, which I knew were not physical and didn't belong in the room. I was propelled through them with amazing speed. There were scenes within the mirrors, and people moving about. I rushed through a series of such scenes. The traveling sensations were very real, indisputable and somewhat frightening.

I "landed" on a hillside. Two women ran over the hills, and I followed them. I had no idea who the women were, but I decided to see whether I could leap from the ground in this state to the top of one of the hills. As soon as I thought of this, I sped up through the air to the top, then backward to where I had been standing. To make sure of my results, I executed the same "leap" once again.

Here I experienced another false awakening in which I told Rob what was going on and explained the previous episode. (Actually I'd returned to the bedroom, I believe, still in astral form, lost the necessary focus of consciousness and hallucinated.)

I left the room almost at once and appeared in a house supposedly owned by friends, Jack and Lydia. This was not their normal house in daily life, though, and I was aware of this. Here I stood talking to Rob again, quite forgetting that he was at work. As I spoke to him, I turned my head and saw another Rob, a perfect double, standing in a room directly across the corridor. Amazed, I told Rob to stand where he was, while I moved closer to the door to check my observations.

"Look, Rob. Come here," I said, and Rob came to the doorway where he saw his own double clearly. They stared at each other, the double looking as amazed as Rob was.

Then I fell into a brief period of unconsciousness. I came to to find myself back in the garden I had seen earlier. A woman beckoned to me. I recognized her instantly as Miss Lizzie Roohan, a neighbor of ours years ago, who had been dead for at least fifteen years. Remembering her death, I was quite surprised to see her and even more intrigued by her appearance. Although she had been in her eighties when she died and in her sixties when I first knew her, she looked like a woman in her middle thirties. We carried on a conversation that I did not remember later. I fell into a normal dream which was also forgotten before the alarm awakened me.

The sensation of intense speed was very real at the beginning of the experience, and during the entire episode I struggled to retain a critical sense which I alternately achieved and lost. The experiment was a success, in that I was convinced I'd left my body from the dream state. But what about Rob's doubles and Miss Roohan?

That night, June 1, 1966, we had our 264th session, and in it, Seth made some references to my experience:

Ruburt's projection from the dream state was legitimate,

though his control was poor. The plants Ruburt saw represented the books upon which he has worked and is working. The Lydia episode contained many ordinary dream elements. [To Rob:] *You were indeed present with Ruburt in some of his travels, but you have forgotten.*

Ruburt saw two of you. He saw your second form as described earlier [in Session 262]. The other was Ruburt's dream form of you, created by himself in the dream state. When you appeared in your form two, he was conscious enough to recognize your arrival and then point out the dream image he had already created. You were able to see it also, because of your own state.

Now, when Ruburt dreams that he has discussed a dream with you, in most cases he has done so. You both converse quite naturally in forms number two. With enough traveling, these conversations can be recorded in both of your dreams. The amount of work to be done here is astounding, but you can both do this, and in so doing, you can increase man's knowledge of the potentials of the dream state.

During this period, of course, we were recording all the dreams we could capture. Usually at least one of mine per night dealt with flying or levitation. During a series of dreams I seemed to be work-ing to perfect my "flying technique," and was taking lessons from others. Then, in the middle of several dreams such as this, I dreamed the following, according to my notes:

"The whole dream was in images. I saw the universe or whole reality, an infinity of spirals and stars, in multi-dimensional depth. Someone told me that most of our cherished ideas about the nature of reality were completely wrong. This was a revelation-type dream, but I couldn't remember much of it at all upon awaken-ing. Someone was guiding me, I believe."

In Session 268, June 15, 1966, Seth mentioned this dream and continued his information on projection.

"More on The Dream Body,
Inner Senses and Projection"
(Excerpts from Session 268, June 15, 1966)

You remember that I listed briefly the three forms used during projections. In the first form, you usually use certain inner senses. In the second form, you use more of these, and in the third form you attempt to use all of them, though very rarely is this successful. You should notice the overall form of perception that you seem to be using. You automatically shield yourselves from stimuli that are too strong for your own rate of development. This kind of balancing can lead to an unevenness of experience, however, in any given projection.

As you know, it is almost impossible for you to be aware of the full perceptions possible, for the ego would not stand for it. Often, even in simple dreams, however, you will feel concepts or understand a particular piece of information without a word being spoken. In some projections, you will also experience a concept, and, at first, you may not understand what is happening. In these, you experience as actual the innermost reality of a given concept.

Ruburt [in the dream given before this session] was in the third form, and he did project beyond your solar system. This was still a projection within the physical universe, however. He was given information that he did not remember. When you explore the inside of a concept, you act it out. You form a temporary but very vivid image production. If Ruburt's experience had been only this, it still would have been pertinent, for when you understand a concept in such a way the knowledge is never forgotten. It becomes part of your physical cells and your electromagnetic structure.

I want to make this clearer, however. Suppose that you suddenly understand the concept of oneness with the universe, and that this inner sensing of concepts is to be used. You would

then construct dream images, a multitudinous variety of shapes
and forms meant to represent the complicated forms of life. You
would then have the experience of entering each of those lives.
You would not think of what it was like to be a bird. You would
momentarily be one. This does involve a projection of sorts, yet
still must be called by contrast a pseudo-projection. A normal
projection would involve one of the three body forms.

Some experiences, then, will be simple attempts to use the
inner senses more fully. They may appear to be projections, and
as we go along, I will tell you how to distinguish between them.

You will be able to look back and see your physical body
upon the bed on some occasions, and in other cases you will not
be able to do this. In the first body form, for example, you can
look back and see the physical body. If you project from this
form into the next, in order to intensify the experience, then
from this second form you will not see the physical one. You
will be aware of it, and you may experience some duality. In
the third form, you will no longer be aware of the physical
body, and you will not see it.

In the third form, your experiences will be most vivid. They
may involve you in other systems beside your own, and you will
have little contact with the physical environment. For this
reason, projections in the third form are the most difficult to
maintain. There are dangers that do not exist when the other
two forms are used.

Using the third form, there could be a tendency for you not
to recognize your own physical situation. It would be difficult
to carry the memories of the present ego personality with you.
This third form is the vehicle of the inner self. The
disorientation that it feels is the same that it will feel when the
physical body is deserted at the point of death. This
disorientation is only temporary, and when at death the form is
severed from the physical body, then all the memories and
identity within the electromagnetic structure become part of the

inner self. This form is sometimes used for purposes of instruction, however, or to acquaint the whole personality with the circumstances that strongly affect it.

Most of your projections will be in the first and second form, in any case. Usually you will project from the physical body into the first form and then, perhaps, into the second. Occasionally, this will happen and you will not know it, despite all your attempts to ascertain your circumstances.

There are ways of knowing when you switch forms, of course, and we shall see that you get this information. You should both have several projections within the first and second forms in the following months if your development continues at its present rate.

I want to mention the difference in experience and sensation between projections from a dream state and those from the trance state and also what Ruburt calls awake-seeming dreams, for there are many things here that you do not know, and they are fairly important.

Some of you may call dream projections hallucinatory. Yet nothing of that kind happened to us before the Seth sessions. The instructions we were given worked. A curious new second life began, adjacent to our normal one. Some may call it a fantasy life, but surely it is no more fantastic or mysterious than the ordinary world in which we all find ourselves.

So at least twice a week I lay down to experiment, my body on the couch or bed, the alarm clock set, my house in order, while I try to "get out" to see what I could find. I seem to have a curious talent for this, and rarely do I fail to leave my body when I've really made up my mind to go. Yet for periods at a time, I just concentrate on the Seth sessions, with Seth on the one side of reality and Rob on the other — two good guardians. Then I avoid out-of-body experiments. A sense of strangeness seems connected with them then. My consciousness, so used to my flesh, says that I've had enough. And I'm afraid to leave my body in the wintertime.

In black and white print, this sounds ridiculous, yet, emotionally, the statement has a logic that speaks louder than all my deliberate suggestions to the contrary. So I experiment between May and November, coming in for the winter when the wild skies of fall are over and the bone-chilling cold settles in.

Not that I've been cold out of my body, because I haven't. But my flesh itself seems to slow down come December, despite all I should know from the Seth Material about the innate vitality that gives the body its life.

20

More on Dream Projections

Some Instructions
I Meet Miss Cunningham "Out-of-Body"

Seth's series of sessions on projection continued through 1966, 1967 and 1968. In 1966, portions of the sessions were also given over to the clairvoyant experiments, and much of Rob's time was taken over in writing up the results. By late 1967, Seth was also devoting some sessions to helping strangers who had written us, as mentioned in *The Seth Material*.

By then, of course, Rob and I felt a strong committment to the sessions. Now we feel that we have a twice-weekly appontment with the universe, and certainly this attitude developed during those projection sessions when we tried during the day to follow the instructions given by Seth. Sessions were held in the bedroom then. Now we hold them in Rob's back studio. Both rooms are to the rear of the apartment and more private than the living room. So even space-wise, there seems to be a connection between those earlier sessions and the present ones in which Seth is dictating his own book.

Now, like then, we close the living room door so we won't hear the phone or be interrupted by visitors. Rob moves my favorite rocker in. We usually take some wine. So from nine until nearly midnight, there we are — humble listeners. Of course, its also possible that we're picking up, hearing and transcribing only cosmic noise. I doubt it, but even then I'd rather spend my life in the quest for meaning, the search for learning, rather than ignore the messages and signals that have appeared within our world. And I do believe that we are in contact with a source quite beyond our normal comprehension.

I do not always take what is said at face value. Telegraph messages alone mean something different than the data presented, the dots and dashes that are only symbols for the information they contain. To make sense to us as physical creatures, any "truth" must undergo transformations, be couched in certain terms or we couldn't understand it. Distortion may be part of the message — or even the medium through which it must come.

This reminds me of a poem I wrote as a freshman in college:

> *A frog sat still and stared with awe*
> *At a watch that lay in the sand.*
> *"Now," he thought, "I am quite sure*
> *There is such a thing as Man."*
>
> *"Our priests," he mused, "have spoken*
> *of Man Who made our pond.*
> *Perhaps He left this as a token,*
> *Between us, to be a bond."*
>
> *So the frog spent all his life*
> *Trying to understand.*
> *While he grew old and feeble*
> *The watch ticked on in the sand.*

Some frogs jeered and scoffed at him.
Others called him great.
He only smiled and went off by himself,
Poor lonely frog, to meditate.

It may be that the frog could have learned more by exploring his own frogness, and, certainly, I felt rather superior to the frog and the nature of his search — that's implied in the poem. Now it seems to me that any lively exploration into reality should lead to exuberence and greater understanding, not sadness and alienation. And I don't believe that our world, like the watch, is simply a discard from another greater reality, though certainly it is a part of one.

The frog did not learn to tell time from his watch, though, and it's difficult to see how this would have helped him if he had. The Seth Material, on the other hand, is more like a map, vitalized through Seth's personality, and as we follow it, we do become aware of other realities that had been unknown to us earlier.

The experience of "coming to life during dreams" with any consistency, having some critical awareness, some rational control, some glimpse of other-dimensional reality — these events in the overall are bound to transform ordinary concepts regarding the nature of consciousness.

And it is always strange to realize that physical reality has that little hold, comparitively speaking, that you can slip out of it so easily, that it is more like bright transparent cellophane than solid wood or rock. You can go in and out of it, through it and back, without leaving a tear. Yet the world is so smooth and unseamed when you're in the body and focused there.

My ESP classes didn't begin until 1967, so Rob and I tried out the projection experiments alone, and only later were we joined by my students. I had given up my gallery work, and was teaching nursery school during part of this time. This was the framework in which most of these sessions took place.

"Instructions for Projection from Trance and Dream States"

(Excerpts from Session 265, June 6, 1966)

Whatever information I can give you will be of great practical benefit. I do not want either of you traveling about unless you know what you are doing. Again I want to mention the matter of subconscious fabrications. Initially, particularly, you will meet with them. You must remember that you are wandering in completely different dimensions, and the rules with which you are familiar simply do not apply.

You may, then, encounter images that are subconsciously formed, quite valid images that belong in another dimension; or constructions created by others in other systems. For any control at all, you must learn to distinguish one from the other. Again, if you meet a disturbing image, you must first will it to disappear. If it is a subconscious construction of your own, it will vanish. But if you do not will it to disappear or realize its nature, then you must deal with it.

I have told you that the form in which you are traveling can be a tipoff to you. If your levitation experience seems to carry you outside of the solar system, then you know that you are in the third form and that your abilities for the time are almost limitless, comparatively speaking. Any image you see here must be accepted. It does no good to call these forms hallucinations, for they are no more hallucinations than the chair in which my friend Ruburt now sits. Ruburt told one of your friends to respect physical reality. 'Whether or not the automobile is a sensory hallucination, it can kill you,' he said. And I tell you that whether or not these projection images are hallucinations, they can be dangerous and you must respect the reality in which they exist. I want to be sure that you realize that some of these constructions will belong to other systems. You are safe as long as you do not meddle. You may explore, and freely, and that is all.

Now, here are my instructions. You may induce a medium trance in whatever way you choose. On occasion, this will be almost spontaneous, as you know. For best results in the beginning, make a projection attempt when you feel slightly drowsy, but pleasantly so. When you have induced the trance state, then begin to examine your own subjective feelings until you find recognition of the inner self.

This involves a recognition of yourself as distinct from the flesh fibers in which you reside. Then, begin to imagine this inner self rising upward. You should experience at this point an internal sense of motion. This motion may be from side to side as you gently shake yourself loose.

It may, instead, be a rushing upward. Whichever motion you experience, there will be a moment when you feel your identity and consciousness definitely withdrawing from the physical organism. Before you begin the experiment, the suggestion should also be given that the physical organism will be well protected and comfortable.

When you feel your consciousness withdrawing, the first step is this: Forget the physical body or what you are to do with it. Will yourself out in a quick motion. There is no need to experience the hallucinations mentioned by Fox [in his book, Astral Projection]. If the projection is a success, you will instantly lose contact with the body using this method. You simply will not be in it.

It will be far from lifeless, of course. Its maintenance is being controlled by the consciousness of the individual cells and organs of which I have spoken. I will give you alternate methods of projection, but I will be concerned now with what you can expect the first few moments after leaving the body.

Once you are out of the body, then you are dealing with a different kind of reality, but the experience is as valid as any other. You may or may not have the sensation of traveling through doors or windows. This is dependent upon the kind of projection involved. The molecular structure of the projecting

self is of a different nature than that of the physical body. There
is no change in the physical nature of the door, for example.
The molecular structure of the traveling self changes.

There is no danger of not returning to the body, generally
speaking. If in your projection you seem to be flying past
treetops, then you are doing so. . . . You can meet and speak
with others on some of these excursions. It is possible, with
training, to arrange such meetings. For any kind of scientific
proof, of course, this would be a necessary preliminary.

Remember that I told you you may visit not only the past,
present or future as it exists or will exist in your terms, but you
may also visit realities that never existed physically. In our early
sessions, I mentioned that intensity regulated the 'duration' of
experience. Now, many events that were only imagined never
took place physically, yet they exist. They simply are not a part
of your definition of reality. You may, therefore, visit a museum
that was planned in the sixteenth century but never built. Such
a museum has a reality as valid as the house in which you live.

I have been speaking of projection from the trance state.
Projection from a dream is something else again, and when
executed successfully, you have a fine example of the self as it
changes the focus of awareness. Here the critical consciousness
can be fully alert while the body sleeps. Spontaneous,
unrecalled projections of this kind happen often. It is beneficial
that they be carried out by the conscious wish of the projector.
You learn, therefore, to manipulate your own consciousness and
to experience its mobility. Quite simply, such projections allow
you practice in dealing with realities that you will meet when
you no longer operate in the physical system.

All through this period I was trying to train myself to come
"awake" while asleep. It serves no purpose to include all of the
many dreams of this nature that I recorded — dreams in which I
managed to regain my critical senses, sometimes only to fall back
into normal dreaming and sometimes to embark upon conscious

experiments. But one experience in particular was very vivid and informative. Excerpts from the following session will show you what I was trying to do.

"Instructions and Awake-Seeming Dreams"
(*Excerpts From session 269, June 20, 1966*)

There are some notes I wanted to give you concerning dreams in which you feel certain you are normally awake. When these dreams are unusually vivid, then the ego is aware and participating, but generally it is not using its critical faculties. As you know, you can become critically alert, but when you do so, you realize that you are not in your normal waking condition.

In awake-seeming dreams you are indeed awake, but within a different psychological framework, indeed, within a different framework of reality. You are operating at a high level of awareness, and using the inner senses. These enable you to perceive an added depth of dimension which is responsible for the vividness and sense of exhileration that often occurs within the kind of dream. The next step, of course, is to allow the ego to awaken its critical faculties while within this state. You are then able to realize that while you are indeed awake as you seem, you are awake while the body is asleep.

When this occurs, you will be able to use your normal abilities in addition to those of the dream condition. You will be certain of your identity, realize that the physical self is sleeping or in a dream state and that the inner self is fully awake. This represents a definite increase in the scope of consciousness and a considerable expansion over the usual limitations set by you upon yourself.

Only then can you fully begin to manipulate the conditions that exist and communicate this knowledge that you receive to the ego. For the time, you see, the ego becomes a direct participator in such experience, at least to a degree.

Almost all of your dream experiences do involve projection of one kind or another. These vary in intensity, type and even duration as any other experiences vary. It takes a good deal of training and competence to operate with any real effectiveness within these situations.

All in all, the intellect plays some part, but the intuitional qualities are most important. There are chemical changes, also, that occur with the physical body when projections happen, and electromagnetic variations. These vary according to the form in which the projection occurs.

The projected form does make some impression upon the physical system. It is possible for it to be detected. It is a kind of pseudo-image, materialistically speaking, but it has definite electromagnetic reality and chemical properties. Animals have sensed such apparitions. They react to the chemical properties and build up to the [perception of] the image from these.

These chemical properties are more diffused in such an apparition than in a physical form, however. The chemical composition of a storm, perhaps, will give you an idea of what I mean. . . . They cause small disturbances in the physical system. As a rule, they are not solid, in the same way that clouds are not solid, and yet they have shape and to a certain extent, boundaries and movement. They definitely have a reality, though you cannot usually perceive it with the physical senses.

Perhaps this diffused quality is the most important difference (from your point of view) between an apparition and a physical form. There is an atomic structure, but in some ways it is less complete than the physical one. There is always a minute difference in the body's weight when the individual is projecting.

While I had a whole string of dreams along these lines, the following episode illustrates almost all of the phenomena mentioned in this session. It happened some months later, on October 19, 1966, and involved Miss Cunningham, the retired teacher. She had finally been taken to another nurisng home, and once again she entered my psychic life as she withdrew more and more from ordinary concerns.

Dream One: I was in a beautiful landscape. There were two huge swings, the playground type, whose ropes reached straight up into the sky. Two boys arrived. They got on the swings, swinging way out over the hillside, over the lower land beneath, back and forth over the land for miles. Then a woman appeared and we began to talk. I told her that the swings fascinated me, but scared me also, because they were so high. Her automobile was parked nearby, and it suddenly occurred to me that I had no idea how I came to this place — which was in Ohio, I knew. This should have been a clue to me that I was dreaming, but instead I explained rapidly that I am an excellent hiker. Finally I got on one of the swings, swinging back and forth over the length of the hilltop, rather than over the edge of the land beneath.

This was followed by two innocuous dreams, also recorded consecutively.

False Awakening or Awake-Seeming Dream: Now I had a false awakening. In the back of my mind all night was the resolution to make sure I recorded my dreams. Here, I was sure I was awake. I wrote the dreams down in my notebook which was on the bedside table, and then, to make sure, I awakened Rob and told him the dreams also. Rob pointed out that the first dream and one of the others were definitely related. Again, I was positive I was awake.

Then the suspicion struck me that perhaps this was an awake-seeming dream, that I was still dreaming and that none of the dreams had been written down at all. I kept struggling to analyze my state of consciousness and finally decided to check the notebook again.

Without moving my physical body and with my physical eyes closed, I reached over and checked my dream book, finding that the page was blank. Really angry at this self-deception, I decided to get out of bed entirely, go into the living room, turn the light on and make sure that I really wrote the dreams down this time. (When I got out of bed here, I believe that I was in my dream body, without realizing it.)

The next thing I knew, I was out in the living room having some difficulty standing on the floor, but bumping up and down a few feet above the rug. This, in itself, should have told me that I was out of my body, but the realization didn't come. As I stood there, trying to figure out what was going on, I heard someone at the door. In came Miss Cunningham, wearing a nightgown and robe. She was mumbling and crying to herself, confused and disoriented. "Mrs. Butts? Mrs. Butts?" she kept saying, exactly as she used to when she came to me for help.

The room was dark, normal in every way, lit to some degree by the streetlights outside. At first I thought that Miss C. was sleepwalking and was worried about awakening her. Something else confused me. I heard very dim jazz music and couldn't figure out where it was coming from. Miss C. was hardly the type to carry a small transistor radio in her robe pocket.

I stood there a moment, wondering how she got in, and decided that I must have left the door unlocked. But how to get her back to her own apartment, I wondered? I completely forgot that she had moved. Now I stood by the bathroom door. She came closer, muttering under her breath, and for a moment the two of us were clearly delineated by the streetlight. Our eyes met. Instantly I realized that I was out of my body, and so was she. Miss C. gave a deep, frightened gasp and disappeared. Instantly, I opened my eyes to find myself in bed, body and all. I was as bewildered as I've ever been. Only one split second ago I'd been in the living room.

Quickly I got up and rushed out to the other room. No one was there. It was 12:30 P.M. I sat down and wrote down the experience and the earlier dreams. As I wrote, I heard dim music. It was coming from the apartment upstairs, and it was exactly the same kind I'd heard earlier. With some excitement I went back to the bedroom. It was quiet and still there. The music could only be heard where I'd met Miss Cunningham.

I'm convinced that I left my body when I decided to go into the living room, and met Miss C. who was traveling in her dream body, wandering about in her old surroundings and coming in for help as she used to do. Unfortunately, my critical sense was fully awakened only toward the end of the experience, though I made several valiant efforts to understand my condition.

In Session 298, October 31, 1966, Seth commented on this experience:

Ruburt's experience with your Miss Cunningham was quite legitimate. He used a most advantageous method of projection without knowing that he did so, and I highly recommend this method to you both. When you awaken — or seem to waken — in the middle of the night, try to get out of the body. Simply try to get out of bed without moving the body and go into another room.

This is a pleasant and easy method. With some experience you will discover that you can maintain control, walk out of the apartment and outside. You may then attempt normal locomotion or levitate. There is little strain with this method. Keep it in mind so that you are alert to the initial favorable circumstances. You may be half awake. You may be in a false awakening. The method will work in either case. You can, if you want to, look back at your body.

You must want to do this, however. Often, you do not want to see the body by itself, so to speak, and so choose methods that make this more difficult. Just this one exercise will sharpen your control greatly. It is an ABC. This experience is also less

*startling to the ego than a more abrupt projection, and the
ordinary nature of the activities — walking into the next room,
for example — will be reassuring. You are more calm in your
own surroundings. Of course, Ruburt was out of his body when
he saw Miss Cunningham, who was in the same condition.*

*Now it is possible for someone within the body to perceive
someone who is not, but it is not usual. The perceiver must be a
person of strong psychic abilities or the projecting personality
must be driven by high emotional intensity to make himself
known.*

During this time, I was experimenting with waking projections
also. The idea behind those was different: I wanted to go someplace in an out-of-body state, record my impressions of what I
saw, and check the results in whatever way I could. With the
dream projections, I was more intrigued by the manipulations of
consciousness involved (the trick of staying between hallucinations
and physical reality) and the methods. These tell far more about
how consciousness works, and I was always intrigued by trying to
continue normal awareness throughout dreaming.

As I mentioned in *The Seth Material*, my waking projections
and the spontaneous ones in the Seth trance yielded enough evidence to convince us that I was legitimately out of my body and
perceiving another location — and not just out of my mind. It is
far more difficult to get objective proof for dream projections, yet
the subjective proof is quite definite. The task of trying to maintain specific states of consciousness is enough work and effort to
convince anyone having the experience that far more than simple
dreaming or imagination is involved.

And some of these dream projections did yield evidence that
was convincing to me. One night while experimenting in the
dream state, for example, I found myself standing in a room about
the size of our bedroom, but it was obviously being used as a
closet. A single bulb hung from the ceiling. The walls were wood-
paneled, in beautiful condition, and shelves were built along two

sides. These were filled with boxes of various sizes, and jars of things like lotions and shoe polish. Clothing was hung on hangers by wall brackets all about. Everything was very vivid. What a waste of a great room, I thought. Then I saw that the room had no windows at all. I knew I was in someone's house, and that my body was in bed. But where was I? Suddenly, I knew that the house belonged to Bill and Beverly Gray, previous tenants in our apartment house. They had moved to a house about a year previously, and I hadn't seen them since.

That's all that I remembered. I must have fallen back into a normal dream state, and when I awakened, it was morning. I wrote down what I had seen, dated the record as usual, told Rob and wondered about calling Beverly to check. She was only an acquaintance, however; we had never been close. So I let it rest.

About two days later I met her downtown, the first time I'd seen her since her move. My first book was already out, and she knew about my work, so I told her of the projection and asked if the room meant anything to her at all. Her eyes widened as she told me that I'd described an inner room in her new house perfectly, down to the bare bulb in the ceiling and the paneling. The room was really far too large for a closet, though small enough for a normal room. She hadn't known what to use it for, and so she'd finally turned it into a closet.

Just lately the same sort of thing happened. Sometime during the night I "awakened" to find myself standing in a bathroom. In this brief but clear moment of critical consciousness, I saw a linen cabinet, open. On the shelf directly in front of me was a stack of towels, all more or less the same size, as if they were of a set. I could see only the front edges, of course, except for the top. They were blue-purple, and the top one had a flower in the center. I could see what was in front of me clearly, but something blocked my vision to the right. I tried to observe what I could, quickly. At first, nothing told me whose house this was, so I asked mentally, and got the words, "Tom's, one of your students."

Again, the next thing I knew it was morning. I wrote down what I remembered. The trouble was, I have two students named Tom. When I mentioned this in class, one had no idea of what kind of towels were in the bathroom. The other said my description seemed to apply to those in his bathroom linen closet. It wasn't until several weeks later, however, that Rob and I visited Tom Height. "Come on, check out the bathroom," he said, as everyone laughed. But the minute I entered, I saw it was the room I'd been in. The closet was right inside the door, and a jut in the wall blocked vision of the rest of the room. The cabinet and towels were identical.

On another occasion, I gave myself suggestions that during the night, I would project to Peg and Bill Gallagher's house. When morning came, I remembered nothing except that I had tried to get there, drifted off in the general area, then lost proper control of my consciousness. A few days later Peg called me with a strange story. A newspaper man, a colleague of hers, told Peg that, though he didn't know me at all, he awakened in the middle of the night convinced that I was in his room. My name kept coming to him over and over, and he sensed my presence. The man has no interest in psychic matters, and told Peg because he knew she was a friend of mine. His experience happened the same night that I tried to get to Gallaghers — and he lives in the same area.

Before I give some further examples of dream projections, here are further instructions and hints from the sessions.

(Excerpts from Session 274, July 20, 1966)

Certain chemical changes must come about in the physical organism before projection can occur. Were it not for these, you would still be imprisoned within the corporal image. You know that dreaming has a definite chemical basis, that chemicals built up during period of waking experience are released through dreams. Not only are these released, but they form a propelling action that allows energy to flow in the opposite direction. As chemical reactions allow the body to utilize energy and form physical materializations, so the excess built up becomes, then, a propelling force, allowing action to flow in what you would call subjective directions.

This same chemical reaction must also occur, only more strongly, before a legitimate projection can occur. This is one of the main reasons why deliberate projections are not more numerous. Usually the chemical access is used in normal dreaming. In periods of exuberant energy and well being, a more than normal excess accumulates. This can trigger a projection. In periods of momentary indisposition, however, the dreaming process may be blocked and the chemical excess accumulated. Again, a good time to try projection.

These chemical excesses are a natural byproduct of consciousness that is bound up in physical materialization. The more intense the characteristic experience of reality, the greater the chemical excess that is built up. Consciousness itself, when physically oriented, burns up the chemicals. The more intense the individual, the hotter the fire, so to speak, and the greater the chemical excesses released.

Released they must be, or the organism would not survive. Periods of intense activity may also generate this additional chemical propellant. Although this is generated through activity, it is released, making projections possible, in alternating periods of quietude and rest. There must be a disciplined focus, therefore, of this propellant. Periods of heightened sexual activity of a strong and deep nature will help. Periods of no sexual activity will also help, however. On the one hand, the chemical excess is built up as a result of great intensity, and in the latter case it is built up because psychic and sexual release has not been granted.

Eggs and asparagus are helpful as far as diet is concerned. I am obviously not suggesting a whole diet of eggs and

asparagus. These plus fish oils are benficial, however, but not
when taken with acid foods. . . .

I still suggest a more thorough examination of your dreams
for many of them contain spontaneous projections. They are
most apt to occur in the early hours, between 3:00 and 5:00
A.M. The body temperature drops at such times. Five in the
afternoon is also beneficial from this standpoint. The drinking
of pure water also facilitates projection, although for obvious
reasons, the bladder should be empty. The north-south position
is extremely important, and, indeed, is a necessity for any
efficient dream recall. . . . Energy is most easily utilized in this
position for one thing, and this cuts unnecessary restructions to
a minimum.

There is a vast difference between ordinary dreams and
projections, whether or not the projections occur from the
dream threshold. Dreams are constructed and sent upon their
way. As you know, they maintain an independence within their
own dimension.

Projections involve many more aspects of the whole self and
are a mark that the personality is progressing in important
ways. The inner senses are allowed their greatest freedom in
projection states, and the self retains experience that it would
not otherwise. When this knowledge becomes apart of the
ordinary waking consciousness, then you have taken a gigantic
step forward.

An almost automatic determination must be established,
however, if conscious projections are to be anything but rare
oddities. With the both of you, the problem is somewhat
different than it might be with some others. These chemical
excesses are used up, for one things, in your own creative work.
You do this automatically. It goes without saying that your own
work will gain immeasurably through the extended experience
of projection. The yoga exercises allow you to draw an
abundance — indeed, a super-abundance — of energy. This

energy results, also, in chemical excesses that can be utilized in projections, without drawing energy away from your other work.

The expectation and knowledge that you are a part of all energy will allow you to realize that all the energy you require will be given. Your attitude toward what is possible determines what is possible for you in very definite terms. . . .

Now, there are also electromagnetic changes [during projections] that can be perceived with instruments. Certain electrical fields will make themselves known under these conditions. The fields have always existed, but they will become apparent to physical instruments only when they are being crossed — in other words, at the very act of projection.

Other hints: A cool body temperature but with room temperature between 73.8 and 75.9. High humidity is poor. The color of a room is important. Cool colors are best. Too warm colors are deterimental, being too closely allied with earthly conditions. In your climate, October, February and March are best. August can be beneficial, according to the weather. Too warm weather is detrimental.

(Excerpts from Session 276, August 1, 1966)

Projections actually involve a change of atomic structure. Consciousness simply changes its form. When projection is first accomplished, there is a strong charge of adrenaline in the body and high activity of the thyroid gland. There is a charge of sexual hormones which are also utilized in projection.

After projection is accomplished, however, there is a marked decline in chemical activity and hormone action, a drop in body temperature and a drop in blood pressure. The rapid eye movements noted by dream investigators cease entirely. The eye muscles are not used. The normal muscular activity that usually occurs in sleep vanishes. The physical body is in a deep trance state. The trance may also be masked by sleep, if the projection happens from a dream threshold.

According to the intensity of the projection and to the systems visited, the body may become more or less rigid when consciousness returns to it. This is simply a reaction to the returning consciousness. There is a subtle difference in the way sugar molecules are utilized. Momentarily, the body uses less sugar. However, the sugar is important in fueling the consciousness on its journey. It also aids in connecting the consciousness to the body.

In other words, there is indeed a connection that is and must be partially physical, between the body and the traveling consciousness, and it is based upon a certain sugar molecule in a form not normally seen. Before conscious projections I would therefore recommend that you take a small amount of starchy or sugar food. A small snack before bed is a good idea from this viewpoint. Alcohol is of some benefit, though not to any great degree. Excellent results can be achieved in a dream-based projection during the day, in a nap.

21

Projections from the Dream State

I'm going to devote this chapter to various kinds of dream projections from our own records and those of my students. I refer specifically to projections embarked upon from the dream state, rather than those in which a trance is induced. Deliberate waking projections will also be excluded.

From the Records of Sue Watkins
(April 12, 1970)

I had a long series of projections in which I talked to Sean [Sue's son] about his health in the physical environment, and suggest that he will find health easy to maintain. In the last projection, I found myself hovering over a long row of shopping-center-like stores. There was a large grocery store near me and a drugstore somewhere beyond. Suddenly the entire grocery store exploded into flames. I could clearly hear explosions in the building. The windows blew out and the color of the flames was fantastic.

NOTE: On April 13 at 6:00 A.M., the huge K Mart at the Mattydale Shopping Center near Syracuse burned in a sudden fire. I saw this on TV when I awoke in the morning. The news film showed the food cans exploding — or rather, the newscaster explained this was what happened. The plate glass windows blew out, and all of this was in the news. I got up at 6:30 A.M. so I don't know if the experience was a projection at the time of the fire or a clairvoyant viewing of it. A drugstore next to the market was undamaged.

(September 11, 1970)

As we were going to bed, I began to feel a tremendous energy in the room. I tried not to be frightened and told myself that the intuitive self sensed something exciting going on, even if the ego was worried. I closed my eyes and the energy became stronger. Then I fell asleep and 'woke up' to find myself projecting in the dark-yet-not-dark of many projections. Seth stood in the doorway, looking as he does in Rob's painting of him. He was short, rather stout, dressed in light shirt and pants. I realized that he took this form because it is reassuring to me.

He said that he was here to take Carl and me on our second trip. He promised three some time ago, and we'd been on one. I turned and looked at Carl's sleeping body. Then I shouted at him until he began to project, grabbed his astral arm and helped him to his feet. Seth stood smiling, then gestured and we followed him. He gave us a lecture that I swore to remember. When I came to, it was dawn. The lecture had been so real that I was certain I'd remember it. Of course I didn't. From now on, I will hereby install a pen point in the end of my nose and sleep with my head on a writing table.

On several occasions Sue found herself in an out-of-body state, explaining the facts of death to the newly dead who did not realize their condition. Obviously, such experiences cannot be proven in scientific terms. I've had several such "dreams," and I know that they are completely different from ordinary ones. For one thing, the critical abilities are functioning and in normal dreams they are not. Like mine, Sue's records are full of notes concerning the effort needed to maintain consciousness at the required level and to prevent falling off into a regular dream state.

Just last week, in a five- to ten-minute period, Rob had an excellent out-of-body with very little distortion. His abilities have developed along the lines of psychic-vision, as explained in *The Seth Material*. His projections have been infrequent, and he never gained conscious awareness of any from the sleep state until this one. "How can I tell if I do have a legitimate projection from sleep? How will I know its not a dream or hallucination?" he used to ask. After this experience he told me that the subjective feeling is its own proof — and of course, it is.

The incident happened on a class night. Rob had been working in his studio and gone to bed around 11:00 P.M. He was vaguely aware of class leaving (at 12:30).

From Rob's Notes
(April 21, 1971)

The next thing I knew, I had the feeling that I was hovering in our dark bathroom. We close the door between the bath and living room to keep Willie, our cat, in the living room at night. I was before the closed door, but wasn't able to penetrate it. I felt no fear or panic. Although I was awake while sleeping and definitely projecting, I didn't realize this at first. The fact slowly dawned on me. This was the first time that the fear element wasn't present for me. I had no actual memory of leaving my body, and I must have fallen off into normal sleep for a moment, because the next thing I knew, I found myself out of my body, hovering just above my sleeping physical image.

Physically, I was sleeping flat on my back with my hands down at my sides. My astral body was in the same approximate position, perhaps six inches above. The state and sensation were remarkably steady and pleasant. I felt fully awake, aware of what I was doing and quite free and weightless. I knew I wasn't dreaming. At the time I remembered asking Jane in the past how you could distinguish between dream projection and dreams. The difference is obvious, when you have the experience at first hand.

I was particularly aware of my lower astral legs, hovering above the physical ones, and took great pleasure in wiggling them about, enjoying the marvelous sense of freedom and lightness they possessed. I knew my physical legs couldn't move this freely, although they are in good condition. My astral legs felt rubbery, so loose and flexible! I could see that they were light-colored, translucent from the knees down — this without my sitting up in my astral form to see them.

As stated, I wasn't at all frightened. I thought this was a fine time to do something, anything while I was at it — a visit someplace else, a trip down the street. . . . As I lay there, I tried to think of some experiment I'd particularly like to try.

All this time Jane was beside me in bed. I was also snoring. I could hear the snoring clearly and was amazed at the loudness of the sounds my body made. I heard the sounds in my physical head, I believe, just beneath me. Now I conceived the idea of using the sound of my snoring as an impetus to leave my body on the bed, while I went soaring off.

I arrived at this idea after several conscious and deliberate attempts to 'get going' once again and leave my body behind. No success. I just remained where I was, hovering. Trying to use my own sounds I began to snore even louder, if possible. I wanted to build up a massive sound-impetus that I would somehow use to propel me. All this time I enjoyed the feeling of floating above my body, but even more, of using my physical body to make noise with. This must imply a kind of dual consciousness here, since I was aware of both bodies.

I don't know if I would have succeeded in getting further or not because now Jane said to me, 'Hon, you're snoring. Turn over.' I heard her very clearly. . . . That ended it. I had no further success, although the pleasant aura surrounding the episode lingered. The whole time I felt that so much was possible with the state, that just beyond my ability at this moment lay wonderful accomplishments. . . . At no time did I see the astral cord.

Before he went back to sleep, Rob told me what had happened. I was amazed, because I hadn't been in bed over five minutes yet. I'd been waiting for his snoring to quiet down or hopefully, stop. When it didn't, I asked him to turn over. The bathroom light had been off only ten minutes at the most and the bathroom door closed. Except for undressing, these were the last two things I did before going to bed. A humorous domestic quandary results. Now I'll have to think twice before asking Rob to turn over if he's snoring. I'll be afraid of disturbing a projection.

In our next Seth session, the 583rd, April 21, 1971, Seth took out time from his book dictation to mention Rob's experience.

Congratulations, he said.

"Thank you."

You tried the experiment when you did, having an ace in the hole, so to speak, in case you became frightened — knowing full well that Ruburt would be coming to bed. You were ready to try again, however, and picked a slow and easy method, pleasant surroundings, to make it easy to become familiar with the sensations before trying anything too adventurous.

"Did I try this before Jane came to bed, before I became conscious of what was happening?"

You began your attempts before Ruburt came to bed, but did not succeed until then. The time sense outside the body can be quite different than the body's. You knew that one successful experience would free you, so you chose the best of circumstances. Remember, you have chosen those circumstances before, in the quick projection into the living room.

The snoring was supposed to be a signal to Ruburt. You knew he would 'awaken' you. This was its original motivation. If you did not like the experiment, you see, it would be terminated. In the meantime, you became delighted and decided upon using the noise as propellant, but Ruburt's usual reaction to the snoring took place.

Rob has had several spontaneous projections but none experimentally produced. The one Seth mentioned happened several years ago, in wintertime. We slept in the living room for the night because the back of the apartment was chilly. Rob had just gone to bed on the opened-up couch. I puttered about, in the same room, ready to join him. All the lights were on. He closed his eyes. The next instant he found himself fully awake and conscious in his studio.

(From his notes:) I was pounding some nails with a hammer, working on some frames. Actually, I'd been cutting masonite and gluing canvas on panels all day. I felt the hammer, saw the nails.

I worked at my drawing table. The light was on, and the windows dark. It was clearly nighttime. After a moment I realized that I wasn't supposed to be in the studio, that I had just gone to bed and should be in the living room. As soon as I made this connection, I snapped back to my body. Jane was beside me, so she had just come to bed. I knew I had not been dreaming and felt a most peculiar sense of suspension and ease.

In this case, I think that Rob projected to the studio, and hallucinated the rest of the events or performed them in the astral body. Had he been more critical at the time, he could have caused the hallucinations to disappear, continued with them or left the apartment.

Experimentation requires constant vigilance and continual checking. The following experience of mine shows some of the issues involved, and can give some of you some hints as to how to proceed. I usually speed out of my body and away from this locaton very quickly. Left to myself, this seems to be my characteristic method. But this allows no walking around the room, no chance to study the actual departure with any clearness; it happens too quickly. So, many of my experiments include the attempt to leave my body slowly so I can study my behavior.

From my records
(March 24, 1970, 2:30 P.M. to 3:45 P.M.)

I lay down to experiment and fell asleep at once to have a confused experience, mixed with dream elements. I found myself getting out of my body with some difficulty, only I was someone else or in someone else's body, a young woman student. I went running out of a house into a landscaped yard, sat down, left that body and went strolling through the yard. Other people were there, and I was jubilant because no one saw me. A young man stood by the steps. I finally said, 'I'm out of my body. Can you see me? Can you?' He said that he could, and didn't seem at all impressed, so I went back into the other body again. I started to wake up and realized that some kind of a projection had been involved, though I wasn't sure how much was contaminated by dream elements. I decided to let myself fall back into a doze to see what else developed and to monitor my consciousness.

Then I realized that I was in an excellent state for experimentation, fully alert and awake, and still in my body which was asleep. This time I decided to try and get up astrally, just walk around the room and observe the various stages of activity. I tried cautiously at first, afraid that I might rouse the physical muscles instead. The second time I succeeded, getting used to the fine distinction between moving the astral body up while leaving the physical one alone. This took quite a bit of concentration. I finally stood up, wobbly, and somewhat groggy with the effort.

I was having trouble getting away from the couch and walking properly. All through this, I was afraid that my body might not be as deeply asleep as I'd earlier supposed, but all of my consciousness was with me in my astral form. My vision wasn't clear, though, and the room looked hazy. I shook my head to clear it and saw to my dismay that the entire living room wall was lying flat on the floor, face up, closed door and all. This told me at once that I was hallucinating and if I didn't watch it, I could fall into a dreaming state. (If I'd just accepted the wall's position as 'one of those things,' I would have lost my critical awareness.) I decided that it might be better to go back into my body and try over.

By now, I was standing with my back to my body, and I just 'fell' backward into it. I got out again fairly quickly, this time able to study the strange sensing involved in distinguishing between the astral self I wanted to sit up and the physcial self I wanted to stay flat. I walked out to the center of the room which now was perfectly normal, but had difficulty walking and remembered that in my case, at least, this sometimes happens when I'm close to my body. I decided to go to Rob's studio, where he was working, to see if I could make him observe me.

I was still walking very slowly, with my astral eyes slitted to cut down the focus of distractions. I closed them to deepen my trance and reached out for the bathroom doorknob. I felt it hard and round, perfectly normal in my astral hand. Then I paused in uncertainty; something didn't seem right. What had I done wrong *now?* I opened my astral eyes fully and stared down at my hand. It circled a 'knob' of air. For just another moment I felt the hardness, the bulk of that knob. Then only air was there. Obviously, I'd hallucinated the doorknob. The door was still several feet away. Disappointed with myself, I returned to my body, determined to plan out a new course of action.

As I was entering my body, I heard Rob in the bathroom. I wondered if he would come in to see what I was doing. This awakened my physical body.

Between the first episode and the second, I was fully alert, awake in my astral body, but still connected with the physical one. In this state I experienced what I can only call ecstasy, involving the entire body. While the feeling was not localized, it certainly felt strongly sexual in nature, and when I left my body, there was a moment when this continued very intensely.

Sue, my other students, and myself are aware that creative, psychic and sexual energy are only various aspects of the same force. At times we may collect this energy sexually, then switch over, transforming the energy from one form to another. The sexual feelings accompany many dream projections and are entirely absent in others. Their presence at all, however, may easily give rise to interpretations based more on social taboos than anything else — and to sexual hallucinations that should be but are not always recognized as such.

Here is another example, also from my own records, in which I struggled to maintain proper consciousness and perfect a projection. Hopefully, these various episodes will illustrate some of the many ways that projections can be brought about from a sleep state.

This experience happened September 27, 1967, after a social evening at home. I'd had several glasses of wine during the evening, and when I went to bed, I couldn't get comfortable, but dozed and awakened often. I went to bed at 11:30 P.M. and recorded this experience at 1:30 A.M.

As I fell off to sleep I had been thinking of Congress Park in Saratoga Springs, New York. Suddenly, I became aware that I had begun a projection, but I wasn't sure exactly how far the process had gone. I found myself seeing Congress Park very clearly, for example, yet I wasn't there yet, and my head kept throbbing in a way that wasn't physical — as if I heard rather than felt the throbs. This was accompanied by a buzzing noise and other loud sounds that I now accept as characteristic of certain kinds of projection. My head felt full of a white light. Everything in my astral visions was opaque white, instead of dark.

I decided to continue the projection though I hadn't faced these particular conditions before — being half in and half out of an environment. Instantly, I found myself walking along the park path, sometimes slightly above it. The night was foggy and dark, as it was in Elmira. My sight was operating perfectly, but it took a while before my hearing worked. (In good projections, all senses are super-perfect). I worked at getting clearer focus and really enjoyed walking down the park paths. I hadn't been in that park for years and was consciously delighted. Now and then I paused to see if anything had changed. So far everything was the same.

At the end of the park basin are a flight of stone steps leading to another street and an old house in which I once lived for a short time. I went there. The front downstairs door was ajar, but to see how well I was doing, I walked through the part that was closed and went upstairs. After wandering through the upstairs hall and seeing no one, I went out to the side porch and stood looking out at the park and enjoying the night air.

All the while, I was very conscious of the white light that was beginning to bother me. It seemed to fill my entire head, growing more and more intense. A funny wooshing sound inside my head also distracted me and my head itself began to feel fantastically light. The more I tried to concentrate in my environment, the stronger these effects grew.

It occurred to me that perhaps the effects were warnings to go back to my body or indications that conditions weren't good. At the same time, there was no way I could check out the projection physically — I'd met no one — and I decided that since I was over 250 miles away from my body, I may as well get whatever evidence I could for myself.

Ignoring the light, I willed myself to go to the house of the Linden family, across town. Instantly I found myself there on the porch. For a moment I wondered if I was in the right place, then I saw that the old side porch had been completely removed and another front porch added. Was this a distortion or hallucination? I willed all hallucinations to vanish, but everything remained the same. This usually means that the environment is a "real" location. It was dark, with no lights on in the house, and I decided to go inside.

At this point the pulsations of the white light inside my head quickened and grew very powerful. I felt for a moment as if my consciousness could really be swept away or as if I could really have difficulty getting back to my body. I kept "testing" the strength of the light during the whole experience, and each time decided to continue despite it. Now I decided I'd better return.

I found myself then in my astral body above my physical one, but in reversed position. My astral hand with its strange sensations and pulsing light was to the south, over my physical feet. For a few moments I kept fluctuating — back to the park then back to my room — with the white light pulsating very strongly. Finally I just wished myself into my body, experienced some difficulty, a brief instant of unconsciousness, and fell back in.

We didn't go to Saratoga physically until the summer of 1970, when we drove through on our way north. When we were there, I had Rob drive around to Linden's. The house was exactly like it had been in my experience, with the side porch removed and a front one added.

Since this book is about the dream state, including dream projections, this is not the place to compare waking, trance and dream projections. I simply hope to show some of the types of projections possible from the dream state. The following experience was Carl Watkins' first projection, January 6, 1969.

It all started when I turned over to switch on the light next to the bed. It flashed a bright red color which I thought strange and unaccountable. I got up to go to the bathroom, but when I began to walk, I felt very dizzy. When I reached the door, I had the odd feeling that I'd left something behind me. When I looked back toward the body, I nearly flipped. I sure had left something — my body! Then I realized that I was in my astral form.

Then I remembered that on first going to bed, I'd felt that someone was in the room. Right then, Sue Mullin [later Carl's wife] now appeared, out of thin air. When I saw her, I suggested that we both go to Jane's house to let her know we were out-of-body, but Sue wanted to talk instead. We talked for some time, but now I can't remember the conversation. I kept watching my body on the bed. It changed position, lying on its back. Before it had faced the window. I was particularly interested in the eyes. Either the shadow in the room was freaking me out or the eyes were wide open but blank. When I turned around to Sue again, she was gone.

Now I had trouble staying out of my body but found that by exhaling I could keep myself in the astral one. Once I went back in my body, got up and thought I did so physically and was in a normal state, but then I saw my body on the bed . . .

Finally I looked up and saw my mother in front of me. She was lying in bed, and I couldn't tell if I was in her bedroom or seeing through the wall or what. I started thinking about what Jane said about people being out-of-body without knowing it and wondered if Mom was out right then. With this, she sat right up and pointed at me. This reminded me of the way that Seth points at people sometimes. Apparently this worried me, for I ran to my body for protection. After this I came awake in my body and wrote down my first out-of-body trip!

The same night, Sue recorded this note:

> From the sleep state I project to Carl's and shout at him until his astral body sits up. I try to get to Jane's.

One of my most delightful dream encounters involved a meeting with Rob in the out-of-body state on May 9, 1969. I had a dentist's appointment later in the day, but in the morning I lay down at 9:30, specifically to try a projection from the dream state. I dozed and awoke at 10:30, remembering nothing. Disappointed but determined, I set the alarm for 11:15 and tried again. Almost instantly I fell asleep.

First I found myself in the studio and Rob was there. He came to bed with me, and we made love. I was surprised he was home, knowing it was Friday when he was out of his body also, and so was I. I told Rob and we discussed it, plus our amazement over out-of-body love-making. Then, laughing and curious, we walked out into the living room together, looking at everything. The room and the morning were all normal. We hugged and joked — the bodies we had certainly seemed real to us. Yet to others we'd be invisible.

This made me think of looking at my physical body. Rob's, we knew, would be at work. I went into the bedroom, but the bed was as I left it, only empty. This really confused me. I called Rob. He couldn't see my physical body either. "My body's got to be in bed," I said. "Why can't we see it?" We discussed what had happened so far, but couldn't solve the mystery. "Could it be that we're really both physical after all?" I asked.

"No," Rob said. "My physical body's at the art department." With that, he simply disappeared. I found myself back in the bedroom. I left the apartment and had two very long adventures in the astral condition, all clear and vivid, and recorded in my notes.

I still couldn't figure out what had really happened with Rob and me, though. Luckily, in the next, 481st session on May 12, 1969, Seth began an explanation. The session also contains further hints for dream projections.

Ruburt's experience involving you was quite legitimate, although you did not consciously remember it. You were, nevertheless, largely responsible for the encounter. Both consciously and unconsciously, you were thinking about Ruburt's dental appointment. You wanted to give him confidence and to reassure him. This acted as the emotional impetus.

Ruburt was writing earlier in the morning, and, without realizing it, he was telepathically aware of your emotional presence. It was this that gave him the idea of a projection experiment. He wanted to see if he could become more aware of your form. You did not want to project per se, necessarily. You wanted to be here to offer comfort. The desire got you here. Your conscious mind was fully taken up with your activities at the art department, giving the inner self full rein.

In the same way do you travel in other realities without being aware of it. You perceived in a 'normal' fashion, which should show you again that perception is not dependent upon the physical image. You have both traveled together in such a fashion from the dream state. There is no reason why you cannot try such experiments, trying to project at the same time.

If you do this from a dream state, then you must set aside two and one half hours, for the first portion will be used as preliminaries. You can also given yourselves such suggestions before you sleep. You might begin by making an appointment to meet each other, say, at three in the morning in the living room.

You will feel more comfortable if the initial journeys are only within your apartment in the beginning. Joseph, you sleep more deeply than Ruburt, so be sure to give yourself the suggestion to awaken normally and record any experience. It might also help you if you place an object to which you are strongly attached in the living room.

For your own purposes, an unfinished painting on your easel would help you project to the studio, for you would wish to study it. You have often done this, without remembering. It would be to your advantage if the two of you traveled together, however. You could help each other retain proper consciousness and purpose during projection. If Ruburt is projecting, he should try to rouse you astrally.

He can be of great help to you, when he develops further.

You can also suggest dreams in which you are flying in an airplane and tell yourself then that you will waken from the dream and project. You will know the plane to be a dream image, but be able to retain it for your convenience if you want, so that you do not fear falling at first.

In such instances, you are withdrawing your perceptive abilities from the physical body. They will seem to operate as usual, but they are more vivid and far-reaching. Your thoughts instantly attain a form that you can then perceive. If you think of a dog, for example, quite unconsciously you form the image of a dog, which you then perceive.

It is because of this instantaneous creation and projection of inner reality outward into form that you experience time within the physical system — to train you, to give you time to learn to handle your own creations. Projection experiments, then, should only be tried when you are in a peaceful state of mind, as Ruburt should know after his black creature experience [described in *The Seth Material*].

Now, there are 'objective' realities that exist within the astral system. There are more than your own thought forms, in other words. Your own thought-forms can be definite aids when you are in the proper mental condition, and they can impede your progress if you are not. For example, a man in a desperate frame of mind is more apt to emphasize the unpleasant aspects of the news and to see bitterness rather than the joy in the faces of those he meets. He will ignore a contented child playing on one side of the street and notice, instead, a dirty ragged child, even though he be further away. So your frame of mind when projecting will largely determine the kind of experiences you have.

The original intensity behind the construction determines its duration. . . . Left alone, any such construction will eventually vanish. It will leave a trace, however, in electromagnetic reality where it can then be activated by *anyone when certain conditions are met or are favorable.*

Denying energy to such a construction can be like pricking a balloon. . . . Then all attention must be taken from it, for it thrives upon attention.

Sue and I are positive that we have met many times during out-of-body states. Sometimes one of us remembers, sometimes the other does. On several instances, however, both of us have remembered and recorded our experiences which were similar *but not identical.* We hope to do much more work here. Rob is now becoming much more familiar with projection, so he and I plan to do some extensive work on our own. Hopefully, through the years, we can amass some kind of evidence that will be of help to others.

I often dream of giving a Seth session for one of my students, and in almost each case, the individual involved records the same kind of dream for that night. This has happened in Sue's case five or six times.

22

~

The Inside of Consciousness

More Projection Instructions
Projections as Strange Sense Experiences

Projections from the dream state intrigue me because in them I believe we encounter the inside of our own consciousness in a most direct fashion. In a way, we are completely on our own, manipulating in a subjective environment, aware of the workings of consciousness when it is not soaked up or fastened upon objective specifics. Such exploration is full of surprises. In these states, consciousness operates within definite conditions, within an ordered system of experience. But we must struggle to discover what these are as opposed to the hallucinary images we set up ourselves against or superimposed upon this reality.

While we may "come awake" spontaneously within a dream, certain procedures do help, and these can induce projections from the dream state. They have been mentioned before in previous chapters, but here I'll give them as briefly and simply as possible. First you must realize that you are dreaming. Suggestion to this effect, given before sleep, facilitates this recognition.

This knowledge automatically changes the dream state into another in which the critical faculties are aroused and operating. Dream actions are no longer taken for granted. Experience is scrutinized. You may "awaken" in your house, for example. If so, check your rooms against their normal arrangement. Anything that does not normally belong there may be an hallucination, part of the usual dreaming process. If you will such images to disappear, they will, leaving you within the basic unhallucinated environment. If you rationalize any such elements or accept them uncritically, you may fall back into normal dreaming.

The next point is to realize that you are alert, conscious and awake, while your body is asleep. You can then explore the environment in which you find yourself or travel to another location. Instead of "coming to" in your home, however, you may instead become alert in another location, a town, another house or unfamiliar place where checking against usual circumstances is nearly impossible.

Here, rely on common sense. If you find a girl in a bathing suit standing on a wintery street, for example, one or the other has to go. If the girl is the main incongruous element, and the rest all fits in, then will the girl to disappear. Keep this up with any other such images that you meet. Again, you'll be left with the basic environment and can proceed as you want. You *can* accept such images and play around with them or watch them to see what develops, but only if you realize they are hallucinations. There are exceptions to this practice, however, as the next Seth excerpt shows.

To travel somewhere else, will yourself there. Often travel seems instantaneous. At other times, you may find yourself swept from place to place, with little control. If you come awake while still within your physical body or close to it, you may or may not see your own body as described earlier. You may also find yourself in non-physical locations or places in which matter does not behave the way it usually does. Seth explains this very well in Session 284, September 7, 1966.

You agree to accept certain data in the physical universe. You agree to form this into certain patterns, and you agree to ignore other data completely. These now, called root assumptions, form the main basis for the apparent permanence and coherence of your physical system.

In your journeys into inner reality, you cannot proceed with these same root assumptions. Reality, per se, changes completely according to the basic root agreements that you accept. One of the root agreements upon which physical reality is based is the assumption that objects have a reality independent of any subjective cause and that these objects, within definite specified limitations, are permanent.

Objects may appear and disappear in these other systems. Using the root assumptions just mentioned as a basis for judging reality, an observer would insist that the objects were not real, for they do not behave as he believes objects must. Because dream images may appear and disappear, then, do not take it for granted that they do not really exist.

There is a cohesiveness to the inner universe and to the systems that are not basically physical. But this is based upon an entirely different set of root assumptions and these are the keys that alone will let you manipulate within other systems or understand them. There are several major root assumptions connected here and many minor ones:

1. *Energy and action are basically the same, although neither must necessarily apply to physical action.*
2. *All objects have their origin basically in mental action. Mental action is directed psychic energy.*
3. *Permanence is not a matter of time. Existence has value in terms of intensities.*
4. *Objects are blocks of energy perceived in a highly specialized manner.*

5. *Stability in time sequence is not a prerequisite requirement for an object, except as a root assumption in the physical universe.*
6. *Space as a barrier does not exist.*
7. *The spacious present is here more available to the senses.*
8. *The only barriers are mental or psychic ones.*

Only if these basic root assumptions are taken for granted will your projection experiences make sense to you. Different rules simply apply. Your subjective experience is extremely important here; that is, the vividness of any given experience in terms of intensity will be far more important than anything else.

Elements from past, present and future may be indiscriminately available to you. You may be convinced that a given episode is the result of subconscious fabrication, simply because the time sequence is not maintained, and this could be a fine error. In a given dream projection, for example, you may experience an event that is obviously from the physical past, yet within it there may be elements that do not fit. In an old-fashioned room of the 1700's, you may look out and see an automobile pass by. Obviously, you think: distortion. Yet you may be straddling time in such an instance, perceiving, say, the room as it was in the 1700's and the street as it appears in your present. These elements may appear side by side. The car may suddenly disappear before your eyes, to be replaced by an animal or the whole street may turn into a field.

'This is how dreams work,' you may think. 'This cannot be a legitimate projection.' Yet you may be perceiving the street and the field that existed 'before' it, and the images may be transposed one upon the other. If you try to judge such an experience with physical root assumptions, it will be meaningless. As mentioned earlier, you may also perceive a

building that will never exist in physical reality. This does not
mean that the form is illusion. You are simply in a position
where you can pick up and translate the energy pattern before
you.

If another individual under the same circumstances comes
across the same 'potential' object, he can also perceive it as you
did. He may, however, because of his own make-up, perceive
and translate another portion of allied pattern. He may see the
form of the man who originated the thought of the building.

To a large extent in the physical system, your habit of
perceiving time as a sequence forms the type of experience and
also limits it. This habit also unites the experiences, however.
The unifying and limiting aspects of consecutive moments are
absent in inner reality. Time, in other words, cannot be counted
upon to unify action. The unifying elements will be those of
your own understanding and abilities. You are not forced to
perceive action as a series of moments within inner reality,
therefore.

Episodes will be related to each other by different methods
that will be intuitional, highly selective and psychological. You
will find your way through complicated mazes of reality
according to your own intuitional nature. You will find what
you expect to find. You will seek out what you want from the
available data.

In physical experience, you are dealing with an environment
with which you are familiar. You have completely forgotten the
chaos and unpredictable nature it presented before learning
processes were channeled into its specific directions. You learned
to perceive reality in a highly specified fashion. When you are
dealing with inner, or basically non-physical realities, you must
learn to become unspecialized and then learn a new set of
principles. You will soon learn to trust your perceptions,
whether or not the experiences seem to make logical sense.

In a projection, the problems will be of a different sort. The form of a man, for example, may be a thought-form, or a fragment sent quite unconsciously by another individual whom it resembles. It may be another projectionist, like yourself. It may be a potential form like any potential object . . . a record of a form played over and over again.

It may be another version of yourself. We will discuss ways of distinguishing between these. A man may suddenly appear, and be then replaced by a small girl. This would be a nonsensical development to the logical mind; yet, the girl might be the form of the man's previous or future reincarnated self.

The unity, you see, is different. Basically, perception of the spacious present is naturally available. It is your nervous physical mechanism which acts as a limiting device. By acting in this manner it forces you to focus upon what you can perceive with greater intensity.

Your mental processes are formed and developed as a result of this conditioning. The intuitive portions of the personality are not so formed, and these will operate to advantage in any inner exploration.

You are basically capable of seeing any particular location as it existed a thousand years in your past or as it will exist a thousand years in your future. The physical senses serve to blot out more aspects of reality than they allow you to perceive . . . yet, in many inner explorations you will automatically translate experience into terms that the senses can use. . . . Any such translation is, nevertheless, a second-hand version of the original — an important point to remember.

The images and forms Seth speaks about in that session would *not* disappear when you banished your own hallucinations, as mentioned earlier. In the next session, Seth explained more about root assumptions and for the first time mentioned psychedelic experience in connection with projection.

(From Session 285, September 12, 1966)

Root assumptions represent the basic premises upon which a given existence-system is formed. These are the ground rules, so to speak. Your physical mechanisms are equipped to function in such a way that reality is perceived through the lens of particular root assumptions, then. Using the physical senses, it is almost impossible for you to perceive reality in any other way.

Physically speaking, you will find nothing to contradict these assumptions, since they are all that you can experience or perceive physically. These root assumptions are the framework of the camouflage system. As you explore other realities, you almost automatically interpret such data in terms of the root assumptions of your own system.

This highly falsifies such information. The inner senses are not bound by those assumptions, however. . . . This is why so many psychic or subjective experiences seem to contradict physical laws. You must learn the 'laws' that apply to other systems.

The root assumptions that govern physical reality are indeed valid, but within physical reality alone. They do not apply elsewhere. There is a natural tendency to continue judging experience against these assumptions, however. With experience, the habit will lose much of its hold. Inner experience must be colored to some extent by the physical system, while you exist in it. In order for such data to rise to conscious levels, for example, it must be translated into terms that the ego can understand, and the translation is bound to distort the original experience. . . .

The whole physical organism of the body has been trained to react to certain patterns, these based on physical root assumptions. The nervous system reacts definitely to visual block images. Such images are received through the skin, as well as through the eyes. The whole system is highly complicated and organized. This is obviously necessary for physical survival. . . .

The organization however is, biologically speaking, artificial and learned. It is no less rigid for that reason. This organizational structure of perception can be broken up, as recent LSD experiments certainly show. This can be dangerous, however. The fact that this does occur shows that the systems of perception are not a part of over-all structure biologically, but learned secondary responses. It is disturbing to the whole organism, however, to break up the strong pattern of usual perception. Inner stability of response is suddenly swept away. Changes that are not yet known occur within the nervous system under these circumstances, both electromagnetic and chemical.

The inner senses alone are equipped to process and perceive other reality systems. Even the distortions can be kept at a minimum with training. Indiscriminate use of the psychedelic drugs can severely shake up learned patterns of response that are necessary for effective manipulation within physical reality; break subtle connections and you disturb electromagnetic functions. Ego failure can result.

Development of the inner senses is a much more effective method of perceiving other realities, and, followed correctly, the ego is not only stronger but more flexible. Even consciousness of physical reality is increased. Such development becomes an unfolding and natural expansion of the whole personality.

These root assumptions are so a part of your existence that they cloud your dreams. Beneath them, however, portions of the self perceive physical reality in an entirely different fashion, free of the tyranny of objects and physical form. Here you experience concepts directly, without the need for symbols. You have knowledge of your 'past' personalities and know that they exist simultaneously with your own.

The practice of psychological time will allow you to reach these portions of the self. The ego is not artificially disorganized by such practice. It is simply bypassed for the moment. The

experience gained does become a part of the physical structure,
but there is no massive disorganization of perception, since the
ego agrees to step aside momentarily.

It is not bombarded, as with the drug experiments, and
forced to experience chaotic and frightening perceptions that
can terrify it into complete disorder. Survival in your system is
dependent upon the highly specialized, focused, limited but
specific qualities of the ego. It should not be rigid. Neither
should it be purposely weakened.

The root assumptions upon which physical reality is formed
represent secure ground to the ego. We always operate with the
ego's consent. It interprets the inner knowledge gained in its
own way, true, but it is immeasurably enriched by so doing.

The ego can exist only within the context of these
assumptions. The primary dream experience is finally woven
into a structure composed of these assumptions, and it is these
you remember. These serve you as basic information but the
information is in symbolic form. Objects, you see, are symbols.
Dream objects are often symbols of realities that the ego could
not otherwise perceive.

Some out-of-body experiences are extremely difficult to cata-
gorize and involve extraordinarily sensuous events that remain
vivid long after their occurrence. Some are suggestive of drug-
induced episodes, except for the greater sense of alertness and self-
control. I have two particular experiences of mine in mind.

One involved spectacular color. I lay down to try a projection
one Friday afternoon last January — my last projection experiment for the winter. Rob was out. It was another dreary day with
veils of light rain falling. I was just beginning the final draft of this
book and told myself that I could have an excellent projection to
use in this section. I specifically requested a projection within the
room, rather than to an outside location.

I fell asleep and dreamed that Rob had just come home and had begun to redecorate the room. Though I was surprised to see him, I accepted without question the fact that he was home early and did not realize I was dreaming at this point. Instead, I found the room transformed with spectacular color such as I'd never seen before — brilliant, shimmering, alive and richer than I ever imagined color could be. Everything in the room took on this fantastic other-color life. I felt myself drink it up, absorb it, in a way that's most difficult to explain. The white walls were replaced by intricate colored wallpaper and drapes of velvet. The colors seemed to have a natural life themselves, glowing from within, throbbing with vitality.

I kept exclaiming about the colors and ran into the next room to see if the effect went through the whole apartment. My image in the bathroom mirror stopped me. I was wearing a lovely head-dress of orange and yellow intertwined threads, each one listening in the golden light that now filled the room. I took it off and examined it, wonderingly, then looked in the mirror again. My own hair shone, each separate hair vigorous and sensuous with color. My skin appeared the same way, giving forth the most subtle tones.

I went back into the front room, now almost realizing my state. "Rob, this isn't really our apartment, is it?" I asked. I looked around again. "I must be dreaming. That plant by the window sill isn't ours. It must be an hallucination."

"You're normally awake," Rob said. "The plant is ours. You just forgot about it." So I accepted his statement and never even wondered that *he* might be a thought-form of mine.

Other adventures followed: Rob disappeared, and I found myself walking along a strange outside corridor, like a public path, only high in the air. Other people passed, all dressed in delightful long flowing trousers and gowns of indescribable colors. Looking down, I saw that I was wearing a beautiful pair of trousers of some clinging, bright material.

The next thing I knew, I was flying above land a good deal

south of here because there was no snow, and a Middle-Atlantic-States-type landscape. Many cars were heading north, and there was some commotion at an intersection below. A woman came out of a house nearby to watch. Some kind of a roadblock was set up. I tried to come closer to the ground to see more clearly, but instead was whisked back through the air to Elmira.

I returned to my body and experienced a false awakening in which Rob spoke to me. I couldn't wait to open my eyes to see what the room looked like and if the colors were still present. Instead, the room was faded by contrast.

"Rob, I had the wildest experience, but unfortunately I'm back now because all that great color is gone," I said; and I told him what happened. As I finished speaking, something caught my eye — the wallpaper. While it was not as colorful as it had been earlier, neither was it the white painted wall that should have been there.

With this realization I really awoke to the ordinary room and checked the clock. The whole experience took place between 2 P.M., the last time I'd looked at the clock, and 3 P.M. Then I realized that my left hand was completely immobile, folded up and locked tight. There was no feeling in it whatsoever. When I tried to move it, it wouldn't budge. I decided that it was a muscular rigidity resulting from the projection and waited quietly for several minutes. Then slowly it regained mobility and feeling.

Actually, I was only remotely aware of the difficulties of my hand. Instead, my mind was filled with memories of the spectacular colors I had seen. For a moment, I was almost enthralled as I partially recalled them out of the nowhere into which they had vanished. I had to go downtown to meet Rob for grocery shopping, so I dressed quickly. But it seemed that all the color had drained away from the world. Walking downtown, I was depressed. It was weeks later before I regained my normal feelings for our apartment. In the meantime, it seemed insufferably dreary. For that matter, so did the rest of the world. I've had normal dreams that were in vivid color, but nothing like that, and at no other time has my usual earthly environment been bathed in such iridescence.

Seth has more to say about hallucinations and objects in Session 287 for September 21, 1966, and perhaps the first part of the following excerpts helps explain my experience. Seth was talking about basic reality in the dream state.

You will sometimes automatically translate this reality into physical terms. Such images will be hallucinatory, but it may take awhile for you to distinguish their true nature. It must be understood, however, that all physical objects are hallucinatory. They may be called mass hallucinations.

There is constant translation of inner reality into objects in the waking state and a constant translation of ideas into pseudo-objects in the dream state. Within a certain range of dream reality, ideas and thoughts can be translated into pseudo-objects and transported. This is what happens when you adopt a pseudo-form in projection, though I am simplifying this considerably.

When you travel beyond a certain range of intensities, even psuedo-objects must vanish. They exist in a cluster about, and connected to, your own system. The lack of these, obviously, means that you have gone beyond your own camouflage system. If it were possible, you would then travel through a range of intensities in which no camouflage existed. Then you would encounter the pseudo-camouflage of the next system. This would or would not be physical matter, according to the system. You would then encounter the heart of the camouflage area. The completely uncamouflaged areas at the outer edges of the various systems should remind you of the undifferentiated areas between various life cycles in the subconscious. This is no coincidence.

As a rule, you see, there is little communication within the uncamouflaged areas. They act as boundaries, even while they represent the basic stuff of which all camouflage is composed. (Without the camouflage, you would perceive nothing with the physical senses.)

The sentence is really meaningless, however, because the physical senses are themselves camouflage. There would be nothing to translate. It is only the inner senses that will allow you to perceive under these circumstances. Theoretically, if you can bridge the gap between various reincarnations, then you can bridge the gap between your system and another.

Once more: The undifferentiated layers are composed of the vitality that forms the camouflage of all systems. Such an area is not really a thing in itself, but a portion of vitality that contains no camouflage, and is therefore unrecognizable to those within any given system. You are in touch with infinity in such areas, since it is only camouflage that gives you the conception of time. . . .

Now, during some projections, you may be aware of nothing as far as surroundings are concerned. There will only be the mobility of your own consciousness. If this occurs, you will be traveling through such an uncamouflaged area. You could then expect to encounter next a more differentiated environment, that seems to become clearer as you progress toward the heart of another system.

The completely uncamouflaged layer would be rather bewildering. You might automatically be tempted to project images into it. They would not take, so to speak, but would appear and disappear with great rapidity. This is a silent area. Thoughts would not be perceived here, as a rule, for the symbols for them would not be understood.

If a certain intensity is reached, however — a peak of intensity — then you could perceive the spacious present as it exists within your native system. You could, from this peak, look into other systems, but you would not understand what you perceived, not having the proper root assumptions. I have used the idea of neighboring systems for simplicity's sake, as if they were laid out end to end. Obviously, such is not the case. The systems [of reality] are more like the various segments of a tangerine, with the uncamouflaged boundary areas like the white membrane between the tangerine sections.

The tangerine, then, would be compared to a group of many systems, yet it would represent in itself but one portion of an unperceived whole. The tangerine would be but one segment of a larger system. You can see, then, why some projections would lead you in a far different direction from your linear sort of travel and why time as you know it would be meaningless.

Nor do such projections necessarily involve journeys through space as you know it. There are systems, vivid in intensity, that have no existence in physical reality at all. It is now thought, I believe, that time and space are basically one, but they are both a part of something else. They are merely the camouflage patterns by which you perceive reality. Space as you perceive it in the dream state comes much closer to the reality.

Projections within your own system will, of course, involve you with some kind of camouflage. If none is present, you will know you are out of the system. The dream universe is obviously closely connected with your own, since pseudo-objects are present. Even there, you are to some extent free from the space-time elements of your own system. Within the dream state, then, you are in the 'outward' areas of the physically oriented universe.

One point: There are other systems all about and within your own. The undifferentiated areas move out like spirals, through all reality. Little resistance is encountered within them. They represent inner roads that connect systems, as well as divide them. The traveler must leave his own camouflage paraphernalia behind him, however, or he will get nowhere.

It is possible, theoretically, to travel to any system in this manner and bypass others, you see. Such a traveler would not *age physically. His body would be in a suspended state. Only a very few individuals have traveled in this manner. Most of the knowledge gained escapes the ego, and the experiences cannot be translated by the physical brain.*

However, it is possible to travel under such circumstances, and some of the data would be retained by inner portions of the self. In a creative individual, some of this information might be symbolically expressed in a painting or other work of art.

[Here Seth went into some material that was highly interesting to Rob:]

Each brushstroke of a painting represents concentrated experience and compressed perceptions. In a good painting, these almost explode when perceived by the lively consciousness of another. The observer is washed over by intensities. The excellent work of art recreates for the observer inner experience of his own, also, of which he has never been aware. As you know, paintings have motion, yet the painting itself does not move. This idea should help you understand experience in terms of intensities and projections or the movement of consciousness without necessarily motion through space.

True motion has nothing to do with space. The only real motion is that of the traveling consciousness.

My own most recent projection was very close to home, compared to the possible journeys Seth mentioned in the previous excerpts. Again, it reminded me later of reported sense experience under the influence of drugs. It was most unusual and I'm sure I'll never forget it.

Last Thursday, May 6, 1971, I took an hour nap in the late morning. No suggestions were given. It was another dark day, and the air was full of moisture. I "came to" in Rob's studio. I was standing before the open window, looking out at the pear tree, but it was the air itself that captured my attention. It was transparent as always but thick as Jell-O.

Astonished, I thrust my hand out the window, and the motion set ripples out, making fairly deep "cracks" near my fingers and more shallow ones farther away. The tree, I saw, was not only held up and supported by its roots deep in the earth, but by the air itself. Why had I ever thought that branches stayed up simply because this was how branches acted? The air itself helped hold them!

I was fully alert and more curious than I can say. Several times I put my hand out as far as it could go and wiggled my fingers. The air stirred, like pudding. There was much greater contrast than usual between the very dark clouds high above and the rest of the air, and colors — dark purple, a greyish white and several green and dark greys — almost appeared like clumps, thick and then thinning.

What would happen to objects falling? I wondered. From everything I saw, I judged that they would glide to earth or drop slowly through that textured air. The effect was far from inert, though. The sky and air moved constantly, perhaps like very heavy jellied water, with the trees stuck in like huge seaweed. I felt as if I could almost walk on the air, but from the motion of my hand through it, I knew it was not normally heavy enough to support me.

Cautiousness and wonder made me pause. For one thing, the air inside the room was normal. For another, I felt as if I was observing a legitimate glimpse of air from the framework of a different kind of perception. Was this in some way air slowed down? And if so, was my "body" in the same state? Was this what air was really like and was it perceived this way by certain kinds of consciousness or at particular stages of molecular activity? All of these thoughts went through my mind, but before I could figure out what other experiments I could try, I snapped back to my body.

The experience was so intriguing that I thought of it often in the days following. That Sunday as we were out driving, the idea suddenly struck me that there might be a force coming up from the earth, in opposition to gravity. The two could be part of one phenomena, of course. It could account for the fact that seeds do push up through the earth, not only attracted by the sun but nudged by this force beneath.

That experience is far more vivid than anything else that happened to me that day or during that entire month so far. It will be remembered long after I forget what else I did that day. It does no good to call such episodes hallucinations. They are, above all, valid psychological events. They enrich normal experience, broaden the usual restrictions of daily perception and encourage creative thought. The same applies to all of the dreams and projections mentioned in this book. These dimensions of experience and consciousness co-exist with normal reality as we know it, and I believe that in them we exercise abilities that are ours by right and heritage.

EPILOGUE

A Personal Evaluation

Quite frankly, I believe that normal dreams are the outside shell of deeper inside experience. The interior reality is clothed in dream images as, when we are awake, it is clothed in physical ones. Dream objects and physical objects alike are symbols by which we perceive — and distort — an inner reality that we do not seem able to experience directly. In certain states of consciousness, particularly in projections from the dream state, we achieve a peculiar poise of alertness. This lets us briefly examine the nature of our consciousness by allowing us to view its products — the events and experiences that it creates when released from usual physical focus.

Consciousness forms its own reality, physical and otherwise. I think there is a "mass" dream experience, however, as there is a collectively perceived physical life and definite interior conditions within which dream life happens. Only inner experimentation will let us discover this interior landscape. Perhaps one day we will move freely within it, alert, conscious and far wiser than we are now.

It is a dimension native to consciousness, I believe, at whatever stage of being, physical or nonphysical. We have our primary existence in it after death and spend a good deal of physical time wandering through it, unknowingly, in sleep. Clues as to our creativity and the nature of our existence can be found there and from it emerges the organizational qualities of normal consciousness as we know it.

Since this book was not devoted exclusively to projections, I did not include those embarked upon from waking or trance states, though some of these provided excellent "evidence." In them, however, my own consciousness was still physically oriented since I "went out" to check the reliability of my perceptions against physical reality.

My students provided me with many projection reports from the dream state. I relied largely on my own simply because I was intimately familiar with the subjective feelings involved in each case and did not want to depend upon reports that were necessarily secondhand.

The nature of this book also meant that the Seth material was chosen exactly because it related to subjective experiences such as dreams and consciousness. Seth also relates beautifully to other individuals in sessions and in give-and-take conversations, as I've tried to show several instances. He comes through as far more than just a voice delivering manuscript.

In extracting material on dreams from our many sessions, I have, to some extent, ripped it out of its living context. Each session, for example, includes Rob's notes which provide a constant physical framework and reference to our daily activities. Seth's monologues are broken up by humorous references or snatches of conversation with Rob. Seth's own book, *Seth Speaks: The Eternal Validity of the Soul*, will be presented using the session format, however, so that the entire flavor of the sessions can be appreciated.

I wanted to show the direction in which we were moving since our first experiences with interior events of this nature, and also generally provide guidelines for others who may wish to do their own investigations. Dream interpretations — which are after the dream event — were not covered in this book, therefore.

Seth's own book will carry his discussions of the dream state still further. I have not read that manuscript through, since it is not quite finished, and I want to avoid conscious involvement with it. Rob tells me, however, that it contains a good deal of new material on the nature of dreaming consciousness.

I do not believe that there are any more dangers facing us in the interior universe than there are in the physical one. We should explore each world with common sense and courage. The interior universe is the source of the exterior one, however, and traveling through it we will encounter our own hopes, fears and beliefs in their ever-changing form.

My book is finished. I sit at the same table now as I did when I began it, looking out at the same streets and mountains. Spring is here again. I wrote yesterday . . .

> *Occult spring*
> *With its apport of flowers*
> *Casts its spell*
> *Upon the land . . .*

And so the exterior world emerges from the interior one even as this physical book materialized from the inner reality of inspiration, creativity and dreams.

STILLPOINT PUBLISHING

*Books that explore the expanding frontiers
of human consciousness*

For a free catalog or ordering information

write:

*Stillpoint Publishing
Box 640, Walpole, NH 03608 USA*

or call

1-800-847-4014 TOLL FREE
(Continental US, except NH)

1-603-756-4225 or 756-3508
(Foreign and NH)